Library of
Davidson College
VOID

Louis Pécour's 1700
Recueil de dances

Studies in Musicology, No. 60

George Buelow, Series Editor

Professor of Musicology
Indiana University

Other Titles in This Series

No. 53 *French and Italian Influence on the Zarzuela: 1700-1770*	William M. Bussey
No. 54 *Compositional Origins of Beethoven's String Quartet in C Sharp Minor, Opus 131*	Robert Winter
No. 55 *Voices and Viols in England, 1600-1650: The Sources and the Music*	Craig Monson
No. 56 *The Cantata in Nuremberg during the Seventeenth Century*	Harold E. Samuel
No. 57 *American Women Composers before 1870*	Judith Tick
No. 58 *Essays in Performance Practice*	Frederick Neumann
No. 59 *Wagner's* Siegfried: *Its Drama, History, and Music*	Patrick McCreless
No. 61 *The American Opera to 1790*	Patricia H. Virga
No. 62 *Dr. Burney as Critic and Historian of Music*	Kerry S. Grant

Louis Pécour's 1700
Recueil de dances

by
Anne L. Witherell

UMI RESEARCH PRESS
Ann Arbor, Michigan

Copyright © 1983, 1981
Anne L. Witherell
All rights reserved

Produced and distributed by
UMI Research Press
an imprint of
University Microfilms International
Ann Arbor, Michigan 48106

Library of Congress Cataloging in Publication Data

Witherell, Anne L.
  Louis Pécour's 1700 *Recueil de dances*.

  (Studies in musicology ; no. 60)
  Revision of the author's thesis (Stanford, 1981)
  Bibliography: p.
  Includes index.
  1. Pécourt, Guillaume Louis, 1653-1729. Recueil de dances.   I. Title.   II. Series.
GV1590.P423W57 1982   793.3   82-13496
ISBN 0-8357-1367-9

Contents

Acknowledgments   *vii*

Introduction   *1*
    The Present Study
    The Eighteenth-Century Danse à Deux

1   La Bourrée d'Achille   *7*

2   La Mariée   *35*

3   Le Passepied   *71*

4   La Contredance   *95*

5   Le Rigaudon   *111*

6   La Bourgogne   *129*

7   La Savoye   *153*

8   La Forlana   *171*

9   La Conty   *187*

10 Conclusion   *201*
    Reconstruction
    Analysis

Appendix A   Rameau's Notation of Five Dances
    from Pécour's 1700 *Recueil*   *207*

Appendix B   Sources of the Music in Pécour's 1700 *Recueil*   *265*

Notes *279*

Bibliography *287*

Index *295*

Acknowledgments

This research was completed with financial assistance from Stanford University and the Harriet A. Shaw Scholarship from Wellesley College.

I am grateful to the librarians at the Stanford Music Library, the New York Public Library Dance Collection, the Library of Congress Music Division, and the Sibley Music Library, and also to the following scholars who generously shared their information and private libraries: Leslie Getz, Meredith Little, Carol Rowan, and Erich Schwandt.

I thank the following publishers for permission to use illustrations from their reprint editions: Gregg International Publishers Ltd., for Rameau's *Abbregé de la nouvelle méthode* and for Kellom Tomlinson's *The Art of Dancing and Six Dances;* Broude Brothers for Feuillet's *Chorégraphie* and for Pécour's *Recueil de dances.*

My readers have been a great help: Leonard Ratner, whose work inspired me to enter this field of study; Wendy Hilton, without whose knowledge and art my appreciation of Louis Pécour would be much poorer; and George Houle, whose dedication to the study of historical dance gave this research a home and its author an advisor whose support has been invaluable.

Ann Sultan's preparation of the manuscript has been worthy of Pécour.

Finally, I would like to thank the members of the Stanford Baroque Dance Group who performed the 1700 *Recueil:* Ross Duffin, Rebecca Harris-Warrick, Ronald Harris-Warrick, Elisabeth Rebman, Beverly Simmons, Carole Terry, Lynne Toribara, and Marlene Wong.

Introduction

The Present Study

This research examines the relationship of music and dance in the earliest published collection of eighteenth-century French ballroom choreographies, the 1700 *Recueil de dances* of Louis Pécour. The *Recueil* contains nine "danses à deux" choreographed to music of Lully, Colasse, and Campra: "la Bourée d'Achille" (bourrée, menuet, bourrée), "la Mariée," "le Passepied," "la Contredance" (gigue), "le Rigaudon des Vaisseaux," "la Bourgogne" (courante, bourrée, sarabande, passepied), "la Savoye" (bourrée), "la Forlana," and "la Conty" (venitienne).

Each dance is reconstructed from the original choreographic notation, beginning with the identification of the step-units[1] and the clarification, when possible, of the timing of each step-unit. This is followed by a discussion of material in early eighteenth-century dance manuals which has a bearing upon the performance of step-units in context, the movement of the arms and head, and the floor patterns. I have also included specific references to the particular dances found in the works of dancing masters other than Pécour.

I have tried to point out those matters which the sources leave to the discretion of the performer and to offer, where I can, advice based upon my experience teaching and performing the dances. The aim of the reconstruction is to document what is known with certainty about the performance of the dances and to identify the problems which arise in the performance of a dance, which are solved incompletely in the sources.

My study of the relationship of music and dance is confined in each chapter to the relationship of each of Pécour's dances to the music to which it is choreographed. More general observations, principles, and conclusions about the 1700 *Recueil* are gathered in my closing chapter. Discussion in that chapter is limited to the documentable aspects of choreography and music: principally, the effect of the French technique and style upon the performance of music for dancing and Pécour's setting of step-units and dance figures or floor patterns to music.

In appendices, I have included the music for the dances, including the basses and inner parts, when possible, and a detailed comparison of the notation of the dances by Feuillet in 1700 with their renotation by P. Rameau in 1725.

The Eighteenth-Century Danse à Deux

A danse à deux is a ballroom dance for one couple, choreographed to a particular tune. The lady and gentleman usually perform the same dance steps simultaneously in symmetrical floor patterns.

The danse à deux was one of the three genres of dancing which might be seen during the course of an early eighteenth-century court ball. The line dances which opened the ball, the bransles, were a holdover from an earlier period. The contredanses, also danced by more than one couple, but with an informal, social focus, were an English import destined to replace the danse à deux in the ballroom later in the eighteenth century.

The form of the early eighteenth-century court ball seems particularly suited to the performance of the danse à deux. At the King's Grand Ball in France, which served as the model for formal balls in the century, the ladies and gentlemen of the court were seated around the dancing area in order of their rank, with the King at the top of the room and the musicians at the foot of the room. After the King had danced the first danse à deux, he took his place at the top of the room, a position known as the Présence, and the danses à deux continued in order of rank, the lady of highest rank dancing with the gentleman of next highest rank after the King.

Each dance began at the foot of the room with a reverence to the Présence, followed by a reverence to the partner. During the dance, the dancer's technique and style were in full view of everyone in the court, but the Présence was in the best position to appreciate the geometry of the dance figures. The dancer's attention was divided between his partner and the Présence.

The technique of the danses à deux had formed the basis of the technique of the theatrical dances in the noble style as well. It was probably the most sophisticated dance technique ever demanded of a non-professional. It necessitated practice and the development, over a period of several years, of the muscles of the legs and instep so that the dancer could maintain with ease the position of equilibrium or balance, pictured on page 3.

The technique is designed to preserve the strength and serenity of the body so that it reflects none of the strain of vivacious footwork, nor of slow, sustained steps. Noble bearing, control, and easy grace are the essential elements of the style. In a sense, the danse à deux may be considered the elevation of the noble life to art, in which an audience of experts appreciates the studied carelessness of execution of choreographies characterized by a deceptive simplicity.

An illustration of the demi-coupé by George Bickham, Jr., for the second edition of John Essex's *The Dancing-Master* (London: [John Essex] and J. Brotherton, 1731), a translation of P. Rameau's *Le Maître à Danser*.

Fig. 26. The Fourth Posture in the Demi-Coupé, showing the Equilibrium or Balance

4   Introduction

The beauty and difficulty of the dances and their personification of nobility made the French dancing master a necessity in all the major courts and cities of Europe. Noblemen and tradesmen alike sought to distinguish themselves from the "common herd" through the quality of movement acquired in the study of the danses à deux (notably the menuet), which was considered a requirement for civilized life.

It is hardly surprising, then, that dance music forms such an important part of the early eighteenth-century repertoire, both for use in the accompaniment of dancing and as a rhythmic reference in sacred and chamber music. The interest in this body of music provided much of the initial impetus for the reconstruction and study of historical dance. In addition to the obvious visual fascination of the dances, musical scholars have wondered if the dance steps might explain some elements of the composition of the dance music: its structure, rhythmic figures, and even the differences in melody and harmony among the various dance types. Similarly performers, with a mixture of skepticism and practical concern, follow the studies under way regarding the extent to which a knowledge of the dances might illuminate such aspects of performance practice as ornamentation, tempo, articulation, and rhythmic freedom.

Students of eighteenth-century music and dance are growing increasingly sensitive to the question of which music may be related to which dances. There are a number of primary sources available for the study of the danse à deux, including manuals which describe the technique, treatises on the art of reading choreographic notation, and the choreographies themselves, written by dancing masters in a number of countries at various times. Although all the sources purport to teach the French manner of dancing, they exhibit many points of disagreement, not only upon matters of detail, but also upon such essential questions as the execution of the technique and the timing of the step-units.

For my study, I was interested in the French original, rather than a foreign copy, and particularly interested in Louis Pécour, a universally acknowledged master and a central figure in France for several decades. Scarcely a dance treatise was published in the early eighteenth century which does not contain some reference to Pécour. Pasch,[3] Bonin,[4] and Taubert[5] in Germany, Weaver,[6] Tomlinson,[7] and Pemberton[8] in England, Minguet[9] in Spain, and Dufort[10] in Italy all pay tribute to Pécour and, for the title page of the 1716 edition of his *Neue und Curieuse Theatralische Tantz-Schul,* Lambranzi had his portrait drawn holding a loure by Pécour. Two works of P. Rameau, the French dancing master in Spain, received Pécour's approbation and contain the most complete account of his career.[11]

From these sources we learn that Pécour made his dancing debut at the Paris Opéra in Lully's first opera, *Cadmus.* Pécour specialized in the noble style of dancing and is remembered for his performances of sarabandes, passacailles, and chaconnes. At the same time he tried his hand at choreography in court ballets, where he met with such success that when Lully died and Pierre Beauchamp(s) retired as principal choreographer for the Opéra, Pécour was named his successor.

It was an awesome task to follow Beauchamp, who had been, among other things, Louis XIV's dancing master, but there seem to have been no complaints about Pécour nor any indication that he remained in the shadow of his predecessor. For the modern scholar, it is easier to study Pécour's work than that of Beauchamp or any of Beauchamp's predecessors, because Pécour's career was fortuitously timed to correspond with the publication of a new system of dance notation. Although Beauchamp himself probably devised this system of notation, it was first published by a man named Raoul Feuillet in his *Chorégraphie* (Paris: 1700). Feuillet also wrote out in this notation a collection of danses à deux by Pécour—the 1700 *Recueil de dances*—and a collection of theater dances of his own composition, both of which were bound and sold with *Chorégraphie*.

The notation was universally accepted in the early eighteenth century. Feuillet and his successor, Dezais, published annual collections of ball dances for over twenty years while *Chorégraphie* was eagerly translated and sold throughout the world. Thus, the tradition of French dancing, Pécour's position in France, the publication of his dances in Feuillet's notation, and, finally, the excellence of the dances themselves, combined to give Pécour's dances, particularly those understandably famous dances published with *Chorégraphie*, the reputation of being all that was to be admired and imitated in the French style of dancing. Therefore, I felt a study of the relationship of music and dance in Pécour's 1700 *Recueil* would be a valuable contribution to the larger study of the relationship of music and dance in the Baroque era.

From *Chorégraphie* and the 1700 *Recueil*, the floor patterns and step-units of the dances may be determined, but because the notation was designed to be used by those already well versed in the style and technique, it is also necessary to study the contemporary dance manuals. Most valuable for the reconstruction of Pécour's dances are two works by P. Rameau, *Le Maître à Danser* and *Abbrégé*, both published in Paris in 1725 with Pécour's approbation. *Le Maître à Danser* supplies information about French dance technique and style and detailed instructions for the performance of the step-unit, the arm-movements for each step-unit, and the variation of the arm movements in the context of the dance, with specific references to dances of Pécour. In *Abbrégé*, Rameau clarifies the cadence, or timing, of the step-units with the music and writes out in a more precise variant of Feuillet's notation five of the dances from Pécour's 1700 *Recueil*. Other contemporary dance manuals have been cited when they discuss a matter Rameau omits or leaves unclear, but because they are not French they do not necessarily describe anything other than local practice.

1
La Bourrée d'Achille

The "Bourrée d'Achille" is composed of a bourrée, a menuet, and a return of the bourrée music with a variation of the first bourrée dance. It is one of a number of ballroom dances from this period in which the metre, tempo, and dance type change during the course of the choreography.

The source of the music is the Prologue of *Achille et Polixène,* an opera begun by Lully and completed after his death by his pupil, Pascal Colasse. Here the tunes appear as a pair of untitled dances.

Pécour adds the titles "bourrée" and "menuet" and the repetition of the second strain to make the tunes genuine examples of two-reprise form. It is also Pécour who arranged the layout of the music:

    ‖ : A : B : ‖   ‖ :   ‖ : A : B : ‖   : ‖   ‖ : A : B : ‖
      bourrée   menuet   bourrée

The layout of the music for a ballroom dance was calculated to serve the choreographer's needs. It was anything but a matter of convention, as one can see in the variety of musical layouts found in those choreographies in Pécour's 1700 *Recueil* which employ tunes in two-reprise form ("la Bourrée d'Achille," "la Mariée," "le Passepied," "le Rigaudon des Vaisseaux," and "la Bourgogne").

The step-units for the "Bourrée d'Achille" and their timing may be seen in the chart below; their performance is discussed in the paragraphs which follow.

Key for Charts of Step-Unit Timing[1]

a	assemblé
b l	balancé
c⊣	coupé simple
c⊣	coupé soutenue
c m	coupé de mouvement
c--oj	coupé avec ouverture de jambe
ch	chassé

8 La Bourrée d'Achille

ct b	contretemps ballonné
ct d g	contretemps de gavotte, de chaconne, de côté
ct m	contretemps de menuet
d ct	demi-contretemps
dc	demi-coupé
dj	demi-jeté
gl	glissade
j	jeté
m2	pas de menuet de 2 mouvements (demi-coupé, pas de bourrée)
m3	pas de menuet de 3 mouvements (demi-coupé, demi-coupé, pas marché, demi-jeté)
p d b	pas de bourrée, fleuret
p d e	pas de bourrée emboîté
p d o	pas de bourrée ouvert
p d rd	pas de rigaudon
p g	pas de gaillarde
p s	pas de sissonne
pir	pirouette
pir s	pirouette avec saut
pm	pas marché
pt	temps or point
s	saut
t	pas tombé
—tc	temps de courante

The letters are placed under the notes in the following manner: In demi-coupés, the letter marks the élevé, as in coupés and pas de bourrée. In all other steps, the letter marks the moment when the foot makes contact with the ground, as in pas marchés, jetés, demi-jetés, hops, assemblés, and tombés. Pas glissés are notated so that the letter corresponds to the first transfer of weight, as in the temps de courante and the coupé soutenue. When the gentleman and lady perform different step-units, the gentleman's part is listed first.

A thorough discussion of the step-units is found in Wendy Hilton's *Dance of Court & Theater: The French Noble Style, 1690-1725,* Princeton Book Co., 1981.

La Bourrée d'Achille

bourrée A ♪|♩ ♩ ♩ ♩ |♩ ♫ ♩ ♩ |♩ ♩ ♩ ♩ |♩.

m.1 | p d b | p d b | ct d g | —tc

Arpt

5 | p d b | p d b | ct d g | c—
 | | | | —tc

La Bourrée d'Achille

10 La Bourrée d'Achille

Pécour 1700, P. 1, Measures 1-8

step-units: pas de bourrée forward
              pas de bourrée forward
              contretemps de chaconne
              temps de courante forward
              pas de bourrée forward
              pas de bourrée forward
              contretemps de chaconne
              coupé soutenue forward/ temps
                 de courante forward[2]

    The dancers begin with the weight on the inside foot[3] and the outside foot in fourth position behind. They perform two pas de bourrée forward, holding hands; a contretemps de chaconne closing the second pas into fifth position behind and letting hands go; and a temps de courante forward. This is followed by two pas de bourrée forward to meet the partner at the top of the room; a contretemps de chaconne down the room closing the second pas into fifth position behind; and a quarter-turn to the right with a temps de courante forward toward the Présence for the lady, and a coupé soutenue forward down the room for the gentleman.

    The temps de courante in this passage should be taken from two feet in fifth position because the signs for the plié and élevé are placed at the beginning of the step symbol.[4] Rameau discusses the temps forward from two feet, which he finds less difficult than the temps forward from one foot, as well as the temps from third [or fifth] position, which follows a step-unit which closes in that position.[5] In Rameau's renotation of the dance, he clarifies his intention to make the temps from fifth position by including the foot position with signs for the plié and elevé connected to the step symbol with the glissé forward by a line of liaison.[6]

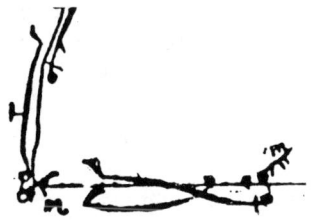

Pécour 1700, P. 2, Measures 9-16

step-units: pas de bourrée forward
pas de bourrée forward
pas de bourrée forward
pas de bourrée forward
pas de sissonne forward[7]
pas de sissonne forward
pas de bourrée backward
coupé soutenue forward

In the second strain of the bourrée, the dancers perform four pas de bourrée forward, circling to meet the partner; a pas de sissonne forward landing from the second saut with the weight on the front foot; a pas de sissonne forward landing from the second saut with the weight on the foot which is behind; a pas de bourrée backward; and a quarter-turn to the right and coupé soutenue forward.

Pécour 1700, P. 3, Measures 17-24

step-units: pas de bourrée forward
pas de bourrée forward
pas de bourrée forward
pas de bourrée forward
pas de sissonne forward
pas de sissonne forward
pas de bourrée backward
coupé simple backward

In the repetition of this strain, the dancers perform the same step-units in a figure comparable to that of measures 9-15. The only change in the step-units is the last pas, which, in measure 24, is a coupé simple backward.

The transitions between bourrée and menuet in measure 24 and later from menuet to bourrée in measure 72 should be performed as notated by Feuillet in the music.⁸ That is, in measure 24, to finish the coupé backward in the bourrée metre, perhaps with a slight ritard, and to begin the menuet tempo with the plié of the first pas de menuet, on the anacrusis.

Pécour 1700, P. 4, Measures 25-40

step-units: pas de menuet of 3 mouvements to the left
pas de menuet of 3 mouvements to the left
pas de menuet of 3 mouvements forward
pas de menuet of 3 mouvements forward

contretemps de menuet forward
contretemps de menuet forward
pas de menuet of 2 mouvements backward
pas de menuet of 2 mouvements backward

To begin the menuet, the dancers perform two pas de menuet of three movements to the left, and, then turning a quarter-turn to the left as they pas, two pas de menuet of three movements forward.

To the second strain of the menuet, the dancers perform a quarter-turn in the air to face each other[9] on the first hop of the first of two contretemps de menuet forward, followed by two pas de menuet of two movements backward on a diagonal path to the left. In performing the pas de menuet backward, the dancers should follow Rameau's directions to leave the left leg extended in fourth position in front on the élevé of the first demi-coupé.[10]

Pécour 1700, P. 5, Measures 41-48

step-units: contretemps de menuet forward
contretemps de menuet forward
pas de menuet of 3 mouvements forward
pas de menuet of 3 mouvements forward

On the repeat of the second strain, the dancers perform two contretemps de menuet and two pas de menuet of three movements forward passing right shoulders on a diagonal path and finishing the last pas de menuet of three movements facing the partner once again after a half-turn made during the course of that pas.

Pécour 1700, P. 6, Measures 49-56

step-units: pas de menuet of 3 mouvements forward
pas de menuet of 3 mouvements forward

> pas de menuet of 3 mouvements forward
> pas de menuet of 3 mouvements forward

As the menuet tune is repeated, the dancers perform four pas de menuet of three movements forward, finishing facing each other (the gentleman facing up the room and the lady facing down the room), in order to present right hands.

> Pécour 1700, P. 7, Measures 57-64

> step-units: pas de menuet of 2 mouvements to the right/
> of 3 mouvements to the left
> pas de menuet of 3 mouvements to the left/
> of 2 mouvements to the right
> pas de menuet of 3 mouvements forward
> pas de menuet of 3 mouvements forward

After the presentation of right hands, the couple dances to the right side of the room and back to the center. The gentleman performs a pas de menuet of two movements to the right behind and behind, as the lady performs a pas de menuet of three movements to the left behind and behind. Then the gentleman performs a pas of three movements to the left behind and behind, as the lady performs a pas of two movements to the right behind and behind. The couple drops hands at this point to perform two pas of three movements forward finishing facing each other (the gentleman facing the left side of the room and the lady facing the right side of the room), in order to present left hands.

> Pécour 1700, P. 8, Measures 65-72

> step-units: pas de menuet of 3 mouvements to the left/
> of 2 mouvements to the right
> pas de menuet of 2 mouvements to the right/
> of 2 mouvements to the left
> pas de menuet of 3 mouvements forward
> pas de menuet of 3 mouvements forward

After presenting left hands, the couple dances a pas down the room and returns in the next pas. The gentleman performs a pas of three movements to the left, behind and behind, as the lady performs a pas of two movements to the right, behind and behind. Then the gentleman performs a pas of two movements to the right, behind and behind, as the lady performs a pas of two movements to the left behind and behind. The dancers drop hands at this point[11] and perform two pas of three movements forward, the first passing right shoulders on a diagonal path, the second turning so that the dancers finish facing each other, the gentleman facing up the room and the lady facing down the room.

After letting go left hands, the diagonal path of the following pas of three movements demands an eighth turn to the left for each dancer. Feuillet notates this with a quarter-turn sign in the lady's part and no sign in the gentleman's, presumably because an eighth-turn which takes you back over the path you have just traveled does not require as much effort as an eighth-turn which continues the direction of travel. Rameau avoids the problem in *Abbrégé* by giving the dancers a circular path.

The bourrée meter and tempo return in measure 72, which is the second measure of the final pas de menuet of three movements. The dancers land from their demi-jeté on the anacrusis of the bourrée tune.

Pécour 1700, P. 9, Measures 73-80

step-units: pas de bourrée forward
pas de bourrée forward
contretemps de chaconne
temps de courante forward
pas de bourrée forward
pas de bourrée forward
contretemps de chaconne
temps de courante forward

In the final bourrée, Pécour employs the same sequence of pas composés that he used in the first bourrée and continues to vary the floor patterns. The dancers advance toward each other with two pas de bourrée forward, execute a contretemps de chaconne to the right followed by a temps de courante forward from fifth position. As these four measures are repeated, the contretemps which is to the left brings the dancers back to the center line, back to back.

Pécour 1700, Pp. 10-11, Measures 81-88

step-units: pas de bourrée forward
pas de bourrée forward
pas de bourrée forward
pas de bourrée forward
pas de sissonne forward
pas de sissonne forward
pas de bourrée backward
coupé to the side sans poser le corps/
    soutenue forward

The four pas de bourrée forward, which begin the second reprise, trace a three-quarter circle which the dancers finish facing each other. This is followed by a pair of pas de sissonne forward, the first landing from the second saut on the front foot and the second landing from the second saut on the foot which is behind; a pas de bourrée backward and, for the lady, a quarter-turn to face the Présence and a coupé soutenue forward. The gentleman, who changes feet at this point, has a quarter-turn to face the Présence and a coupé sans poser le corps to the side with a demi-coupé into fifth behind and a pas marché ouvert, opening to second position and pointing the toe, without a transfer of weight. The gentleman's pas is revised in *Abbrégé* to a quarter-turn and pas de bourrée emboîté.[12]

Pécour 1700, P. 11 (cont.), Measures 89-96

step-units: 2 jetés forward
pas de bourrée forward
2 jetés forward
pas de bourrée forward
pas de sissonne forward
pas de sissonne forward
pas de bourrée forward
closing coupé soutenue

In the repetition of the second reprise, Pécour replaces with pairs of jetés the first and third of the usual four pas de bourrée forward which finish facing the partner. The dancers continue with a pas de sissonne forward, landing from the second saut with the weight on the front foot and a quarter-turn away from the Présence and a pas de sissonne forward, landing from the second saut with the weight on the front foot; a pas de bourrée forward and half-turn in the direction of the partner to face the Présence and a closing coupé soutenue.

In the bourrée, strict repetitions of the pas composés and their directions have an interesting effect upon the floor pattern. An ingenious sequence of pas composés introduces a leapt pas and a change of direction at the beginning of the third quarter of each phrase. With each repetition of the phrases, Pécour's floor pattern presents a different possibility inherent in the sequence.

Such regularity and repetition are not typical of Pécour's court dances, but they are characteristic of a certain sort of bourrée, of which the "Bourrée d'Achille" is one example and the bourrée from "la Bourgogne" is another. It is significant that both these bourrées appear as one section of a choreography in conjunction with dances which have a more complicated relationship of music and dance. The independent duple dances in the 1700 *Recueil*, "la Savoye," "la Mariée," and "le Rigaudon des Vaisseaux," rely to a greater extent upon the overlapping of musical phrases and dance figures for their interest.

The arm movements in the bourrée may follow the Rameau-Beauchamps conventions of opposition, in order to reflect the regularity of the sequence. Holding hands at the opening of the dance is a departure from convention, which has the effect of establishing, from the outset, a human, rather than an ethereal affect. In the first four measures and in the subsequent repetitions, I have omitted the opposition at the end of the contretemps de chaconne, in order to emphasize the opposition to the following temps de courante.

The menuet of the "Bourrée d'Achille" is particularly interesting when seen in light of the menuet ordinaire, for which early eighteenth-century dancing masters, including Taubert,[13] Tomlinson,[14] and Dufort,[15] as well as Rameau,[16] give detailed instructions. The menuet ordinaire is a generic menuet for one couple with a fixed order of floor patterns and a limited vocabulary of pas composés, which could be danced to any menuet tune. Some of Pécour's figures and pas composés in the menuet of the "Bourrée d'Achille" resemble the practice of the menuet ordinaire. One must also consider the possible use of the menuet ordinaire's arm movements and removal of the hat in the performance of the menuet of the "Bourrée d'Achille."

The order of events in a menuet ordinaire is the introduction of the lady, a series of Z or reversed-S figures, in which the dancers pass on a diagonal path, the presentation of the right hand, the presentation of the left hand, more Z figures, and the presentation of both hands and closing. All of the sources agree on this order of figures, although the exact shape of each figure and the number of pas included in a figure vary.

The figures of the menuet from the "Bourrée d'Achille" suggest the first Z figures in measures 25-48 (accompanied by the first statement of the tune) and the presentation of the right and left hands in measures 49-72 (accompanied by the second statement of the tune). The initial bourrée serves the purpose of the introduction and the last bourrée serves the purpose of the final Z's and closing, with only the presentation of both hands conspicuously absent. The sweeping floor pattern in measures 81-84 of the final bourrée is dramatic enough to suggest that the dancers are indeed about to present both hands.

The menuet of the "Bourrée d'Achille" also resembles the menuet ordinaire in its use of certain pas composés at specific points in the figures. Both the menuet ordinaire and choreographed menuets are composed primarily of pas de menuet and a few ornamental steps. The menuet in the "Bourrée d'Achille" uses the pas de menuet of two movements and the pas de menuet of three movements, which are those described in detail by Rameau,[17] and the ornamental contretemps de menuet.

In the French sources, pas de menuet to the right are associated with the pas of two movements, and pas de menuet to the left are associated with the pas of three movements. In both Rameau's *Abbrégé*[18] and Feuillet's *Chorégraphie,*[19] all examples of pas de menuet to the right are illustrated by pas of two movements, and those to the left by pas of three movements. This tendency may also be observed in the menuet ordinaire of Tomlinson[20] and Taubert.[21]

This may be seen as the explanation of the pas in measures 57-60 and 65-66 of the "Bourrée d'Achille," where the dancers, having presented hands, perform steps to the side. Whereas it may well have been Pécour's intention to make the strain more elaborate by having the gentleman and lady perform different pas,[22] it is also significant that he achieves this effect by following an established menuet tradition.

In measures 67-68, however, the lady performs a pas of two movements to the left. This is one of the few errors in Feuillet's notation which Rameau leaves uncorrected.[23]

In the 1700 *Recueil* notated by Feuillet, all pas de menuet forward are pas of three movements; in the Seconde Partie of *Abbrégé*, Rameau notates them as pas of two movements. This seems to indicate a change of fashion in intervening twenty-five years, and might also be evidence of a gradual decline in the dance technique of the French nobility. Rameau writes that, since the pas de menuet of three movements "is not suited to everyone, because it demands a very strong instep, it is not very much used; and its execution has been simplified by the use of an easier manner consisting of two movements only...."[24]

Laying aside the question of Rameau's implication that the pas de menuet of two movements is the simplified evolution of the pas of three movements and the entire matter of dance technique at the French court after the death of Louis XIV, it is clear that by 1725 the pas de menuet of two movements is used almost exclusively for pas de menuet forward. Pas of three movements forward are changed by Rameau to pas of two movements, not only in menuets, but also in passepieds.[25] This is one of the rare instances in the reconstruction of the 1700 *Recueil* in which the dancer must decide if he wishes to reconstruct the dance as it was performed in 1700 or 1725.

In the early eighteenth century, there was no international standardization of the cadence of the pas de menuet, and one can easily recognize the differences in cadence of the menuet steps of Taubert, Tomlinson, Dufort, and Rameau. Taubert reports with some irritation that Parisian dancing masters cannot agree among themselves upon the pas de menuet and that fashion changes rapidly.[26] Furthermore, local traditions of French dancing established by German dancing masters who have studied in Paris reflect this confusion.

There should be little question about the cadence of the pas de menuet for the "Bourrée d'Achille," however, because Rameau uses passages from this dance as examples of the timing of the pas de menuet of two movements and the contretemps de menuet in his "Traité de la Cadence."[27] Rameau writes that Pécour has checked this Traité in particular as well as the notated dances in the Seconde Partie, and that they represent Pécour's intentions.[28] Thus, for the purposes of this study, I have employed Rameau's cadence for the pas de menuet.

There is no evidence that opposition of the arms accompanies a pas de menuet, although it is used with some ornamental steps which can be introduced into the menuet ordinaire, such as the balancé.[29]

Most of the directions for the lady concern her carriage, which is to be erect, upright, easy, and natural, avoiding all stiffness or affectation. She might shade her shoulder while holding her skirt between her thumb and first finger, but she makes no port de bras, reserving the movement of her arms for the presentation of hands.[30]

For the gentleman, Rameau,[31] Dufort,[32] Bonin,[33] and Taubert[34] describe different arm movements closer to the body, while Tomlinson[35] confines his discussion to the logistics of the removal and replacement of the hat in the course of the menuet ordinaire.

In the reconstruction of a figured menuet, one must consider whether the gentleman should remove his hat or employ the arm movements for the pas de menuet in the menuet ordinaire, or both. These are decisions which were dictated at the time by fashion and taste. I have given below the directions for and the uses of the arm movements and the removal of the hat, so that the dancer may decide for himself.

Rameau gave the following directions for the menuet arm movements:

> The manner of moving the arms gracefully in the *Menuet* is as important as the execution of the *pas,* because the arms move with the body and are its principal ornament.
>
> Therefore, the arms should be held at the sides of the body as shown in Fig. 34, the hands being neither open nor closed, because should the thumb press against one of the fingers, this fixed position would stiffen the upper joints and prevent the arms from moving with the smoothness proper to the occasion.
>
> Having the arms disposed as directed, you allow them to fall to the bottom of your coat pockets as you make your first *demi-coupé* with the right foot, the hands turned inwards (see Fig. 35).
>
> But as you execute the second movement with the left foot, the elbow bends slightly so that the hands are imperceptibly raised as shown in Fig. 36. Afterwards you open them very gently, gracefully extending them until you have concluded your *pas de menuet;* and do likewise in every *pas de menuet* you perform, whether it be forwards, backwards, or sideways.
>
> I must observe that although I have made use of three different illustrations, that is merely for the better explanation of the different positions, and to cause the reader to appreciate all the *temps.* Hence, all these successive movements make but one, and are all included in a *pas de menuet.*

Rameau's illustrations for the arm movements follow on pages 19, 20 and 21.

Thus, the movement begins with a fall of the arms from the shoulders, palms turning toward the body on the first demi-coupé. Then, in a continuous movement throughout the rest of the pas de menuet, the forearms are drawn up from the elbow and extended out to the sides as the hands are rotated out a quarter-turn until the palms face each other.

La Bourrée d'Achille 19

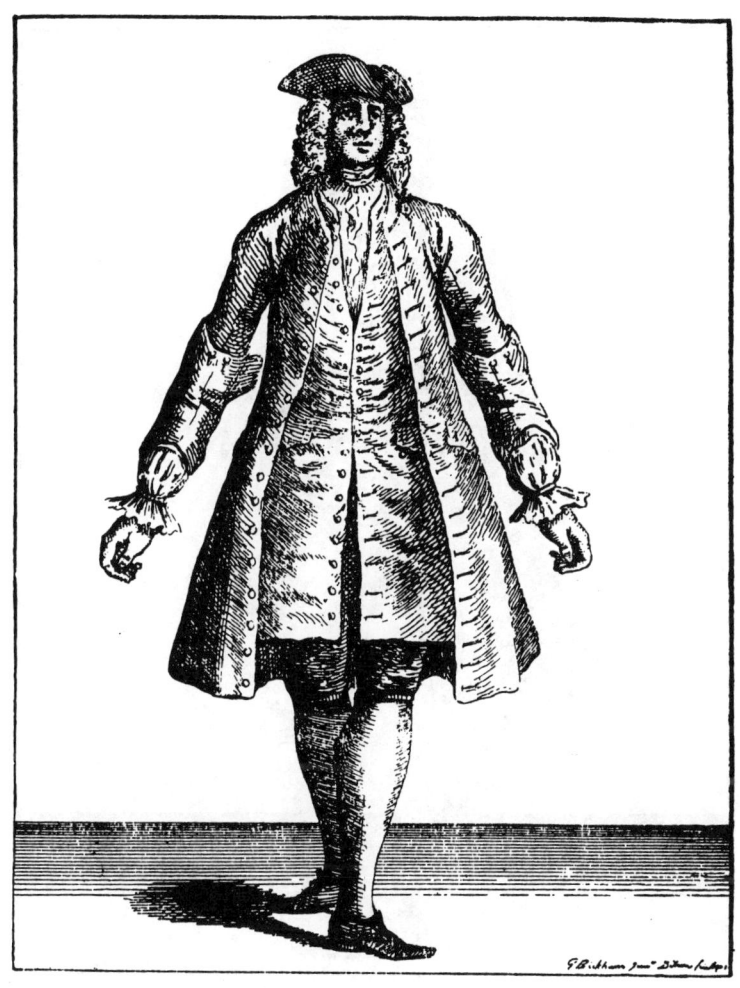

Fig. 34.—The First Position of the Arms in the Menuet

Fig. 35.—The Second Position of the Arms in the Menuet

Fig. 36.—The Third Position of the Arms in the Menuet

All the writers who discuss arm movements for the menuet agree upon this method of execution. Taubert has seen variations of the cadence performed, but he points them out as errors, holding the timing given by Bonin and himself (and later by Rameau and Dufort) to be the only correct one.

Rameau indicates that the arm movements should accompany all pas de menuet in every direction. Taubert adds that the movements are made with the free arm while leading the lady with the other hand. Rameau does not discuss this situation, so at the presentation of the hands, either the continuation of the port de bras for the pas de menuet with the free arm or its interruption may be considered authentic solutions.

I find the presentation of hands more striking if one is not distracted by movements of the free arm. If the gentleman has removed his hat at this point, arm movements with hat in hand seem unnecessarily cumbersome.

The technique of removing and replacing the hat in the course of the menuet is the same as that employed in the bows before dancing, discussed in *Le Maître*.[36] The writers who give directions for the removal of the hat during the course of the menuet (Taubert[37] and Tomlinson[38]) have the gentleman place his hat on his head in preparation for the Z figures and remove it for the presentation of right and left hands. Tomlinson is most specific, explaining that before the presentation of right hands the hat may be removed with the right hand and transferred to the left or removed with the left hand. He instructs the gentleman, upon removing his hat, to let the arm fall "naturally and slow down to the side," and when changing the hat to the right hand in preparation for the presentation of left hands, to hold the hat at arm's length.[39]

Not all of the writers on the early eighteenth-century menuet discuss the removal of the hat, and those who do admit that it is a practice which is subject to fashion and local custom. Neither Rameau nor Dufort mentions removing the hat in chapters on the menuet, although Rameau devotes a chapter to the technique of raising and replacing the hat before discussing the bows.

Tomlinson feels that keeping the hat on the head throughout the menuet is flat and disrespectful, while taking it off and putting it on with a good air "gives a singular Grace to the *Dance*."[40] He hastens to add that this is only his opinion.

Taubert reports that even in France there is disagreement on this point. He presents three arguments for the removal of the hat before presenting the hand: it is easier when learning, the gentleman can warn the lady of the presentation of hands, and finally, ladies in Germany are accustomed to it and would take it as an affront if it were not removed. His advice to the student is to remove the hat in deference to the lady, whatever the fashion.[41]

I do not know if leaving the hat on during the course of a menuet would have been considered a mark of disrespect at the French court or, conversely, if its removal would merely mark the dancer as a foreigner. Its effect is to make the presentation of the hands seem to be a natural extension of courtly behavior rather than an abstract gesture.

Epaulement, or the shading of the shoulder in order to face the partner, is an essential element of the menuet ordinaire which adds grace to the figured menuet as well. Rameau points out places in the figures of the menuet ordinaire where the shoulders should be shaded, but adds that an attitude of slightly shaded shoulders and heads turned to look at the partner should be maintained throughout the dance.[42]

In the menuet, the shoulder is shaded only to facilitate looking at the partner. The direction to look at the partner during the menuet is universal, and Taubert even goes so far as to say that the partner must be held in view, "as much as convenience and the well-being will tolerate."[43]

In the menuet from the "Bourrée d'Achille," certain épaulements suggested by Rameau are choreographed into the figure by Pécour. For example, Rameau asks the dancers to shade right shoulders as they pass on the diagonal of the Z figure.[44] In the opening figure of the menuet from the "Bourrée d'Achille," the pas de menuet to the side make épaulements unnecessary. This is also true in the reversed-S figures of Tomlinson's menuet.[45]

Epaulements may be introduced by the dancers at the beginning of the pas de menuet forward upon passing the partner in measures 29-30, so that the turn away is not so abrupt, and in the contretemps de menuet which pass on the diagonal in measures 41-44. They may be introduced at any other point where subtle shading contributes to the beauty of the figure and to the ease of seeing one's partner, provided the dancer heeds Rameau's warnings to avoid affectation.[46]

24 La Bourrée d'Achille

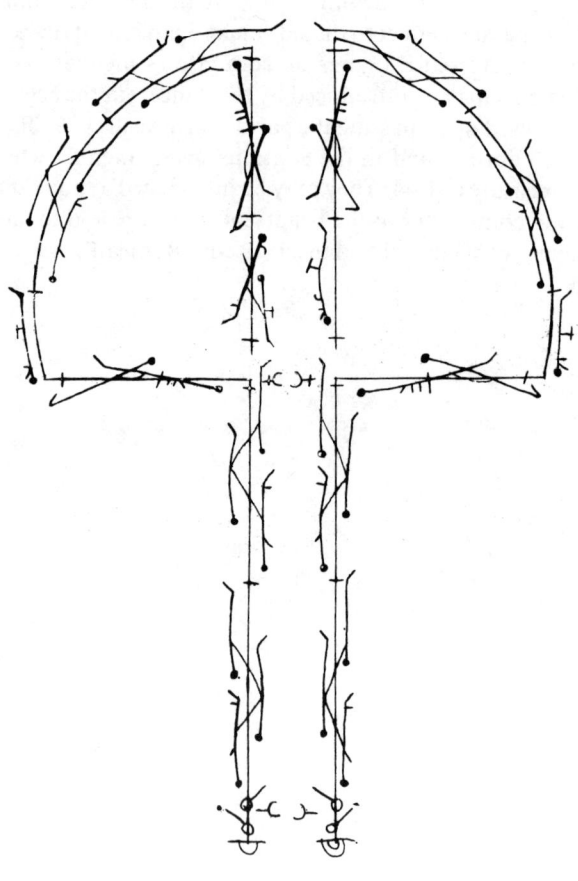

La Bourrée d'Achille

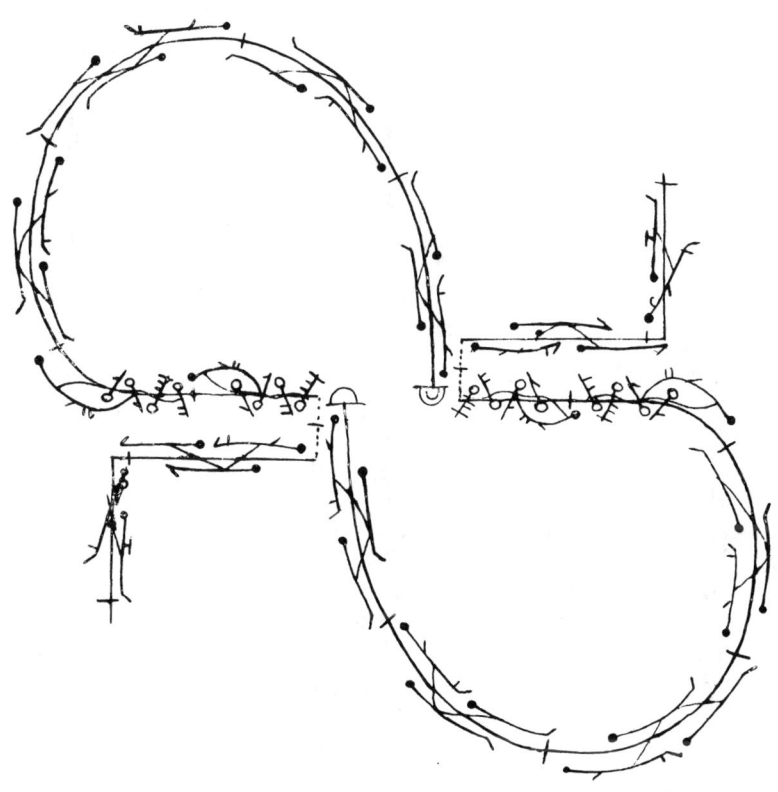

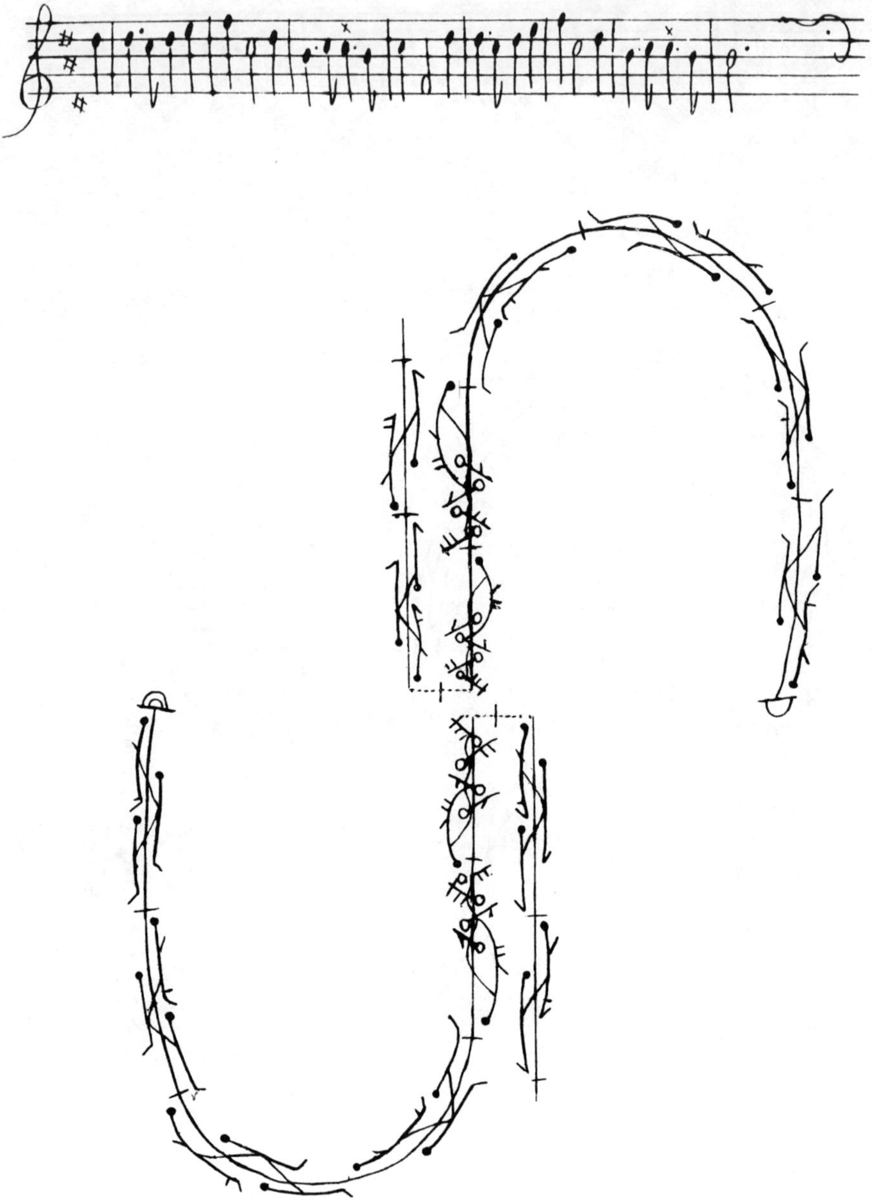

La Bourrée d'Achille

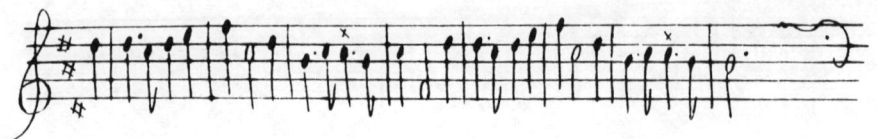

La Bourrée d'Achille

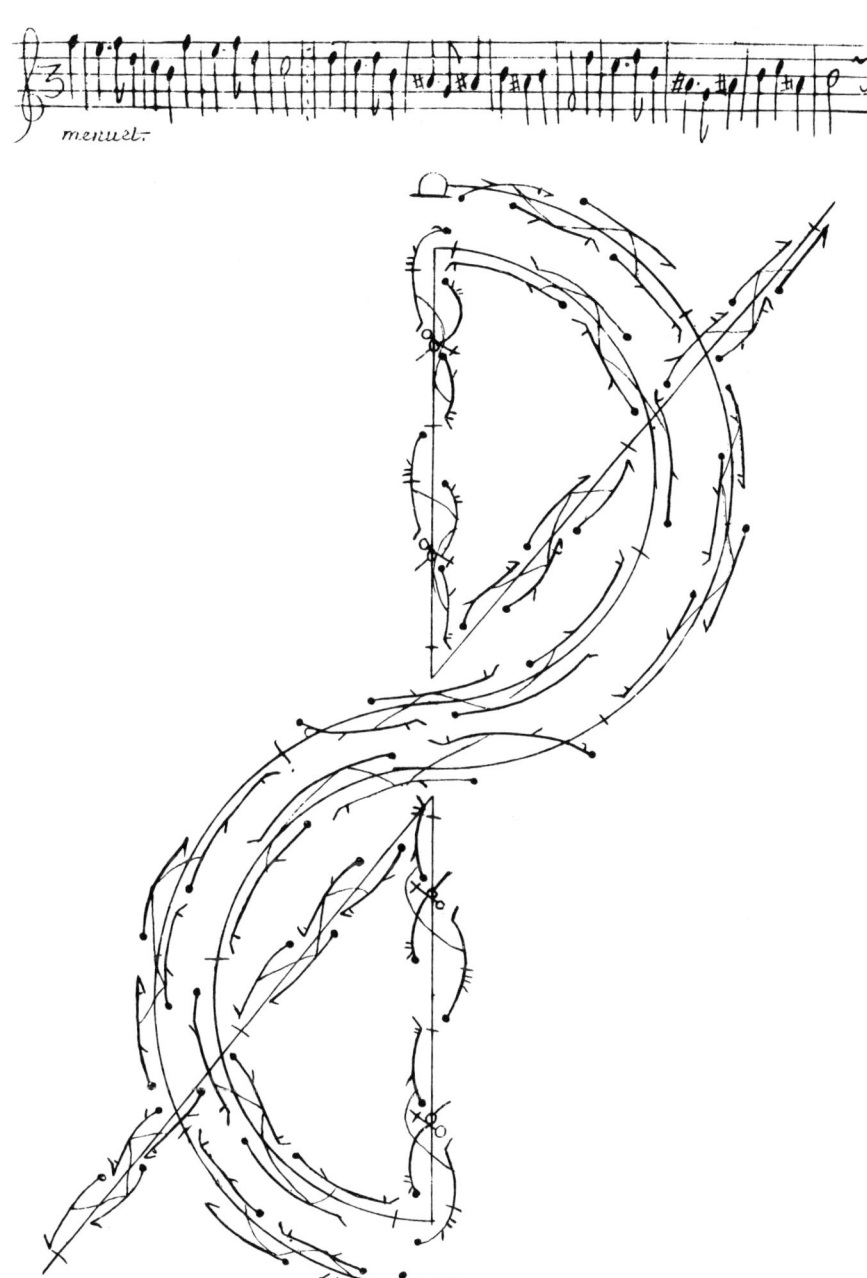

menuet.

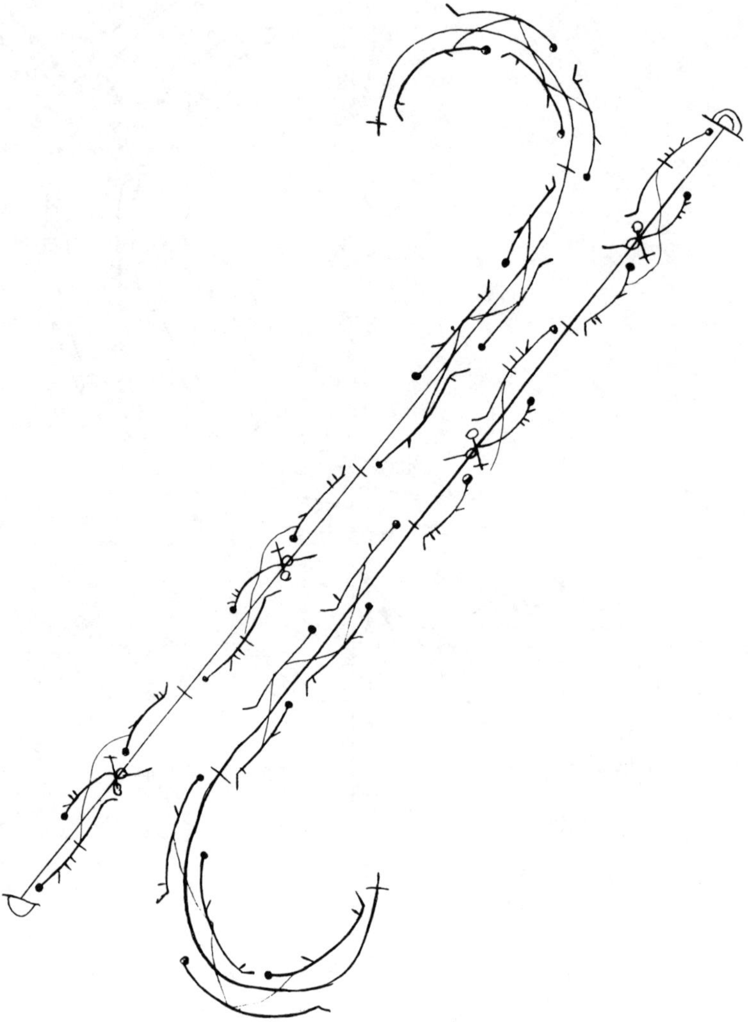

28 La Bourrée d'Achille

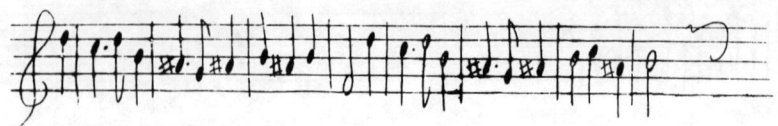

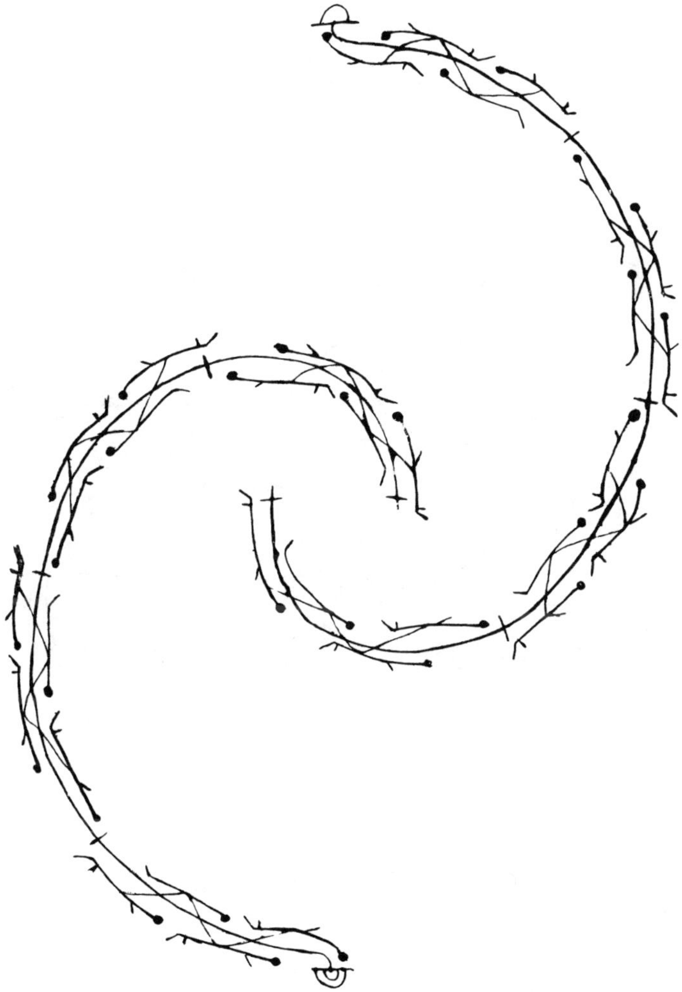

La Bourrée d'Achille

La Bourrée d'Achille

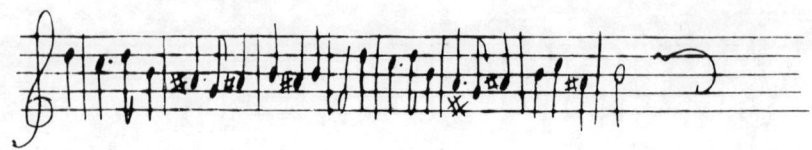

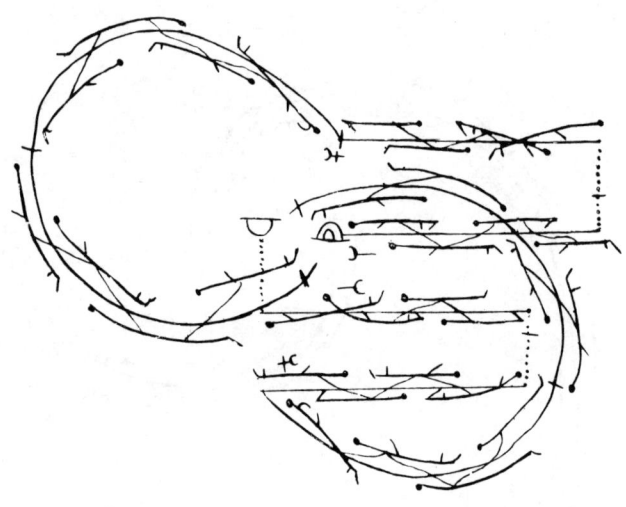

La Bourrée d'Achille 31

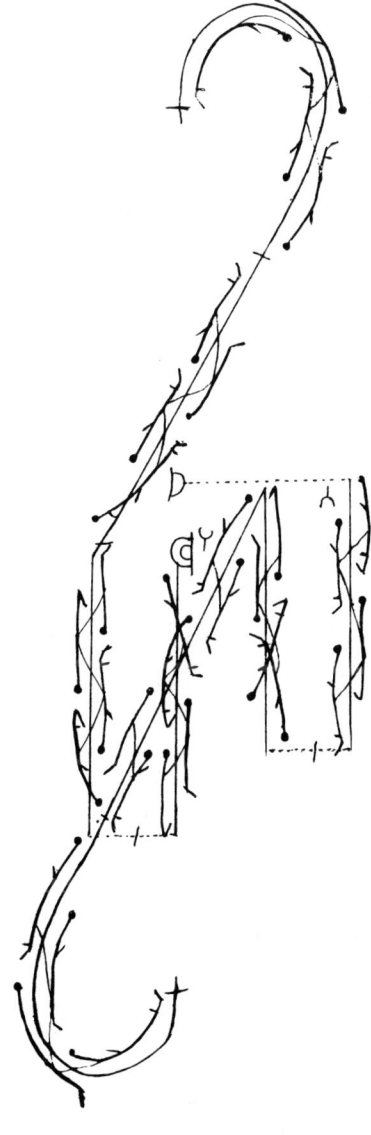

32   La Bourrée d'Achille

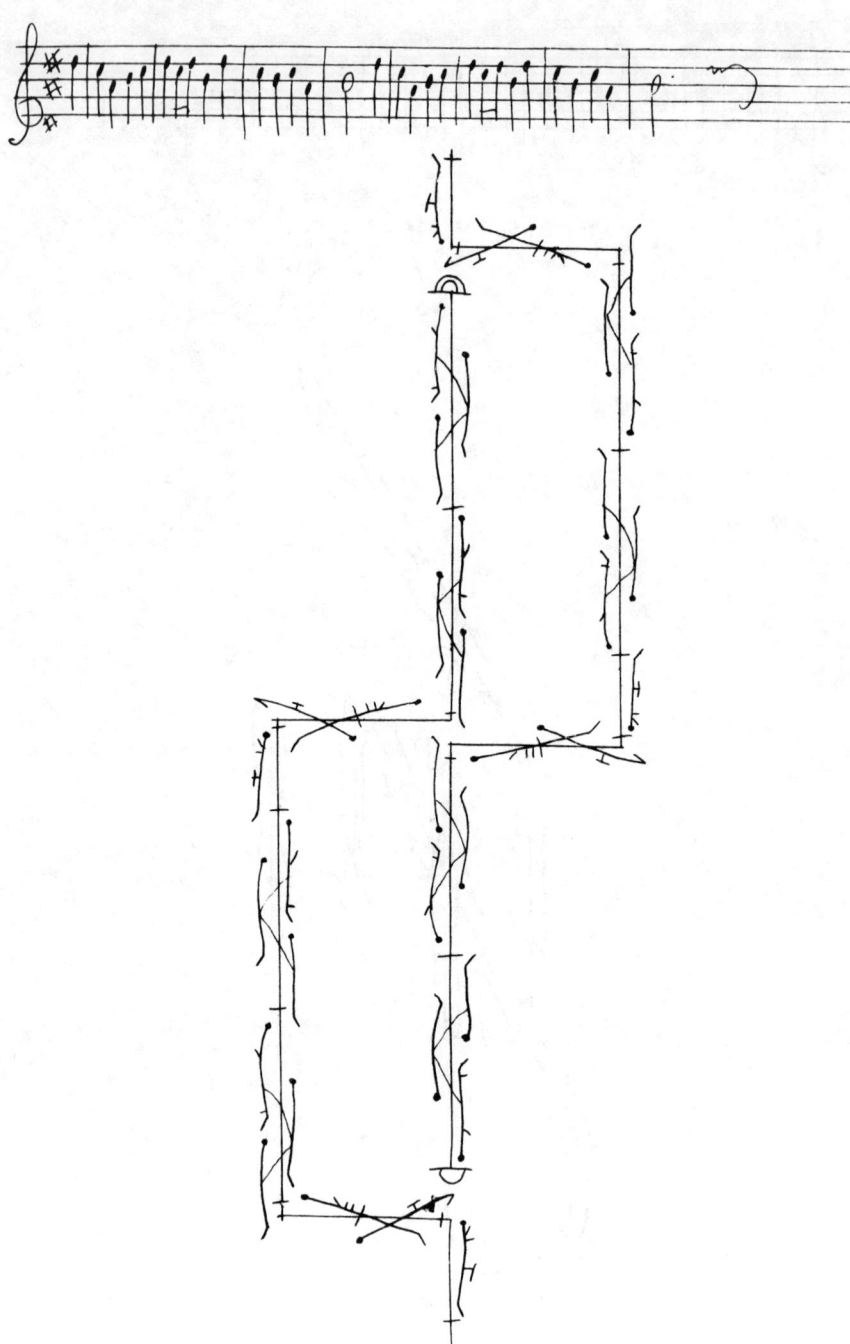

La Bourrée d'Achille 33

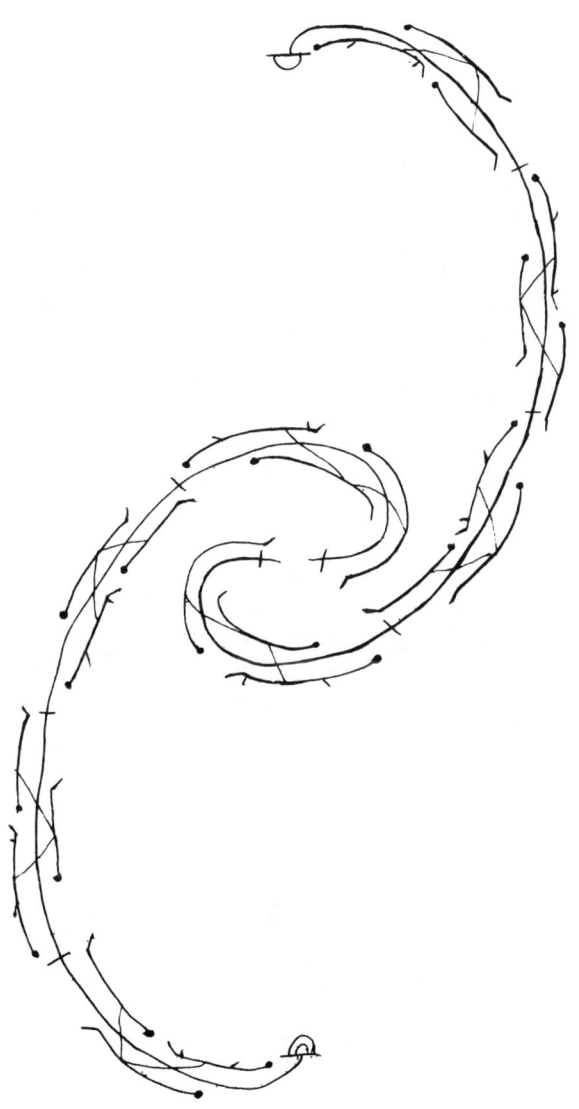

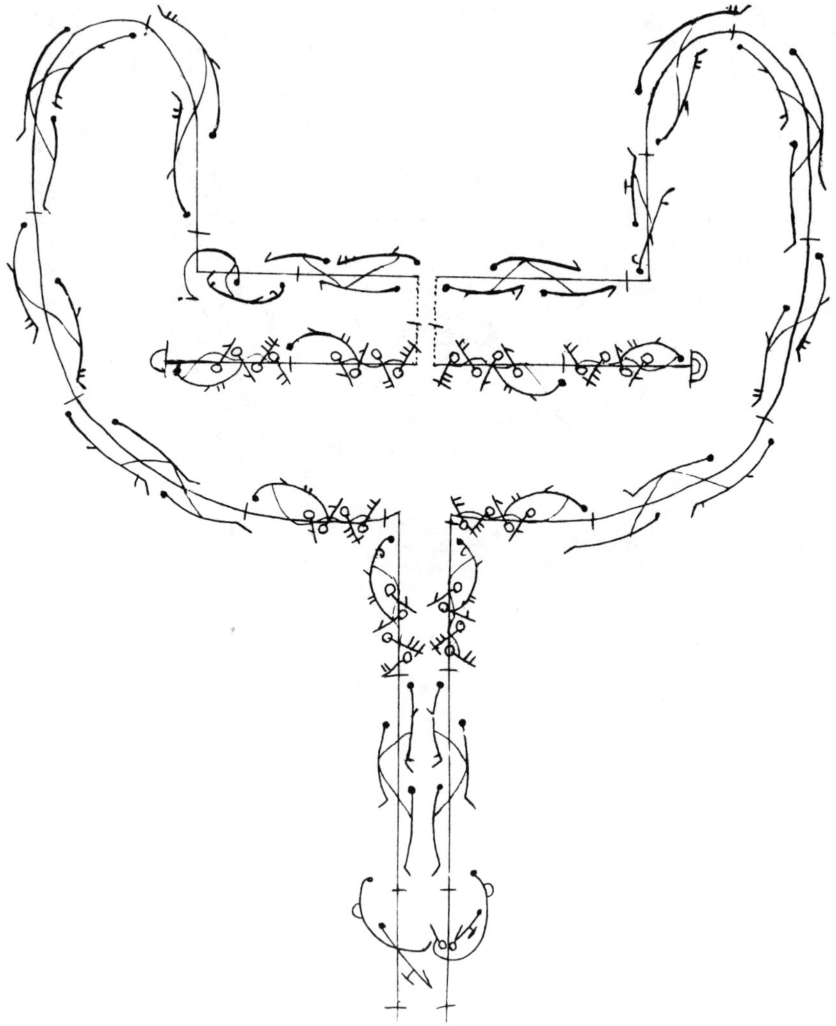

34 *La Bourrée d'Achille*

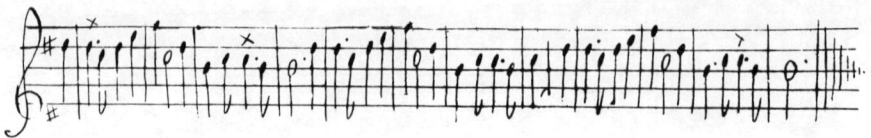

2

La Mariée

"LA MARIÉE"

La Mariée

Pécour 1700, P. 12, Measures 1-14

step-units: coupé simple to the side
pas tombé to the side
contretemps ballonné forward
coupé simple to the side
pas tombé to the side
contretemps ballonné forward
pirouette
pirouette with point to the side

pas de bourrée to the side
contretemps de chaconne
contretemps de chaconne avec pied en l'air
pas de sissonne bâtu
pas de bourrée emboîté
contretemps ballonné forward

The dancers begin "la Mariée" with the weight on the outside foot, and the inside foot in fourth position behind. They make a quarter-turn to face the partner and a coupé simple to the side, crossing the demi-coupé in fifth position before and opening the pas marché to second; a pas tombé to the side falling into fifth position behind followed by a demi-jeté to second position; and a contretemps ballonné forward. Then the dancers make a half-turn in the direction of the Présence and repeat the first three step-units on the opposite foot with the back to the partner, continuing to travel sideways toward the Présence.

At the top of the room, the dancers make two half-turn pirouettes, the first turning in the direction of the Présence to face the partner, the second turning in the direction of the Présence to finish with the back to the partner, pointing the free foot to the side toward the Présence at the end of the turn.

The dancers continue with a pas de bourrée to the side behind and before; a contretemps de chaconne crossing the second pas marché in fifth position behind; a contretemps de chaconne replacing the second pas marché with a pied en l'air moving in front; a pas de sissonne bâtu turning a half-turn in the air in the direction of travel on the first assemblé; a pas de bourrée emboîté; and contretemps ballonné forward.

In the pas tombé, the dancer rises to demi-pointe, shifts the weight of the body out of equilibrium, and falls, landing on the free foot. Feuillet notates this sequence of events with the single sign ●⎯⎯⎯⎯⏋ . The landing from the fall occurs on the beat and the time to rise and shift is taken from the preceding measure, a phenomenon analogous to the treatment of the plié and place in the notation of the demi-coupé.

The necessity of rising before the fall may also affect the performance of the end of the step-unit which precedes a pas tombé. In the opening measure of "la Mariée," the pas marché of the coupé should be made not onto half-toe, but with the heel on the ground, so that the dancer can make a definite rise in order to fall. The rise before the shift and fall is not an élevé from a bent to a straight knee, but a raising of the heel off the floor while the knee remains straight. Rameau devised a new sign for raising the heel, which he uses in his notation of this passage.

38   La Mariée

Rameau, *Abbrégé,* Part II, P. 10

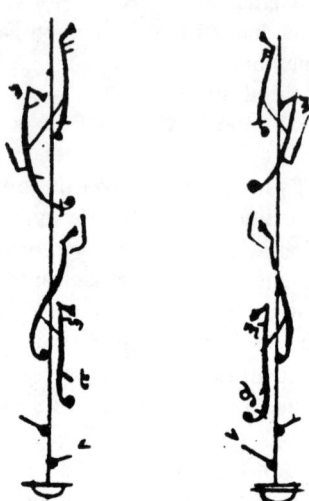

    A shift in the dancers' focus from the partner to the Présence is inherent in the pirouette and pirouette with point as the dancer looks out over the foot which he points to the side. In Feuillet's notation, a double line of liaison connects the second pirouette with the point. A double line indicates that the steps are performed in half the time taken to perform the same steps connected by a single line. Thus, in this instance, the point would arrive on the second quarter-note of the measure rather than on the second half-note. A literal reading of this double line may seem to rush the pirouette in practice; however, an arrival during the second quarter-note which allows the dancers to pause and fix their attention on the Présence for more than a quarter-note can help to define the direction of the opening strain.

    The pied en l'air on the last pas of the contretemps de chaconne in measure 11 is the beginning of a continuous movement from the hip facilitating a half-turn in the air in the direction of travel to face the partner. Although the end of this contretemps is altered in this manner in order to introduce a half-turn and pas de sissonne bâtu, the timing of the contretemps is not affected. The dancer must resist the temptation to delay the first pas marché for a firmer, but more plodding preparation for the turn in the air. The pied en l'air should take the time of the second pas marché.

    The pas de sissonne which follows is ornamented with a battement or beat. The beat into fifth position before, finishing the assemblé in fifth position behind, is the culmination of the movement begun with the pied en l'air in the previous measure. The presence of a battement does not alter the

La Mariée 39

timing of the pas de sissonne, in which the dancers land first on the downbeat and then on the beginning of the second half-note of the measure. The question is the timing of the battement: before, during, or after the landing on the downbeat.

Rameau describes two kinds of battements, those made from the hip and knee in which one foot remains on the ground and the free foot beats against it, and those made from the hip joint alone which are made in the air with both legs moving to make the battement.[1] According to this description and the notation of the dance, I think this pas de sissonne bâtu is an example of the first kind of battement and, thus, the battement should occur at the time of the landing on the downbeat or shortly thereafter, when one foot is on the ground. If Pécour had intended the battement to be performed in the air before the down beat, I think he would have notated this step-unit as an entrechat in the following manner:

Tomlinson describes the same step at the beginning of his chapter, "Of the CLOSE beating before and falling behind in the third position...,"[2] as quoted below. His text does little to clarify the timing of the battement.

> The *Close beating before* & c. which we are now about to explain, differs from the before described Step of this Name, in its being done to the first Note of the measure, and, instead of resting the remaining two Notes, as in the aforesaid to the second, there are the *upright Spring* and *Coupee* to the third; and, instead of the *Close*'s ending either in the first or third Position with the Knees straight, as in the former, it here comes down behind with the Knees bent, after its beating before. This Step is to be performed as follows, *viz.* commencing either with the right or left Foot from the third Position (y), by sinking or bending not only the foremost Foot on which the Body rests, but likewise the hind Foot without Weight; or from thence it begins, by making the *Close* in the like Manner, as aforesaid, in treating of this Step in the Rise or Spring from the above named Sink; but, instead of the *Close*'s lighting in the first or third Position, as in the foregoing, the beginning Leg beats before against that on which the Body rested at first (z), and comes down in the third Position, as at commencing, only the Weight is equally upon both Feet (a), and the Knees are bent, **marking the first Note**.

(y) See the first and second Figures in Plate V.
(z) See the first or inclosed Feet of the first and second figures in Plate IV.
(a) See the hind Feet of the two said Figures in Plate IV.

40 La Mariée

Pécour 1700, P. 13, Measures 15-28

step-units: 2 demi-coupés bâtus
2 demi-coupés bâtus
glissades
coupé soutenue to the side sans poser le corps
pas de bourrée turning to the side
assemblé
pas de sissonne
pas de bourrée to the side
temps to the side

pas de bourrée to the side
contretemps ballonné forward
pas de sissonne forward
pas de bourrée to the side
contretemps ballonné forward

The repetition of the first strain of music begins with a pair of beaten demi-coupés into fourth position behind and fourth position in front in each of the first two measures. The dancers advance toward the Présence with a pair of glissades, crossing first into fifth position behind and then into fifth position before; and a coupé soutenue to the side, crossing the glissé into fifth position behind without transferring the weight; a pas de bourrée to the side turning a full turn in the direction of the Présence during the course of the pas; and an assemblé with a quarter-turn in the air to face the Présence.

The dancers continue with a turning pas de sissonne, landing from the second saut with the weight on the foot which is behind, a pas de bourrée to the side, behind and behind; and a temps to the side away from the partner.

This is followed by a pas de bourrée to the side behind and behind toward the partner; a contretemps ballonné forward; a pas de sissonne forward landing from the second saut with the weight on the foot which is behind; a pas de bourrée to the side, behind and before; and a contretemps ballonné forward with a quarter-turn in the air away from the partner before landing from the first saut.

The sequence of events in the performance of two beaten demi-coupés in one measure should be: plié, beat the free foot against the back of the ankle, place the free foot in fourth position behind, rise onto the foot in fourth position behind, then plié on that leg, beat the free front foot against the front of the ankle, place the free foot in fourth position in front, rise onto the foot in fourth position in front. The steps must be timed so that the élevés of the demi-coupés occur on the downbeat of the measure and on the beginning of the second half-note of the measure. The elaborate preparation for each élevé (plié, beat, place) emphasizes the fact that the dancer must spend most of the measure in a plié in order to get two demi-coupés in before the next down beat. It appears that the dancer has more leisure before the first élevé of the series of four because the last step-units in the preceding phrase is a contretemps ballonné, which lands in a plié on the beginning of the second half-note of the measure. I feel, however, that the beat should be executed immediately before the place in the same time as the beats before the succeeding three demi-coupés, so that the dancer has time to finish the first strain and to define the beginning of the more concentrated activity of the second strain.

Although Feuillet notates each glissade as a demi-coupé and glissé, the first step could be performed either as a demi-coupé or as a demi-jeté, acording to both Rameau[3] and Tomlinson.[4] In *Abbrégé,* all the glissades are notated with demi-jetés. Thus, it would seem that the individual performer could choose to do either, provided his execution was smooth.

The pas de bourrée turning in measure 19 begins with a half-turn in the direction of the Présence and a demi-coupé, finishing with the back to the partner. The dancers continue the circle in another half-turn, taking the next pas marché into second position facing the partner and finishing with a glissé into fifth position behind.

The glissé at the end of the pas is unusual. In the descriptions of pas de bourrée in the manuals of dance technique, a glissé is found only in the pas de bourrée ouvert, a variation of the step-unit which also includes a rise on the last pas.[5] Surprisingly, the sign for the glissé never appears in the notation of the pas de bourrée ouvert.

Other examples which show a glissé on the last step of a pas de bourrée do appear in the charts of Feuillet and his translators, Taubert and Weaver, and those of Tomlinson. These are reproduced below:

Feuillet, *Chorégraphie,* P. 69

Taubert, *Rechtschaffener Tantzmeister,* P. 770

42   La Mariée

Weaver, *Orchesography,* Tables, P. 22

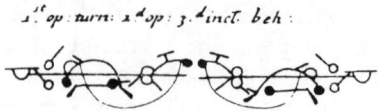

Tomlinson, *The Art of Dancing,* Tables E and I

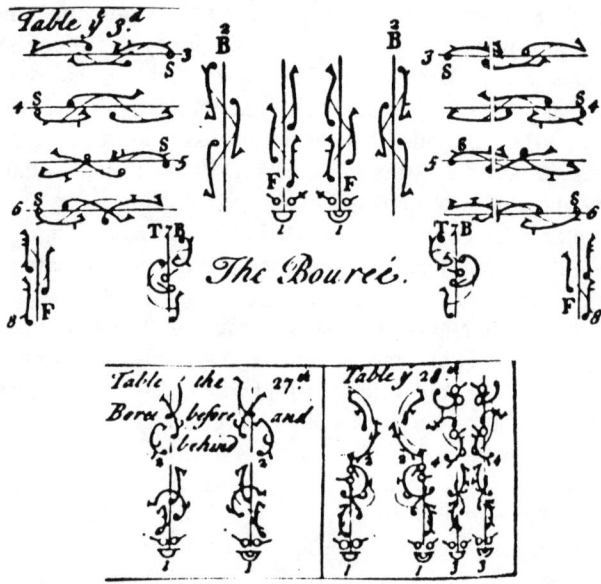

In all of these examples, the pas glissé closes into fifth position at the end of a pas de bourrée to the side before and behind, behind and before, or turning. Thus, Pécour's use of a glissé in "la Mariée's" turning pas de bourrée reflects the preceding coupé sans poser le corps with an unusual, but not unprecedented variation of the pas de bourrée.

Rameau's notation of this step-unit in his renotation of "la Mariée" does not have a glissé. It does clarify the position of the free foot during the second half-turn before the first pas marché, a refinement of notation already found in Feuillet's charts.

Feuillet, *Chorégraphie,* P. 70

Rameau, *Abbrégé,* Part I, P. 59

Rameau, *Abbrégé,* Part II, P. 11

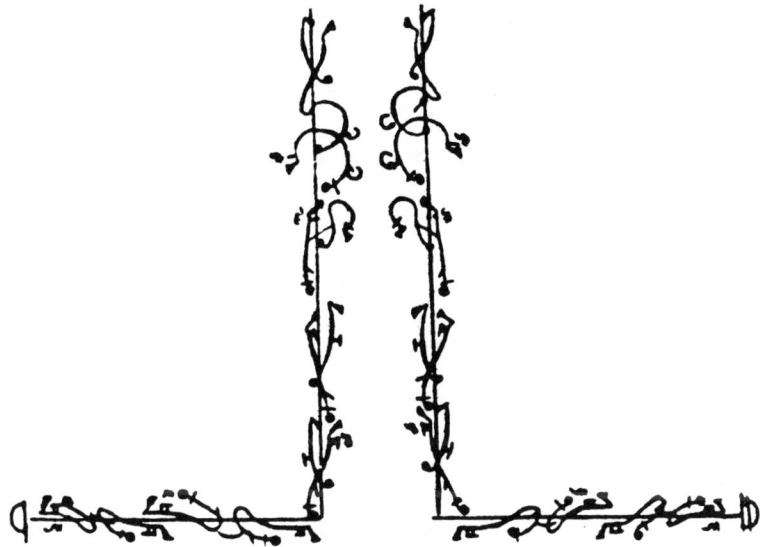

On the first assemblé of the pas de sissonne turning in measure 21, the dancers make a half-turn in the air in the direction of the partner, landing in fifth position with the right foot in front. On the second saut, the lady lands with the weight on the left foot, which is behind. On the second saut, the gentleman performs another half-turn in the air, completing the circle begun in the assemblé, and lands with his weight on the left foot, which is in fifth position behind.

The dancers' point in measure 23, which marks the end of their progress away from each other, is a temps in which there is no transfer of weight. According to both Rameau[6] and Tomlinson,[7] the plié occurs before the downbeat and the élevé and point occur together to mark the beginning of the measure. The dancer holds this position for the entire measure, an effect which Rameau finds most graceful, "especially when succeeding another livelier step."[8]

44   *La Mariée*

Perhaps as a result of the intricacy and variety of Pécour's choreography, Rameau selected the first five measures of "la Mariée's" first strain and its repetition for the only extended examples in his "Traité de la Cadence,"[9] reproduced below:

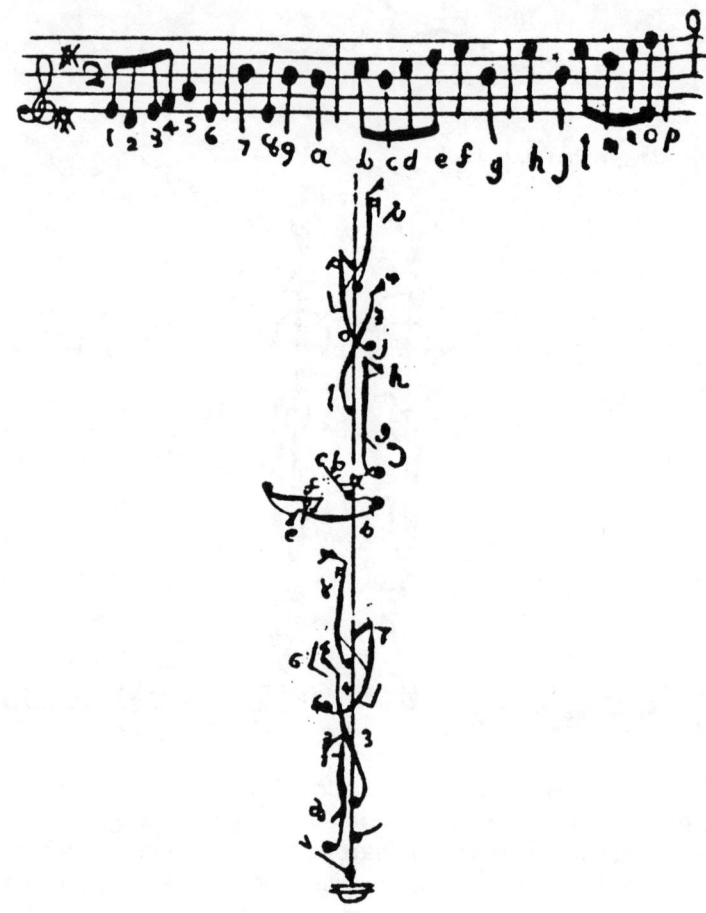

La Mariée   45

Pécour 1700, P. 14, Measures 29-40

step-units: contretemps ballonné forward
 coupé simple/pas de gaillarde to the side
 chassés to the side

 coupé soutenue forward
 pas de gaillarde to the side
 chassés to the side

46   La Mariée

                coupé soutenue forward
                temps de courante forward
                contretemps ballonné forward
                contretemps ballonné forward
                pas de bourrée forward
                pas de sissonne forward/modified pas de sissonne

    The dancers begin the second strain with a contretemps ballonné forward toward each other, making a half-turn to the left in the air before landing from the first saut. Then the dancers take both hands as the gentleman performs a coupé simple to the side crossing the demi-coupé into fifth position before and the lady performs a pas de gaillarde to the right.[10] Both dancers finish with the weight on both feet in preparation for the chassés to the side down the room which follow.

    The dancers let go hands at the end of the chassés to make a half-turn in the direction of the Présence and a coupé soutenue forward away from the partner; a pas de gaillarde into second position; and a pair of chassés down the room.

    Then the dancers make a half-turn in the direction of the Présence and a coupé soutenue forward toward the partner; and, following a circular path, a temps de courante forward presenting right hands; a pair of contretemps ballonnés forward; a pas de bourrée forward, and, for the gentleman, a pas de sissonne forward, landing from the second saut with the weight on the foot which is behind. The lady's last step-unit is also a pas de sissonne, modified so that she can change feet for the next figure. The dancers drop hands at the conclusion of the pas de sissonne.

    Careful examination of the step-unit in measure 33 reveals that Feuillet has placed the sign for the élevé after the free foot has been brought into first position, making a fine notational distinction between this step-unit and that in measure 30, in which the élevé is notated before the foot is brought into first, following the established tradition of notating the pas de gaillarde. I have chosen to emphasize the balanced pattern of the phrase and perform both step-units as pas de gaillarde which introduce chassés, seeing the exigencies of changing feet as the rationalization for the gentleman's coupé in measure 30. If the step-unit in measure 33 is not a pas de gaillarde, then what is it? The notation is similar to that of a beaten demi-coupé, but the beaten demi-coupé does not seem possible in this context. If it were to be performed as a demi-coupé, the élevé and transfer of weight would have to occur on the down beat; and second position with the weight equally distributed, necessitated by the chassés in the following measure, is not the gracious sort of pose which Pécour likes to have the dancer hold for the better part of a measure.

    In *Abbrégé,* Rameau employs different step-units in this passage, exchanging one form of symmetry for another. In measure 30, both dancers perform a coupé and, in measure 33, both dancers perform a pas de gaillarde. The adjustment which is necessary to allow the lady to make a coupé in measure 30 is made in the last measure of the preceding strain, where she performs a saut and point instead of the contretemps ballonné. Thus, the chassés are no longer introduced by the same step-unit, but the visual symmetry at the beginning of this strain is more perfect and the dancers are not obliged to change feet in the course of the strain.

This passage contains the only chassés in the 1700 *Recueil*. Their use in "la Mariée" is cited by Rameau, who also provides the following description:

> This pas is flowing, because in hopping you gain ground to perform the figure required by the dance. It has a gay effect when several are made in succession, for the dancer appears to be always off the ground, and with but a half spring.[11]

The chassé begins with a low spring from two feet in an open position;[12] one foot replaces the other in the air and lands first, the displaced foot landing later in the original starting position, which Tomlinson compares to the Posture of *Defence* in fencing.[13] In chassés to the side, second position is used.

Generally, a pair of chassés is made to one measure of music. The first landing of the first chassé is timed to coincide with the downbeat, and the first landing of the second chassé marks the beginning of the second half-note of the measure.[14] Although this timing follows the eighteenth-century principle of landing on the beat, the timing of the chassé has proven to be understood more easily in theory than in practice, particularly by those whose training in later ballet technique has accustomed them to marking the down beat with the chassé's second landing.

The lady's pas de sissonne at the end of this page is performed in the following manner: after finishing the pas de bourrée on the left foot, she brings the free right foot into third position behind for the plié and then brings it out to the side and back into fifth position behind for the landing on the first assemblé, landing from the second saut on the right foot which is behind. This variation is also illustrated by Rameau in his chart of pas de sissonne.[15]

Pécour 1700, P. 15-16, Measures 41-52

step-units: pas de bourrée emboîté turning
contretemps ballonné forward
pas de bourrée forward
contretemps ballonné forward
pas de bourrée forward
contretemps ballonné forward
coupé soutenue/pas de bourrée forward

coupé soutenue to the side
coupé avec ouverture de jambe to the side
coupé simple to the side
pas de bourrée turning backwards
pas de sissonne backwards/modified pas de sissonne

The dancers begin the repetition of the second strain with a pas de bourrée emboîté turning a quarter-turn to the right. They take left hands and continue in a circle with a contretemps ballonné; pas de bourrée; contretemps ballonné; pas de bourrée; and contretemps ballonné forward. Then the gentleman makes a coupé soutenue forward and the lady makes a pas de bourrée forward to face him, letting go hands at the end of the measure.

Traveling up the room, the dancers take both hands and make a coupé soutenue to the side crossing the pas glissé into fifth position in front; and a coupé to the side avec ouverture de jambe. The dancers return down the room with a coupé simple to the side crossing the pas marché into fifth position in front; a pas de bourrée backward letting go hands and turning three-quarters of a turn during the course of the pas to finish facing the Présence; and a pas de sissonne backward for the gentleman, landing from the second saut with the weight on the foot which is behind, as the lady makes a modified pas de sissonne, landing from the second saut on the foot which is behind.

The turning pas de bourrée emboîté which opens this strain enables the dancer to look at the partner over the left shoulder in preparation for the presentation of left hands. The quarter-turn occurs on the demi-coupé. The characteristic pause in third position after the first pas marché is particularly striking in this turning pas de bourrée emboîté, because it occurs after the turn but before the step forward in the fresh direction. Pécour uses this effect to great advantage in the last page of this dance.

The coupé simple to the side in measure 50 is introduced by a battement. It is preceded by a step-unit which ends in the second position, and the beat follows the principle employed in beats between pas de bourrée emboîtés. Thus, the dancer does not bring the free foot into first position on the preparatory plié at the end of measure 49, but brings it in sharply to beat in first position after the plié and out to place in second position before the élevé on the down beat of measure 50.

This coupé simple is followed by a pas de bourrée backward with a three-quarter turn in the direction of travel so that the dancers face the Présence at the end of the step-unit. The first half-turn is made on the demi-coupé, which is placed so that the dancer continues to travel down the room. The remaining quarter-turn is made on the first pas marché, which is taken into first position. The final pas marché is made to fourth position behind.

The lady's pas de sissonne which concludes the strain is modified so that both dancers can begin the next figure on the right foot. As the gentleman makes his pas de sissonne backwards, the lady brings her free right foot out and lands in the assemblé with the right foot in fifth position in front. She lands from the second saut with the weight on the foot which is behind.

> Pécour 1700, P. 17-18, Measures 53-66
>
> step-units: pas de bourrée to the side
> contretemps ballonné to the side
> pas de bourrée to the side
> contretemps ballonné to the side
> pas de bourrée forward
> contretemps ballonné forward
> coupé simple forward
> pas de rigaudon
> coupé de mouvement
> coupé backward avec ouverture de jambe to the side
> coupé de mouvement
> pas de bourrée backward
> pas de sissonne backward/modified pas de sissonne

As the music begins a second time, the dancers perform the first six step-units (pas de bourrée, contretemps ballonné, pas de bourrée, contretemps ballonné, pas de bourrée, contretemps ballonné), clockwise in a circle, finishing the last contretemps ballonné facing the Présence. The dancers continue with a coupé simple forward, finishing in first position on demi-pointe; and a pas de rigaudon, landing from the first saut with the weight on the left foot.

The dancers make a quarter-turn and coupé de mouvement toward each other; a beat, quarter-turn to face the Présence, and coupé backward avec ouverture de jambe to the side; a quarter-turn and coupé de mouvement forward away from the partner; a beat, quarter-turn, and pas de bourrée backward facing the Présence; and a pas de sissonne backward landing from the second saut with the weight on the foot which is behind for the gentleman as the lady makes a modified pas de sissonne, landing from the second saut with the weight on the foot which is behind.

Before embarking upon this passage, the dancer must choose between the version notated by Feuillet in 1700 and that notated by Rameau in 1725, which exhibits a contrast in focus. In Feuillet's notation, the first four step-units are performed to the side: a pas de bourrée behind and before, a contretemps ballonné, pas de bourrée before and before, and contretemps ballonné. Although there is no turn sign on the next step-unit, the angle of the foot

50 La Mariée

symbol indicates that the pas de bourrée and contretemps ballonné which follow are to be made forward. The dancers do not take hands.

In the later version in *Abbrégé,* the gentleman takes the lady's left hand in his right at the beginning of the figure. Rameau includes an illustration of the dancers holding hands in an unusual manner with the hands higher than the elbow at a level slightly below that of the shoulder. The plates reproduced below illustrate, first, a couple holding hands in the customary manner, followed by the illustration from this passage in "la Mariée."

Rameau, *Le Maître,* Part I, Chapter 22.

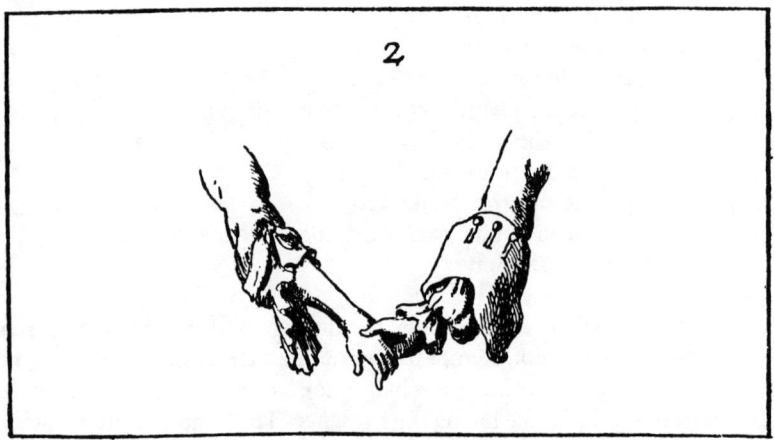

Fig. 27 (2). The Manner of taking Hands

In Rameau's notation, the dancers perform all of the first six step-units to the side, crossing each pas de bourrée behind and behind. The pas de bourrée crossing behind create a more expansive, open circle, which is reflected in the high, rounded arms.

In this passage, Feuillet scrupulously notates the coupé simple to first position with dots to indicate that the step-unit finishes in demi-pointe. This refinement is not found in Rameau's notation of the passage. In the analogous step-unit in measure 73, Feuillet uses the dots in one part only, and in the other example of a coupé to first position in preparation for a pas de rigaudon in this collection, in "le Rigaudon des Vaisseaux," Feuillet does not use the dots. I suspect that this is an example of inconsistent use of notation, rather than any difference in the performance of the steps.

Rameau, *Abbrégé,* Part II, p. 14.

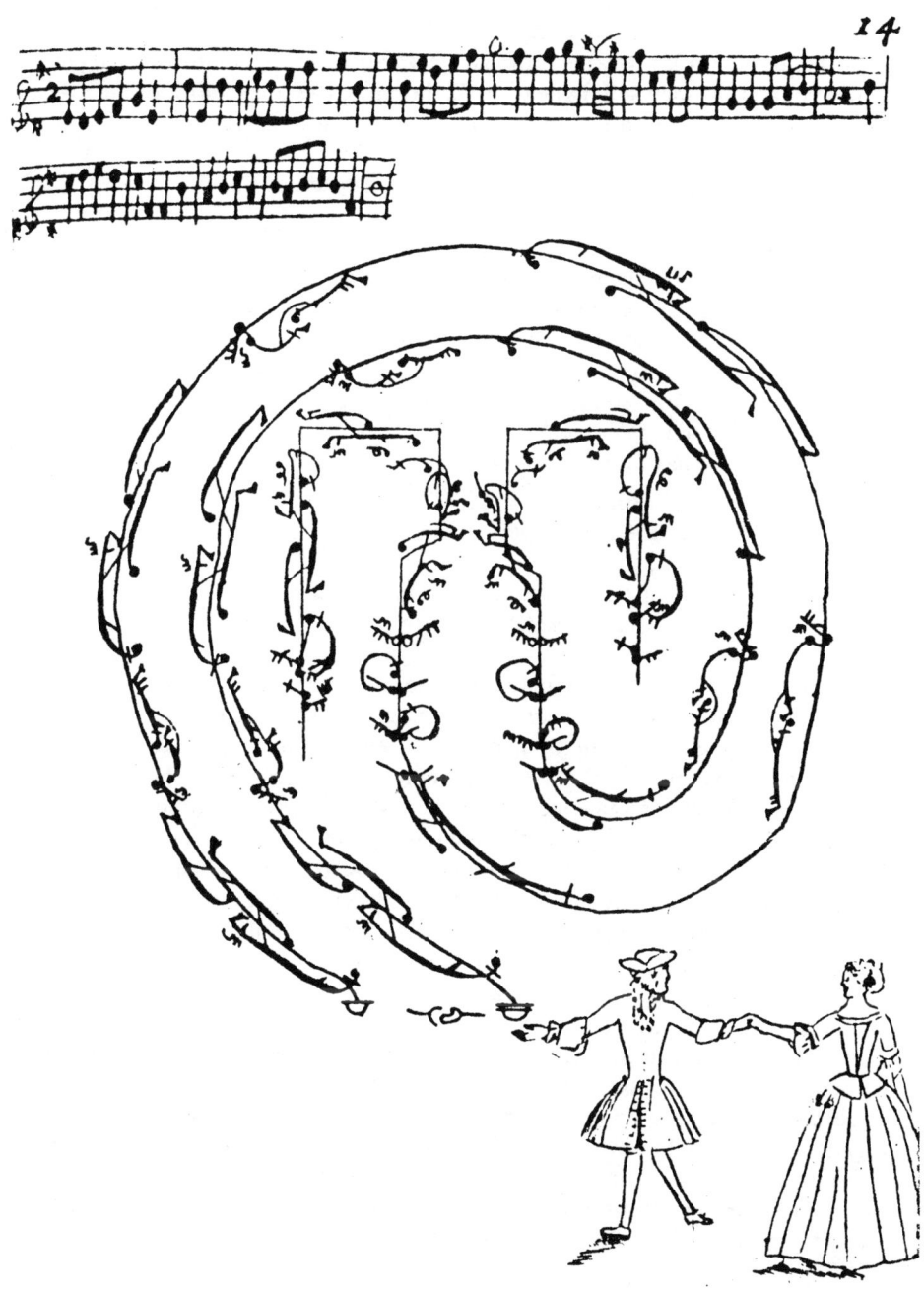

52   La Mariée

After the pas de rigaudon, the dancers return to a symmetrical floor pattern which they begin on opposite feet. At the end of this figure, the lady makes a modified pas de sissonne so that the dancers can begin the next figure, another circle, with the same foot. The lady performs the same modified pas de sissonne that she used in measure 52, bringing the free front foot out and back into fifth position in front for the landing on the assemblé.

Pécour 1700, Pp. 18 (cont.)-19, Measures 67-80

step-units: pas de bourrée to the side
contretemps ballonné to the side
pas de bourrée forward
contretemps ballonné forward
pas de bourrée forward
contretemps ballonné forward
coupé soutenue forward
pas de rigaudon

glissades
coupé avec ouverture de jambe to the side
glissades
coupé soutenue to the side/coupé soutenue
    sans poser le corps to the side

On the repetition of the first strain, the dancers perform the first six step-units in a counterclockwise circle, finishing the last contretemps ballonné facing the Présence (pas de bourrée, contretemps ballonné, pas de bourrée, contretemps ballonné, pas de bourrée, contretemps ballonné). The dancers continue with a coupé soutenue forward to first position on demi-pointe;[16] and a pas de rigaudon, landing from the first saut with the weight on the inside foot.

Then the dancers perform a pair of glissades crossing first behind and then before; a coupé avec ouverture de jambe to the left; and return with a pair of glissades crossing first behind and then before; and a coupé soutenue crossing behind to the right. The lady's coupé soutenue is made sans poser le corps in preparation for the quarter-turn and coupé soutenue toward the partner which concludes the strain.

In this figure, the dancer faces a discrepancy between Feuillet and Rameau analogous to that found in measure 53-58 of this dance. In Feuillet's notation, the dancers make a pas de bourrée behind and before and a contretemps ballonné to the right side, followed by a pas de bourrée, contretemps ballonné, pas de bourrée, and contretemps ballonné forward.

In Rameau's notation, all six step-units are taken to the side, crossing each pas de bourrée behind and behind. The dancers take hands in the same elevated position used in the circle in the preceding figure. The dancers do not let go hands until the coupé soutenue forward in measure 80.

Tomlinson points out that a pair of glissades "is seldom if ever without the Half Coupee sideways following it."[17] This observation is borne out by "la Mariée," where glissades in measure 17 are followed by a coupé to the side sans poser le corps, and, in this strain, by a coupé to the side avec ouverture de jambe. Rameau describes this combination of step-units, found also in "la Contredance," measures 13-16, in "la Savoye," measures 3-4, in the following passage:

> ...this *temps* [the ouverture de jambe] is made very slowly after a *pas* which has been executed quickly. This affords a variety that denotes a good taste in dancing by investing the slow *pas* with gravity and the quick one with lightness.[18]

The dancer does not transfer the weight of the body on the pas glissé of the coupé soutenue forward which closes this strain. This can only be determined from the beginning of the next strain in Feuillet's notation, where the foot which had just made the pas glissé must be free to perform the contretemps de chaconne.

Pécour 1700, P. 20, Measures 81-92

step-units: contretemps de chaconne
pas de bourrée ouvert
demi-contretemps backward
modified contretemps ballonné
pas de sissonne forward
pas de sissonne forward
coupé simple forward

pirouette avec saut
pirouette avec saut
contretemps de gavotte sans poser le corps
    forward/contretemps de gavotte sans poser
    le corps backward
contretemps de gavotte backward/contretemps
    de gavotte forward
pas de sissonne backward/pas de sissonne
    forward

To open the second reprise, the dancers make a contretemps de chaconne away from each other with a quarter-turn in the air to face the Présence on the saut and the second pas marché crossed into fifth position behind, a pas de bourrée ouvert, a demi-contretemps backward, a modified contretemps ballonné forward, a pair of pas de sissonne forward landing from the second saut of each pas with the weight on the front foot, and a quarter-turn and coupé forward toward the partner.

The dancers continue with a half-turn pirouette avec saut in the direction of the Présence, landing with the weight on the foot which made the demi-coupé in the preceding measure, bringing the free foot into first position on the landing. This is followed by another half-turn pirouette avec saut completing the circle, landing with the weight on the same foot. The gentleman brings his free foot around to fourth position in front as the lady brings her foot to the fourth position in back.

The gentleman then makes a contretemps de gavotte forward without transferring the weight on the last pas marché, a contretemps de gavotte backward, and a pas de sissonne backward landing from the second saut with the weight on the foot which is behind. At the same time, the lady makes a contretemps de gavotte backward without transferring the weight on the last pas marché, a contretemps de gavotte forward, and a pas de sissonne forward landing from the second saut with the weight on the foot which is behind.

The pas in measure 84 is composed of a hop on the inside foot, bringing the outside foot around to fourth position en l'air behind in landing, and a jeté forward. The position of the free leg on the first saut distinguishes this pas from the conventional contretemps ballonné.

The performance of the pirouettes avec sauts in measures 88-89 should follow Rameau's directions in *Le Maître à Danser*.[19] He describes each pirouette as a hop with a turn in the air landing on the foot on which the initial plié has been made. The foot which does not bear the weight contributes a graceful, leisurely quality to the pas, participating in the initial plié, while resting the toe on the ground, and then stretching the knee and extending the leg during the saut. The extended leg follows the body in the turn to close in first position after the weight-bearing foot has landed from the saut.

The cadence of the pirouette avec saut is not given by Rameau, and the pas itself is not discussed by Tomlinson, Dufort, or Taubert. However, Feuillet's "Traité de la Cadence" in the 1704 *Recueil* includes an analogous pas without the turn, which is reproduced below.[20]

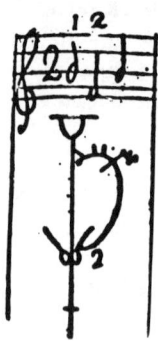

This cadence effectively serves pirouette avec saut, which lands from the saut on the downbeat while moving the extended leg to close at the beginning of the second half of the measure.

Pécour generally choreographs a pair of pirouettes. In this case, after the first pirouette, the extended leg does not bear any weight upon closing, but rests with the toe on the ground while making the initial plié of the second pirouette. The weight is transferred upon closing the extended leg at the end of the second pirouette.

The preparation for the pirouette avec saut is made with the weight on one foot. Thus, the dancer should transfer no weight on the last pas of the coupé in measure 87. The plié for the first pirouette avec saut is made with both knees, in the fourth position and with all of the weight resting on the foot which is behind.

Feuillet indicates this with a pied en l'air sign on the pirouette itself. Rameau's less ambiguous notation of this passage uses a coupé sans poser corps in measure 87,[21] and the preparatory plié with both knees as one leg supports all of the weight is clearly described in his chapter about the pirouette.[22] Both notators indicate that the foot which closes into first position to complete the first pirouette avec saut should bear no weight.

Pécour 1700, P. 21, Measures 93-104

step-units: pas de bourrée backward
                pas de bourrée emboîté turning
                pas de sissonne forward
                pas de bourrée emboîté turning
                coupé simple
                pas de rigaudon + pas marché

                contretemps de côté
                modified contretemps de chaconne
                pas de sissonne bâtu backward/pas de
                    sissonne forward
                pas de bourrée backward/pas de
                    bourrée forward
                closing coupé soutenue

The dancers open the final strain with a pas de bourrée backward curving away from the partner, a pas de bourrée emboîté turning a half-turn to the right on the first two steps, a pas de sissonne forward landing from the second saut with the weight on the foot which is behind, a pas de bourrée emboîté turning a half-turn to the left on the first two steps, a coupé simple forward to first position, and a pas de rigaudon with a pas marché opening the outside foot to second position after the final saut.

The dancers continue with a contretemps de côté crossing the first pas marché into fifth position in front, pointing the toe to second position for the second pas marché but transferring no weight, a modified contretemps de côté in the opposite direction with the final pas marché à pied en l'air to second position for the gentleman, and a pas to fourth position in front for the lady. The gentleman completes the strain with a pas de sissonne bâtu backward, a pas de bourrée backward, and a closing coupé soutenue, as the lady executes a pas de sissonne forward, a pas de bourrée forward, and a closing coupé soutenue turning a half-turn to face the Présence on the first pas.

The turning pas de bourrée emboîté in measures 94 and 96 are executed in the same manner as that in measure 41 described above. The timing and the uninterrupted motion of the steps before the hesitation produce the impression of a single half-turn rather than the two quarter-turns which are notated.

The contretemps de côté is a variant of the contretemps de gavotte taken to the side in which the first pas marché is crossed in fifth position. Rameau describes the contretemps de côté in *Le Maître,* Part I, Chapter 38, where he states his preference for making the initial plié in second position with the weight on both feet.

In measure 99, the pas marché into second position after the pas de rigaudon facilitates this plié. Analogous adjustments to prepare the contretemps de côté may be found in "la Contredance" (measure 23, 29, and 31), "le Rigaudon des Vaisseaux" (measure 16), "la Savoye" (measure 14), and "la Conty" (measure 32).

The gentleman's pas de sissonne bâtu in measure 102 is identical to that in measure 12 described above, with the exception of the half-turn on the initial saut, which does not reappear in the final strain. In both cases, one must decide if the leg with the pied en l'air in the preceding measure should participate in the plié before the initial saut of the pas de sissonne.

In measure 12, it seems clear that the free leg does not plié and that its continuous motion contributes momentum to the turn in the air. Similarly, in measure 102, the pas de sissonne is much more difficult to perform if the gentleman stops the motion of the free leg in second position en l'air before the plié. I feel the pas is most successful if the dancer continues to move the free leg out to second position and perhaps even a bit behind as he makes the plié on the other foot.

Rameau writes that "la Mariée," "being known all the world over, may be justly termed one of the finest dances ever seen."[23] Certainly "la Mariée" was among Louis Pécour's best-known dances, and one which was widely admired in its day. It is cited frequently, not only by eighteenth-century dancing masters, but also by writers in other disciplines like Johann Mattheson, who hands down the curious theory of the derivation of the title, "la Mariée," from its dedication to and appropriateness for ladies of stout build, which he admits is probably conjecture.[24]

This dance also became the center of a small craze, as other choreographers sought to capitalize on the popularity of Pécour's original by publishing other choreographies with variations upon the title. These choreographies include Feuillet's "La Nouvelle Mariée," published in his annual collection for the year 1708, and two which appear only in manuscript sources, "La nouvelle mariée" and "La seconde et nouvelle mariée," Paris, Bibliothèque Nationale, Msfr.14.884, pp. 49-64.

The phenomenon of an original "la Mariée" and at least three choreographed reflections explains the reference by Louis Bonin,[25] who seems to consider "la Mariée" not just a standard nor even a household word, but the beginning of a new dance type.

"La Mariée" is the only dance in Pécour's 1700 *Recueil* which Rameau mentions by name in *Le Maître à Danser*. While serving as an indication of the relative importance of "la Mariée" in the 1700 *Recueil*, Rameau's references also provide additional information concerning the execution of the dance, which I have outlined below.

In Part I, Chapter 39, Rameau writes that, of the several different kinds of chassés, the easiest (those made de côté beginning in the second position) are those most used in ballroom dances such as "la Mariée," "L'Allemande," and "La Babette." Rameau's description of the performance of such a chassé appears earlier in the present chapter on page 47.

In the second part of *Le Maître*, Rameau describes the movements of the arms and their standard, formulaic use with each step-unit. He also describes passages in which the standard arm movements for a step-unit must be altered as a result of the step-unit's context within the phrase. Two of these exceptions are drawn from "la Mariée."

The first example concerns the arm movements for the beaten pas de sissonne en tournant in measure 12. Rameau's instructions are given below:

> In the case of *pas de sissonne* made *en tournant*, the opposite arm must be used for the turn—there are many such examples in ballroom dances. For instance, at the end of the first strain of *La Mariée*, where there are *two contretemps de côté* with the right foot; the left arm, which is in opposition, in extending causes you by its movement to make the half turn to the left. But as the right foot crosses behind, the right arm also bends, in contrast with the left foot in front.
>
> As a general rule, in *pas en tournant*, the arm of the side to which you turn gives you impetus, for by its motion it obliges the body to turn on the side towards which it extends.[26]

His general rule that extending the arm may be used to facilitate the turn is also the basis of his reference to the use of arms in the chassés in measures 31 and 34 of "la Mariée."

> Having given you all the simplest ways of executing all kinds of *chassés* in social dances, it is also necessary to explain the method of moving the arms in different ways.

> I shall begin with those used in *La Mariée* which, being known all the world over, may be justly termed one of the finest dances ever seen.
>
> These *chassés* occur at the beginning of the third strain, where they are preceded by a *coupé;* therefore, in this *coupé,* you bend both arms and extend them at the first movement of the *chassé.* But at the second, in which you rise on the foot contrary to that which has driven the other, the arm on the side of the rising foot bends, because at the end of this pas there is generally a *pas en tournant;* and, as I have already said in the chapter on *pirouettes,* the arm makes it easy for the body to turn on the side to which it is extended, and for this reason this opposition is made. For, if it were as in the *Allemande,* where several are made in succession, there would be no opposition. It is true that there is no movement of the arms in the *chassés* of that dance, because it is quite characteristic.[27]

In addition to the information in *Le Maître* concerning the arm movements for "la Mariée," Rameau renotates the dance in *L'Abbrégé,* providing an illustration for an unusual elevation of the arms while taking hands which literally keeps the dancers at arms' length in this passage. This illustration is reproduced earlier in the present chapter (page 51).

A dance as widely known and well-liked as Pécour's "la Mariée" naturally leads one to wonder what might account for this popularity. Examining the dance with this in mind, I find no single explanation, but among its noteworthy qualities there is something to satisfy almost every taste and many depths of understanding.

"La Mariée's" technical challenges make it both remarkable and appealing. Every dance in Pécour's 1700 *Recueil* places technical demands on the dancer, but in "la Mariée" some of these demands are more readily obvious: a brilliant, quick, strong technique is necessary just to execute the notated steps. Its ornamental battements and its leaps with turns in the air place it among those court dances whose technique approaches that demanded of professional theater dancers. This technique contributes to "la Mariée's" character of a brilliant finale.

Once the dancer has mastered his beats and turns, he can also appreciate Pécour's attention to intensity in the construction of the line. One of the most gratifying phrases to dance, in this regard, is that which opens the first repetition of the first strain of music, beginning in measure 15. Here, the beaten demi-coupés in place produce an explosion of bright activity leading to glissades up the room and a slow coupé, in which forward motion and rapid movement are momentarily held back, to be released again in the turning pas de bourrée. The line of movement which began with the beaten demi-coupés does not really pause until the assemblé in measure 20.

This assemblé brings up Pécour's choice of step-units to end phrases in "la Mariée." Rameau and Tomlinson mention only two step-units which they feel inherently possess the finality of a phrase-ending: the assemblé[28] and the temps or point.[29] Each of these step-units is used in the course of this musical strain to mark an internal pause: the assemblé, in measure 20, and the temps, in measure

23. However, for the ends of six of the seven musical strains,[30] Pécour employs either a pas de sissonne or a contretemps ballonné. In my opinion, this choice contributes significantly to "la Mariée's" ebullient quality, giving the impression of dancers who have the energy to bound on into the next strain.

This phrase also introduces the turning pas de bourrée, a step-unit of increasing fascination in the course of "la Mariée." In its first appearance, the turning pas de bourrée affects one principally as a release of the movement held back in the preceding coupé. When it next appears, as a pas de bourrée emboîté in measure 41 opening the repetition of the second strain of music, Pécour emphasizes, instead, its dramatic possibilities as a change of direction. For a moment, the dancer appears to use the step-unit to drop hands and turn away from his partner, but then it becomes clear that he does this only to give his partner his other hand and repeat the preceding figure in the opposite direction.

Later in that strain, in measure 51, another turning pas de bourrée is used when the dancer finally does turn away from his partner to face the Présence. Here, as in its first appearance in measure 19, the turning pas de bourrée is the penultimate step-unit of the phrase.

The turning pas de bourrée emboîté reappears in "la Mariée's" final strain in a figure which serves both as an intensified expression of the dancer's choice between his partner and the Présence, and as one of Pécour's loveliest floor patterns to watch. The dancers begin facing each other with a pas de bourrée backwards, backing away from each other on an arc which approaches a line from the Présence through the center of the room. With the pas de bourrée emboîté in measure 94, the dancer turns his back on his partner, the lady facing the Présence and the gentleman facing down the room. The movement in this direction is immediately checked by a pas de sissonne and then, in measure 96, the dancers employ another pas de bourrée emboîté to turn to face the partner again in order to dance toward the partner and the center of the room along the line they approached in their arc in measures 93-95.

The matter of the dancer's focus on his partner or the Présence is an element in every danse à deux. "La Mariée" demands a particularly indulgent Présence, because he is denied even a slight glance over the shoulder until the point of the toe in his direction at the end of the pirouette in measure 8. The dancers do not face the Présence at all until they are well into the repetition of the first strain of music, on the assemblé in measure 20. This fact lends further importance to that assemblé and makes this an even more satisfying phrase for the Présence.

In this dance, as a whole, the dancers seem to solve the problem of partner versus Présence by delighting the Présence with engaging patterns and intricate steps while directly acknowledging him rarely. After the illuminating results of the turning pas de bourrée in the last strain, one senses that the final turn to the Présence is really only a convention in "la Mariée."

60   La Mariée

In choosing this Lully tune, Pécour set himself the additional hurdle of choreographing a fourteen-measure musical strain which is divided into sections of five, four, and five measures. His solution, in the opening fourteen measures, is the superimposition of a danced strain of six, two, and six measures.

The pair of pirouettes at the top of the room with the hesitation while pointing to the Présence is the two-measure keystone. The first six-measure group is composed of an unusual three-measure tombé sequence and its repetition, traveling sideways up the room. The last six-measure group is composed of the three step-units traveling back down the room and the three performed in place after the turn to face the partner again.

This phrase is one in which the dance, at first glance, only adds complexity to an already asymmetrical musical situation. For the first fourteen measures the boundaries of the internal phrases which one hears never correspond to those which one sees. It is a phrase which is not easily appreciated by an audience of laymen, but one which might delight that audience of dancers for whom it was written. It is a credit to Pécour's taste and good sense that he does not attempt to top this feat in the next three statements of the musical strain, the choreography of each of which reflects the musical structure with increasing clarity.

La Mariée

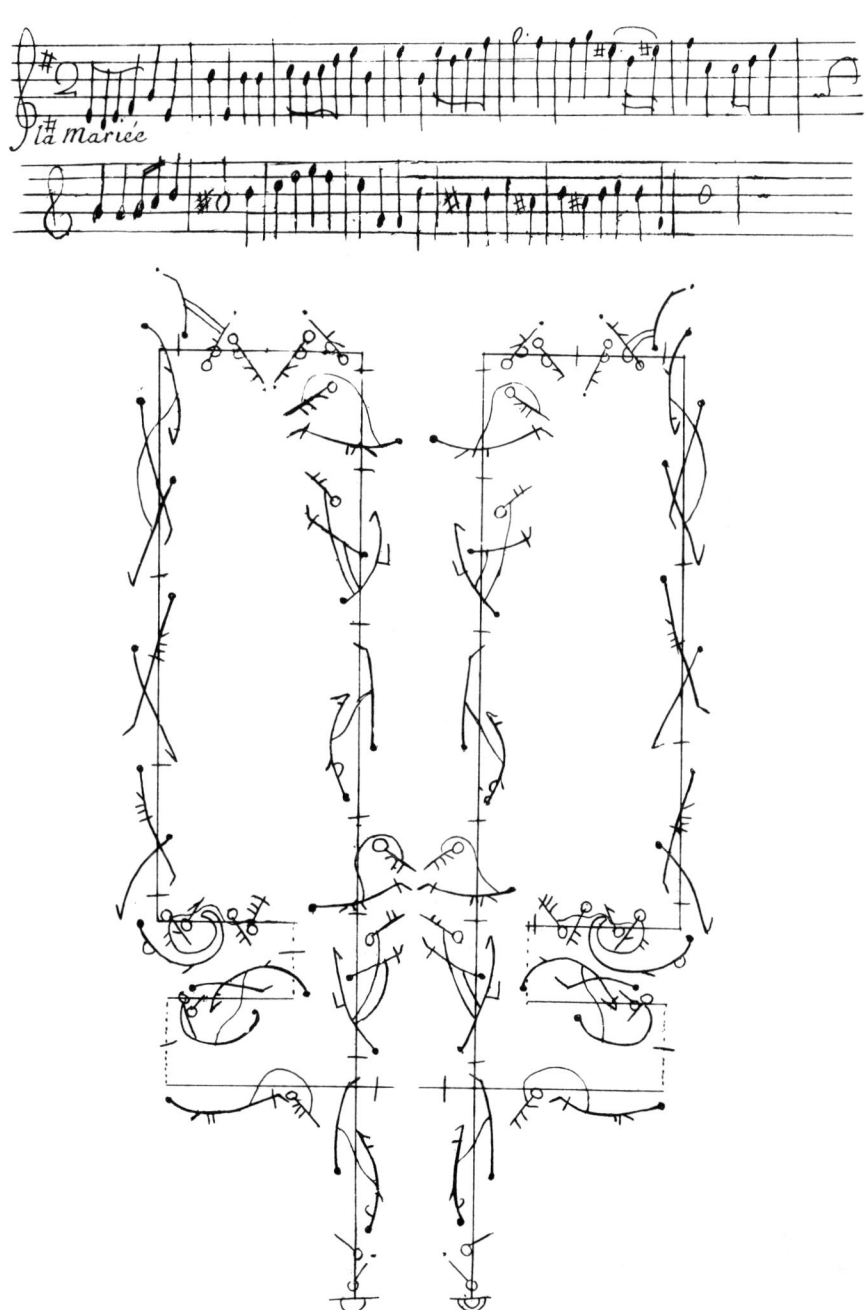

La Mariée

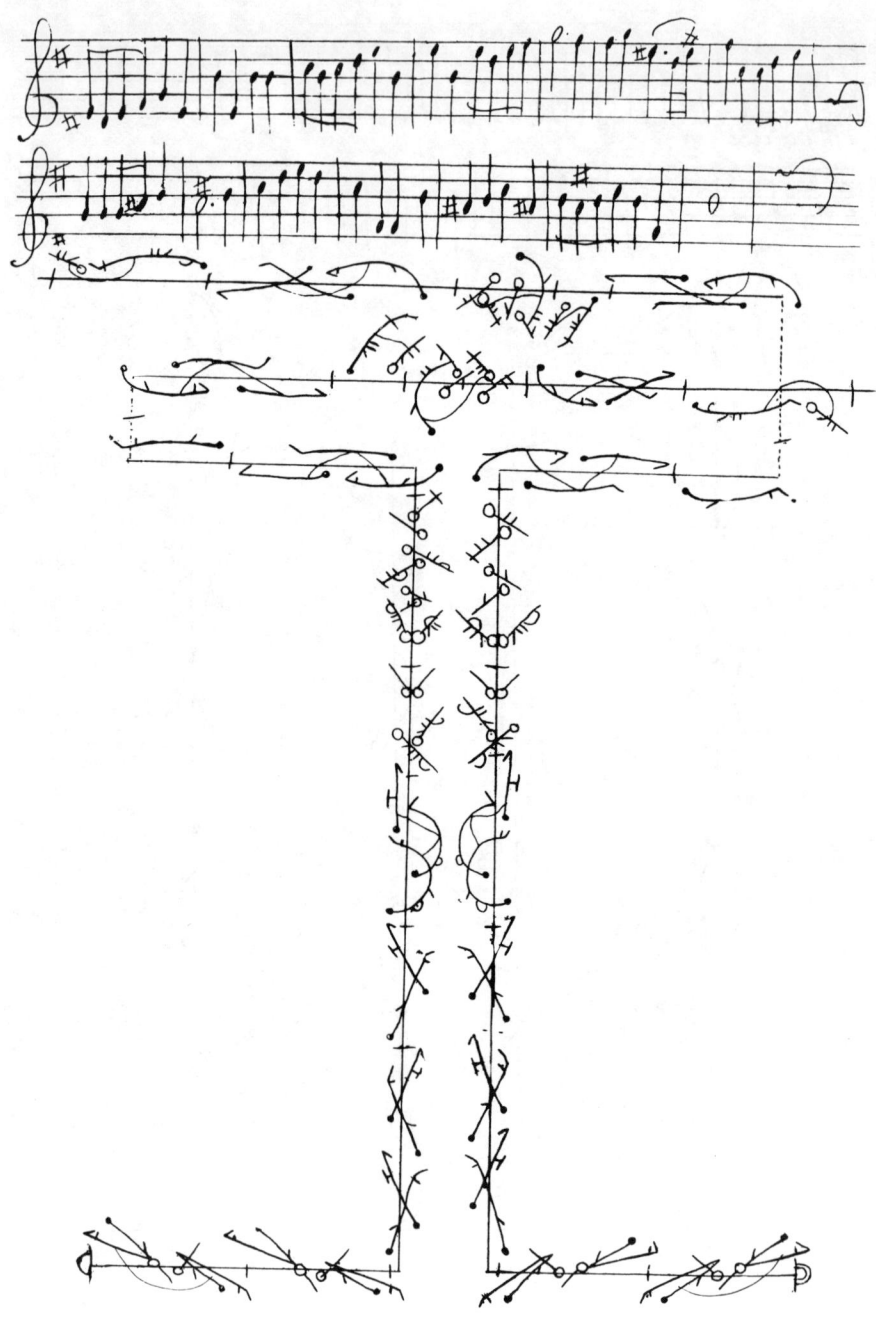

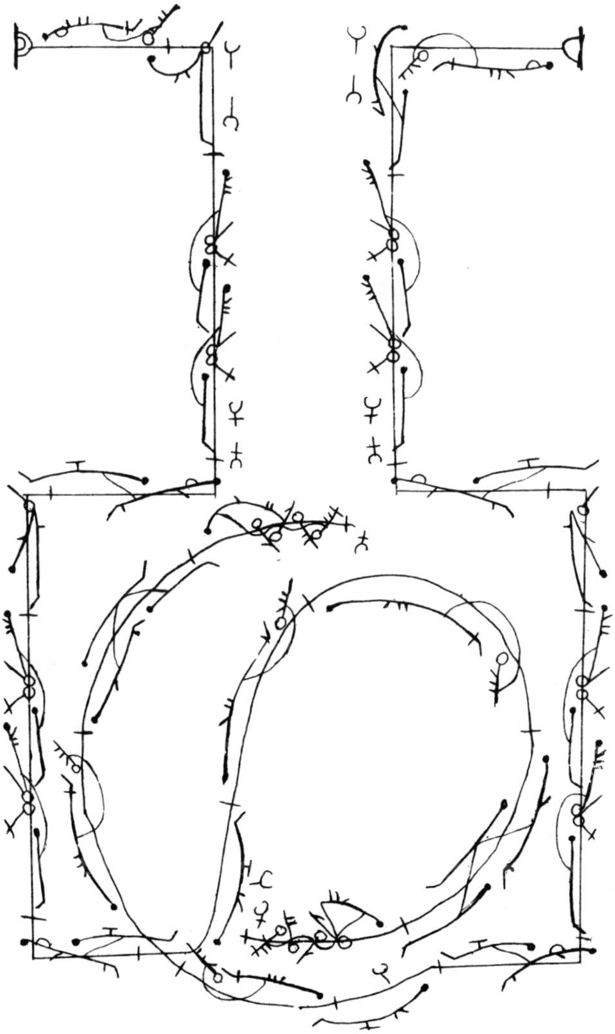

La Mariée 63

64   *La Mariée*

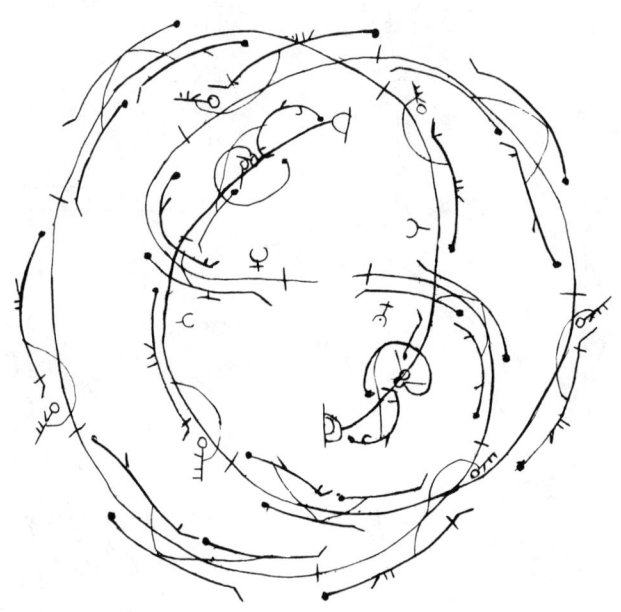

La Mariée

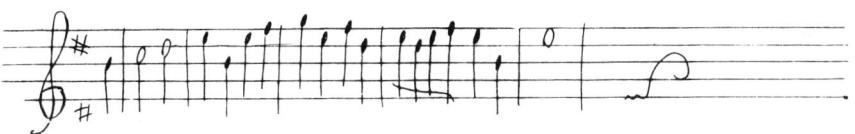

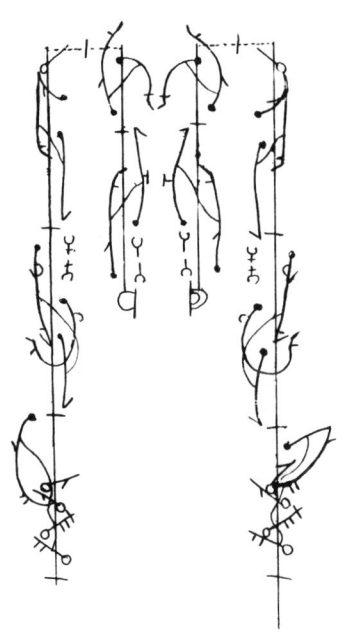

La Mariée

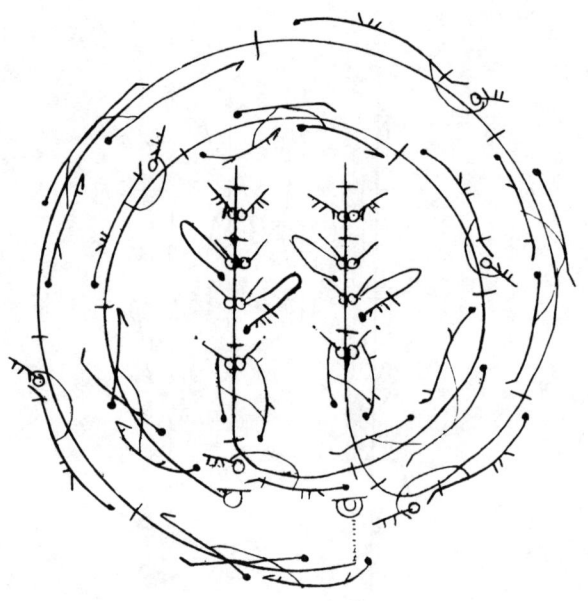

La Mariée   67

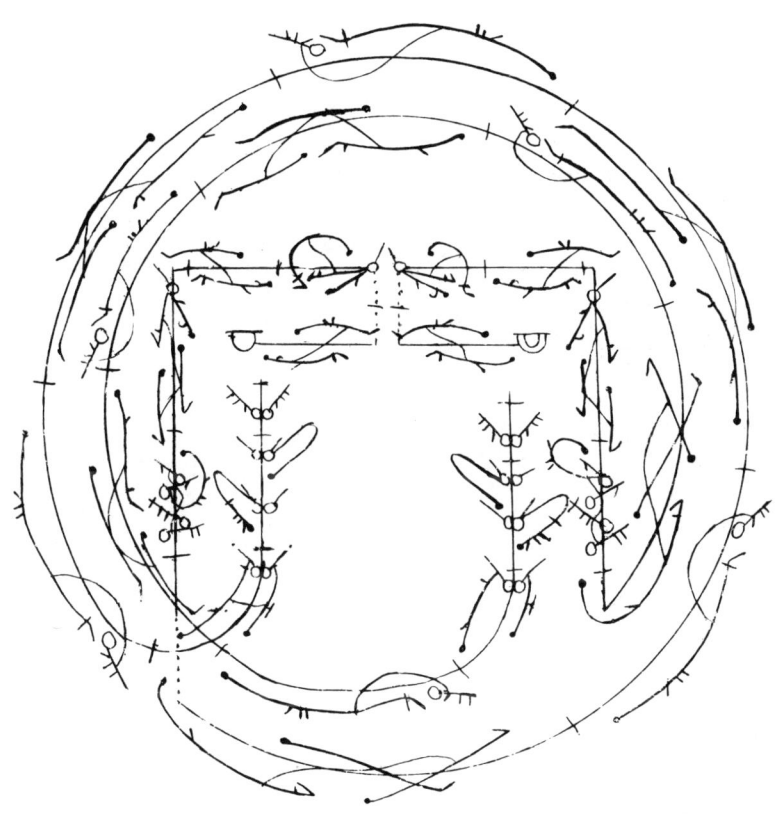

68 *La Mariée*

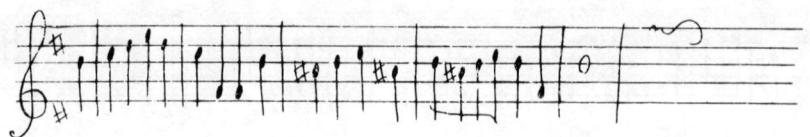

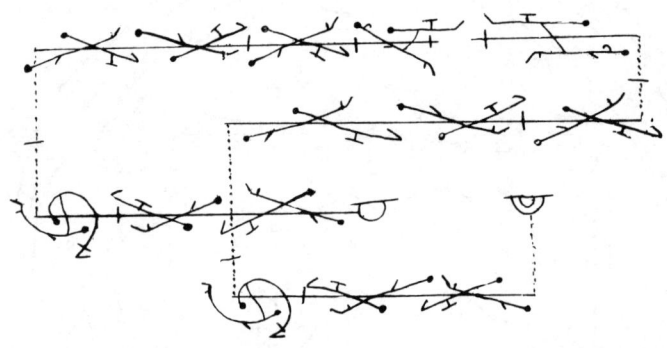

La Mariée 69

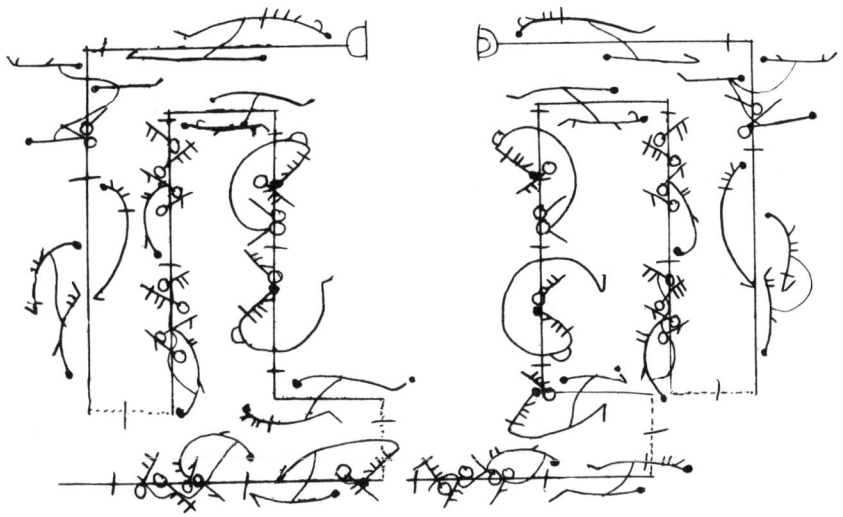

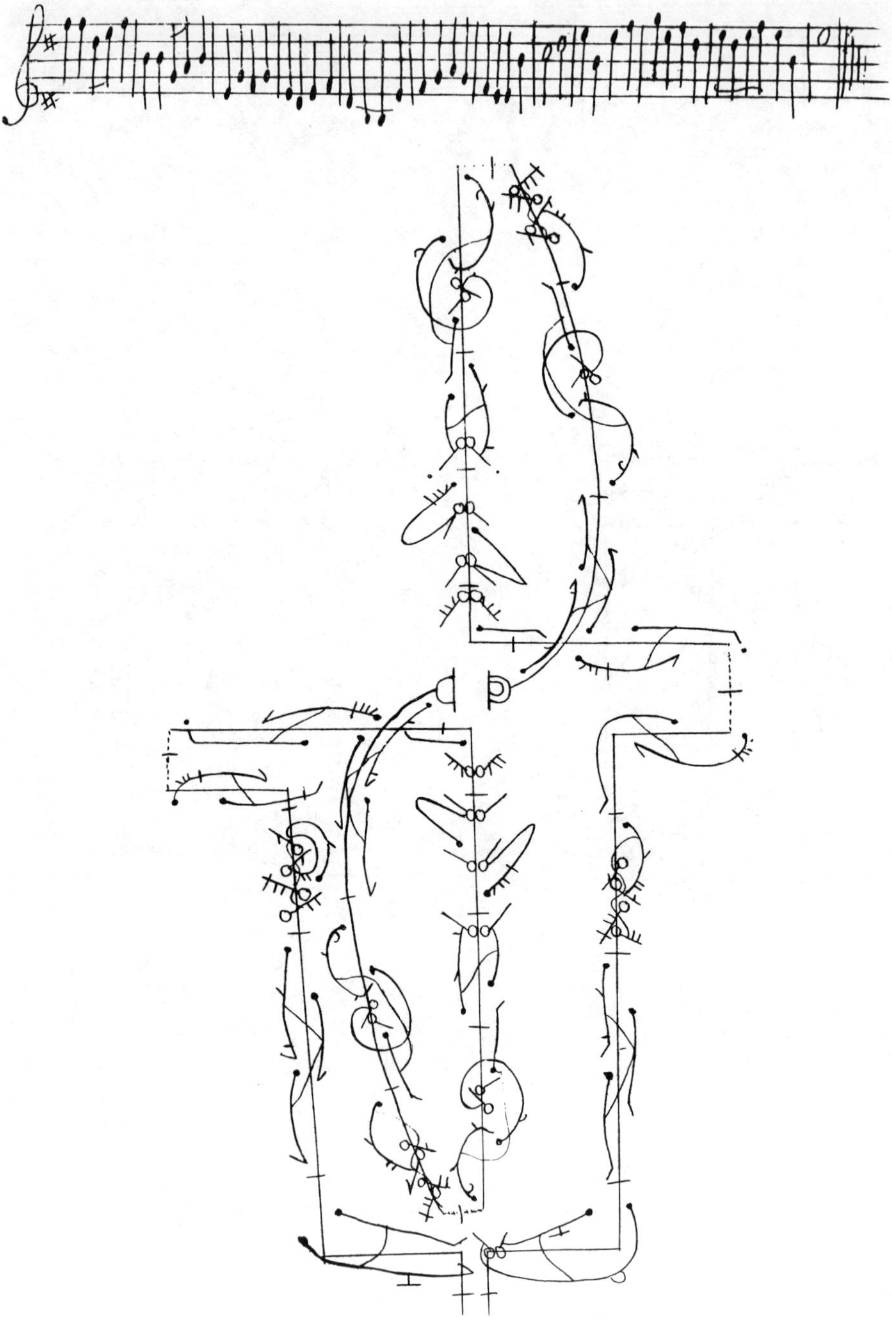

La Mariée

3

Le Passepied

The passepied is unique among the French court dances of Pécour's time, because it is defined in terms of another dance, the menuet. Brossard even says that the passepied is a menuet.[1] Although most theorists do not go that far, the passepied, as a dance, has remained in the shadow of the menuet, which was danced for a longer span of time and is, consequently, better documented.

"Le Passepied" by Pécour was one of the most popular figured passepieds. It was renotated by Rameau in France,[2] mentioned by early eighteenth-century German dancing masters,[3] and included in at least one later eighteenth-century Spanish source.[4] One may assume that it is the sort of passepied described by writers as a menuet or as something very like a menuet.

After a description of the performance of "le Passepied," I will examine both its similarities to the menuet and its distinguishing characteristics and consider whether this dance is distinct enough to merit a separate identity.

le Passepied

A	♪♫♫♫♫ ♫♫♫♫ ♫♫ ♫♫♫♫ ♫♫♫♫♩									
• m.1	{m3 / m2}	{m2 / m3}	ctm	m3		• m.65	b	1	m3	m2	m3
• Arpt										
m.9	{m3 / m2}	{m2 / m3}	ctm	m3		• m.73	b	1	m3	m2	m3
B	♪♫♫ ♫♫ ♫♫♫♫ ♫♫ ♫♫♫♫ ♫♫ ♫♫♫♫♩									
⎧ m.17	m3	m3	m3	m3		m.81	ctm	m3	ctm	m3
⎨ Brpt										
⎩ m.25	m3	m3	m3	{m2(?) / m3}		m.89	m3	m2	m3	m3

Le Passepied

2ᵉ Passepied

A'										
• m.33	b	1	m3	m2	ctm	∗ m.97	b	1	m2	m3	b	1
A'·rpt										
m.41	m3	m3	m3	m3		m.105	m3	m3	m3	m3
B'										
m.49	m3	m3	m3	m3		• m.113	ctm	m3	ctm	m3
B'·rpt										
m.57	m3	m3	m3	m3		■ m.121	ctm	m3	ctm	c1.

Pécour 1700, P. 22, Measures 1-16

step-units: pas de menuet of 3 mouvements to the side/
of 2 mouvements to the side
pas de menuet of 2 mouvements to the side/
of 3 mouvements to the side
contretemps de menuet forward
pas de menuet of 3 mouvements forward
pas de menuet of 3 mouvements to the side/
of 2 mouvements to the side
pas de menuet of 2 mouvements to the side/
of 3 mouvements to the side
contretemps de menuet forward
pas de menuet of 3 mouvements forward

    To open the dance, the dancers perform a pas de menuet to the side away form the partner, followed by a pas de menuet to the side toward the partner. The gentleman has a pas de menuet of three movements to the left behind and behind, followed by a pas de menuet of two movements to the right behind and before. The lady has a pas de menuet of two movements to the right behind and behind, followed by a pas de menuet of three movements to the left behind and behind. Both dancers continue with a contretemps de menuet and pas de menuet of three movements forward.

    During the repetition of the musical phrase, the dancers repeat the steps and floor pattern of the preceding figure.

    Dances which begin with a pas de menuet pose a problem, because both dancers must make their first step onto the right foot, making strict symmetrical opposition impossible. The dancers begin "le Passepied" in the fourth position with the inside foot in front. Feuillet notates the starting position so that both dancers have the weight on the front foot. This is probably an error; Rameau corrected it in his notation of the dance in *Abbrégé,* where the starting position is the same, but each dancer begins with the weight on the left foot, leaving the right foot free for the first pas de menuet.[5]

Pécour 1700, P. 23, Measures 17-32

step-units: pas de menuet of 3 mouvements forward
              pas de menuet of 3 mouvements forward
              pas de menuet of 3 mouvements forward
              pas de menuet of 3 mouvements forward/
                 of 3 turning to the side
              pas de menuet of 3 mouvements forward
              pas de menuet of 3 mouvements forward
              pas de menuet of 3 mouvements forward
              pas de menuet of 2 mouvements forward/
                 of 3 mouvements forward

During the second reprise and its repetition, the dancers give both hands and circle each other in three pas de menuet forward. On the fourth pas the dancers drop one hand as the lady makes a turning pas in place and the gentleman continues his pas de menuet forward. At the fifth pas the lady joins the gentleman in pas forward, tracing a larger circle down the room which finishes, at the end of the eighth pas, with both dancers facing the Présence.

Upon giving hands at the beginning of this figure, the gentleman turns in toward the partner so that his back is toward the Présence and finishes his first pas de menuet facing the Présence, with the lady facing down the room. At the end of the second pas forward, their positions are reversed. The third pas forward travels only a quarter-circle so that the dancers finish the pas with the Présence on the lady's right.

On the fourth pas, the lady executes a half-turn left on her first demi-coupé, a quarter-turn on her second demi-coupé into second position. She finishes the pas to the side crossing the pas marché into fifth position behind with a demi-jeté to second position. The purpose of this step is not to travel, but to drop one hand and allow the gentleman to catch up to her so that the couple may continue the rest of the figure side by side. With a quarter-turn left on the first demi-coupé of the fifth pas, the lady resumes pas forward with the gentleman, which continue through the seventh pas.

In the eighth and final pas of this figure, we find a device which is also employed in the passepied of "la Bourgogne" to get the dancers from a figure in

74 Le Passepied

which they circle together to a position in which they are both facing the Présence. The dancer on the inside of the circle crosses in front on the first demi-coupé and completes a pas to the right, while the partner on the outside of the circle continues his pas forward until he is even with the partner and facing the Présence.

In this instance, the lady on the inside has a pas of three movements to the left, while the gentleman's part is notated by Feuillet as a pas of two movements forward. I believe this is an error. When the figure is repeated in measures 49-64, the outside dancer finishes with a pas forward of three movements. In analogous places in the passepied in "la Bourgogne," the inside dancer has steps of two movements to the side, but the dancer on the outside continues pas of three movements forward.[6]

In *Abbrégé*, all the pas forward are pas of two movements,[7] but it is still significant that the outside dancer does not change the type of pas. It would seem an isolated instance of pure caprice to change the type of pas in a series of pas de menuet forward.

Pécour 1700, P. 24-25, Measures 33-48

step-units: balancé to the side
      pas de menuet of 3 mouvements left
      pas de menuet of 2 mouvements right
      contretemps de menuet forward
      pas de menuet of 3 mouvements left
      pas de menuet of 3 mouvements left
      pas de menuet of 3 mouvements left
      pas de menuet of 3 mouvements left

The second passepied tune begins with a balancé to the side, first to the right and then to the left; a pas of three movements to the left behind and behind; a pas of two movements to the right behind and before; and a contretemps forward. Rameau explains that in menuets and passepieds a balancé takes the time of one pas de menuet with the élevé of each demi-coupé on the downbeat of a measure.[8]

During the repetition of the first reprise, the dancers perform four pas of three movements to the left before and before, tracing a circular path and finishing the fourth pas facing the Présence, in a floor pattern analogous to that found in measures 53-58 and 67-72 of "la Mariée."

Pécour 1700, P. 26, Measures 49-64

step-units: pas de menuet of 3 mouvements forward
      pas de menuet of 3 mouvements forward

              pas de menuet of 3 mouvements forward
              pas de menuet of 3 mouvements turning to the side/
                of 3 mouvements forward
              pas de menuet of 3 mouvements forward
              pas de menuet of 3 mouvements forward
              pas de menuet of 3 mouvements forward
              pas de menuet of 3 mouvements forward

In the second reprise of the second passepied, the dancers perform the same pas and floor pattern that they did in the second reprise of the first passepied (measures 17-32), described above. This time, however, the lady is on the outside of the circle and the gentleman makes the turning pas. As noted above, Feuillet notates the eighth pas of this figure as a pas de menuet of three movements for each dancer.

              Pécour 1700, P. 27, Measures 65-80

step-units: balancé to the side
              pas de menuet of 3 mouvements left
              pas de menuet of 2 mouvements right
              pas de menuet of 3 mouvements forward
              balancé to the side
              pas de menuet of 3 mouvements left
              pas de menuet of 2 mouvements right
              pas de menuet of 3 mouvements forward

As the tune of the first passepied begins again, the dancers execute a balancé to the side, first to the right and then to the left; a pas of three movements left behind and behind; a pas of two movements right behind and behind; and a pas of three movements forward. The dancers repeat this sequence of pas and floor pattern with the repetition of the musical reprise, except that in measure 80 they let go hands and make the last pas of three movements forward on a curved path so that they finish facing each other with the Présence on the gentleman's left and the lady's right.

              Pécour 1700, P. 28, Measures 81-96

step-units: contretemps de menuet forward
              pas de menuet of 3 mouvements turning to the side
              contretemps de menuet forward
              pas de menuet of 3 mouvements forward
              pas de menuet of 3 mouvements forward

76   Le Passepied

>pas de menuet of 2 mouvements right
>pas de menuet of 3 mouvements forward
>pas de menuet of 3 mouvements forward

During the second reprise of the first passepied and its repetition, the dancers turn a quarter-turn in the direction of the partner and perform a contretemps down the room; a pas of three movements turning, during the course of which the dancers make three quarter-turns and finish facing the partner; a quarter-turn in the direction of the partner and a contretemps down the room; and a pas of three movements forward following a path curving away from the partner to finish facing the Présence. The dancers continue with a second pas of three movements forward toward the Présence; a quarter-turn to face the partner and a pas of two movements to the right behind and behind; and a quarter-turn right and two pas of three movements forward, circling to finish facing the partner, the gentleman facing down the room and the lady facing up the room.

The turning pas of three movements in measures 83-84 is performed in the following manner: the gentleman makes a quarter-turn right, placing his first demi-coupé so that it crosses in fifth position in front. With another quarter-turn right, he places his second demi-coupé in fourth position behind to make a demi-coupé backwards facing the Presénce, followed by another quarter-turn right to face the partner on the pas marché opening to second position down the room. He lands from the following demi-jeté crossing in fifth position in front.

The lady makes a quarter-turn left, placing her first demi-coupé opening into second position down the room. She makes another quarter-turn left to face the Présence and takes the second demi-coupé backward into fourth position. Feuillet has inadvertently omitted the turn sign from the following pas marché, but the angle of the foot indicates that the lady should make another quarter-turn left to face the partner and make the pas marché crossing in fifth position behind, followed by the demi-jeté into second position down the room.

In *Abbrégé*[9] this pas has been altered, so that the full turn is made in a pair of half-turns of the first two demi-coupés instead of the quarter-turn arrangement found in the 1700 *Recueil*.[10] In the 1700 version the turn takes more time, an effect which I prefer, but it seems to me that this particular decision may be dictated by the taste of the individual dancer. The change in *Abbrégé* seems to be neither the correction of a mistake nor a change of fashion, but an indication that Pécour had changed his mind.

Pécour 1700, P. 29, Measures 97-112

step-units: balancé to the side
pas de menuet of 2 mouvements right

pas de menuet of 3 mouvements forward
balancé to the side
pas de menuet of 3 mouvements left
pas de menuet of 3 mouvements forward
pas de menuet of 3 mouvements forward
pas de menuet of 3 mouvements forward

The dancers begin the second passepied tune with a balancé to the side, a pas of two movements to the right behind and behind, and a pas of three movements forward following a diagonal path forward to the center of the room. The dancers continue with a second balancé to the side, a pas of three movements to the left behind and behind, and three pas of three movements forward tracing a half-circle, so that the dancers finish facing the partner, as in the beginning of the figure, but at a greater distance.

Pécour 1700, P. 30-31, Measures 113-28

step-units: contretemps de menuet forward
pas de menuet of 3 mouvements forward
contretemps de menuet forward
pas de menuet of 3 mouvements forward
contretemps de menuet forward
pas de menuet of 3 mouvements forward
contretemps de menuet backward/contretemps
   de menuet forward
two coupés/pas de menuet of two
   mouvements forward + close

To begin the second reprise of the second passepied tune, the dancers make a half-turn to the right in the air during the initial hop of a contretemps forward, a pas of three movements forward, a contretemps and another pas of three movements forward. In this figure, the dancers trace a half-circle path to finish facing the partner in the place where the partner began the figure. As notated by both Feuillet and Rameau, the circular path begins at or near the beginning of the first contretemps so that the pas marché on the second beat is not directly up the room for the gentleman (nor down the room for the lady), but at an angle to the right. This necessitates either slightly more than a half-turn in the air or a continuation of the turning motion into the pas marché after the landing from the first saut.

The repetition of the second reprise begins in the same manner as the preceding figure, with a half-turn to the right in the air during the first hop of a contretemps forward, and pas of three movements forward. The gentleman then performs a contretemps backward and a closing pas as the lady continues with a contretemps forward and closing pas.

The pied en l'air at the end of the gentleman's pas of three movements in measure 124 indicates the movement of the free right leg while the left leg is engaged in landing from the demi-jeté on the sixth beat of this measure and the initial saut of the contretemps, which lands on the downbeat of the following measure. Upon landing from the demi-jeté, the right foot is brought forward into first position. In the rebound of the left leg into the air on the next saut, the right knee is straightened with the left and it continues to travel forward and then to make an ouverture de jambe which, upon landing on the left leg in a plié, continues back to make the pas of the contretemps backward. Thus, the gentleman's motion at the beginning of the contretemps backward is identical to that in the half-contretemps backward in "la Contredance" in measures 27-28.

The closing pas of this dance is a standard closing pas for passepieds which is also found at the conclusion of "la Bourgogne": two coupés backward for the gentleman, the second moving in toward the lady, and a pas de menuet of two movements forward for the lady with a half-turn on the final pas marché and a close into first position.

Clearly, the great similarity between "le Passepied" and the menuet lies in the pas composés, while significant differences are the matters of tempo and the focus of the floor patterns. Most remarkable, perhaps, is the similarity of pas composés. With the exception of the courante, menuet, and passepied, which have their own characteristic pas composés, all danses à deux are composed of a common vocabulary of about twenty pas composés, which may be adjusted to any tempo or metre.

The courante is invariably constructed upon a framework of temps de courante and a series of demi-jetés and coupés,[11] while the menuet is composed of pas de menuet and a few ornamental pas, of which the balancé and contretemps de menuet are most common.

The passepied is also composed exclusively of pas de menuet and of ornamental pas which can be introduced into the menuet ordinaire. Furthermore, in 1700, pas de menuet to the side in "le Passepied" exhibit those peculiarities found in the pas de menuet to the side in menuets: pas to the right are pas of two movements, and pas to the left are pas of three movements.[12] The distinguishing characteristic of the passepied noted in the vast majority of dance and musical sources is its faster tempo.

The phenomenon of two dances which employ the same few characteristic pas composés at different tempi invites speculation upon the origin of the dances. I have avoided this topic here, because the origin of a dance-type is a study fraught with problems whose solutions are not absolutely necessary in the reconstruction of Pécour's choreographies.

The principal stumbling block for researchers who seek the roots of eighteenth-century court dances in folk dances (or conversely, the roots of modern folk dances in the court dances of Versailles) is the fact that the performance of peasant dances in the seventeenth and eighteenth centuries is not documented. Consequently, one cannot know with certainty which elements of a modern folk dance were present in an earlier folk dance bearing the same name.

It is true that, for a variety of reasons, writers from Pécour's day to the present have connected some of the ball dances of the court of Louis XIV with regional French folk dances. The passepied is said to come from Bretagne, and the menuet is said to come from Poitou.

Rameau's comment concerning the relationship of court and folk dance in early eighteenth-century France is reproduced below:

> ...the majority of these different *pas* [composés] derive their nomenclature from the different dances common to our provinces, which have conferred on them all those properties which art permits and whose name they bear.[13]

In this passage, Rameau speaks primarily of an etymological link between folk and court dance. "Art" is the determining factor concerning those physical properties of the folk dances which might be allowed in court. Without a knowledge of the folk dances, one can only wonder whether the similarity of pas composés in the court passepieds and menuets stems from a hypothetical common folk dance which had variants in Poitou and Bretagne, or from the regulated art of dance technique taught by Beauchamp and his followers.

The reconstruction of the same pas composés as part of dance types at different tempi also raises the practical question of how the change of tempo affects the execution of the pas. None of the dancing masters of the period deals with the problem specifically with respect to the pas composés common to the menuet and passepied.

One modern approach to this question has been to take the tempo markings provided by eighteenth-century theorists for passepied and menuet music and see what happens to dance technique as a result.[14] This has not been an entirely successful experiment for the dance, because the tempi given by many of the theorists seem remarkably quick. Most of the tempo markings are considerably later than Pécour; and those of Pécour's contemporary, l'Affilard, have been called into question as being twice too fast as interpreted by many modern scholars.[15] In fact, the tempo markings may be more valuable as evidence concerning the later eighteenth-century use of dance as expression[16] or an evocation of passion or mood than they are practically applicable to the dances as they were performed by Louis XIV and his court.

For the purposes of this study, I will limit myself to a consideration of the variations in technique which are allowed and prohibited by Rameau in French

80 Le Passepied

ballroom dancing, as an indication of the possible differences in the performance of the pas composés in the menuet and passepied. The first inviolable element of his technique seems to be the carriage of the body, a mark of the dancer's nobility when standing, walking, or bowing which was not altered in noble dancing. The eighteenth-century nobleman cultivated a strong, serene posture which the dance technique was designed to preserve. The salutary effect of the study of regulated French technique upon one's general physical deportment was considered one of its principal values, not only in France, but in other countries as well.

Different postures were used in character and grotesque dances of the theatre, but these were performed by professional dancers and not by the nobles, who are warned by writers like Michel de Pure to keep their dancing within acceptable limits.[17] This attitude would seem to rule out, in the performance of "le Passepied," any reflection in the body of the quicker tempo, or certainly of the rash affect of the tempo as described by Mattheson.[18]

At least as essential to the French technique is the definition of the rhythm by means of the "movement" or plié and élevé. A common byproduct of dancing to very fast tempi is the elimination of the plié. Rameau does describe pliés of different depths in his treatment of the pas composés in *Le Maître*, although he is not very systematic about it.[19] From this and the importance of horizontal movement in the floor pattern in the passepied, discussed below, it seems reasonable that, in the passepied, the pliés might be both quicker and slightly shallower than those in the menuet. At the same time, the necessity of making a distinct plié, place, and élevé limits the speed at which the passepied might be danced.

A slight difference in the depth of the plié seems to be a sufficient adjustment for the performance of a pas de menuet at a passepied tempo. The contretemps de menuet, however, presents problems which suggest that its performance may differ in a more significant manner depending upon the tempo.

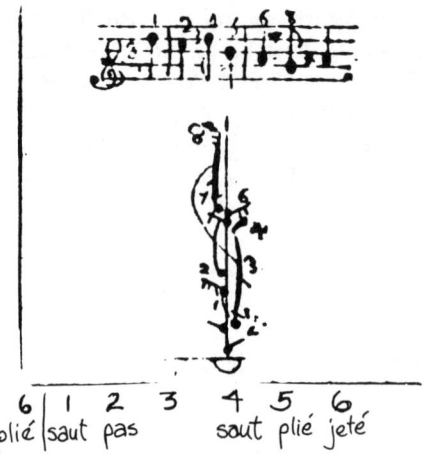

Rameau gives this timing for the contretemps de menuet[20] and the following description:

> It contains three different kinds of *sauts* or hops. One is made before the *pas*, the second after the *pas*, and the third during the *pas*.
>
> The first occurs when you have concluded your *pas de menuet*. As you finish it with the left foot, you transfer the weight of the body to it and bring the right to the first position. Then you bend the left knee and rise on it with a little hop which is commonly termed *sauter à cloche pied*, and that is the hop before the *pas*.
>
> The second occurs when, leaving the weight of the body on the left foot, you bend the left knee a second time and, keeping the knee bent, slide the right foot to the fourth position front and rise on it with a little hop. This is the hop after the *pas*.
>
> The third and last occurs when, having the weight of the body on the right foot, you bend the right knee and bring the left foot to the right foot, then, rising, you pass it gently forwards and fall on it with a hop. This is the hop during the *pas*.[21]

The description of the first three beats is open to more than one interpretation. One might take the pas on beat 2 with a straight knee, as one does in the contretemps de gavotte,[22] and plié again on beat 3 before the saut which lands on beat 4 (see Figure A). Alternatively, one might take the pas while still in a plié, straightening the knees only upon rising, during beat 3, into the saut which lands on beat 4 (see Figure B).

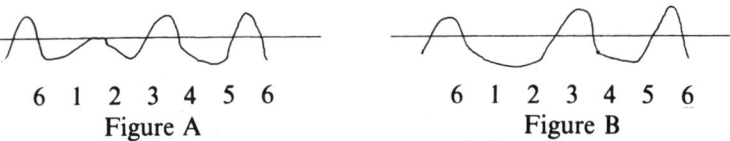

6 1 2 3 4 5 6   6 1 2 3 4 5 6
    Figure A   Figure B

Unfortunately, there is no way of knowing exactly how Pécour intends the pas to be executed. Rameau is consistent in that he does not mention a separate plié before the hop which lands on beat 4, and he does not notate one in the table reproduced above nor in any of the contretemps de menuet which appear in dances in the second part of *Abbrégé*.

The most convincing argument for straightening the knee on the pas, based upon the French sources, is that, when Feuillet notates the contretemps de menuet, he places the sign for the plié before the saut which lands on beat 4 not at the end of the first step symbol, but on the beginning of the foot symbol (see below). This may indicate that the pas forward occurs before the plié.[23]

Feuillet, *Chorégraphie*, Supplement des pas

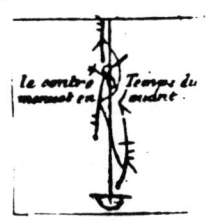

Tomlinson is not much help, because his timing of the contretemps de menuet is different, with the pas arriving on beat 3.[24] He does mention a plié before the saut which lands on beat 4, but any argument that in order to plié you must straighten the knee is weakened by the fact that, in the second half of the contretemps, there is no question that you plié into beat 5 before rising into the jeté, even though there is another plié sign on the step symbol with the jeté.

In the passepied, I have found that making the pas while continuing the plié begun on the downbeat, as diagrammed in Figure B, is the most successful solution. From a practical point of view, when using Rameau's timing in a passepied tempo, even the smallest dancer with the subtlest plié seems to "hop and fret" himself[25] when attempting to move from a straight knee on beat 2, into a plié on beat 3, and rising immediately into the air before beat 4.

In a slower menuet tempo, however, a plié which lasts for more than two full beats seems interminable, and straightening the knee on the pas seems preferable. I have found no evidence in the sources to indicate that the contretemps de menuet actually was performed in different ways at different tempi. Neither Feuillet nor Rameau makes a distinction in his notation between contretemps de menuet in passepieds and those in menuets. In this instance, I have merely taken advantage of the ambiguity of the sources to solve a practical problem.

The figures of "le Passepied" serve a different purpose than those of the menuet. There is no hint of the plot of the menuet ordinaire that can be observed in the "Bourrée d'Achille." In "le Passepied," hands are given or let go as a part of the geometrical design.

The figures explore the effects which are possible in a dance composed of traveling pas, including turning while traveling forward, as in measures 81-88, and the spiral arrangement introduced in measures 17-32, in which the couple traces a circle while holding both hands, then letting go one hand while moving into another circle in which the gentleman and lady travel side by side down the room. The balancé, which does not travel, provides contrast both in its conventional use to the side facing the Présence opening a phrase, as in measures 33, 65, and 97, and the passage in measures 101-4, in which the lady disappears behind the gentleman at the end of the pas of three movements and reappears first on one side and then on the other as they perform a balancé to the side, back to back.

Certain floor patterns emerge as organizing elements in "le Passepied." They are repeated during the course of the dance and are recognizable even when the pas composés change.[26] These patterns and their repetitions which can be identified easily in the choreographic notation are also indicated in the chart on pages 71-72 of this chapter.

In "le Passepied," the dance patterns follow the musical divisions with a few significant exceptions. The music consists of two passepied tunes with the same phrase structure, $\|:4 + 4:\|:8:\|$, each played twice with all repeats in the order, Passepied 1, 2, 1, 2.

Until the second statement of the second passepied tune, four and eight pas patterns in the dance coincide with musical phrases of eight and sixteen measures. In the first statement of the tunes, the repetition in the second passepied of floor patterns from the first passepied underscores the similar phrase structure.

In the second statement of the second passepied tune, the dance reaches what may be considered a climax of disparity between music and dance phrasing. In the first strain, the dancers' balancés seem to divide their strain into groups of $3 + 3 + 2$ pas composés against the statement and repetition of parallel $4 + 4$ groups of musical measures.

The last strain of the second passepied tune contains a musical hemiola in the fourth and fifth measures of an eight-measure musical phrase. Eighteenth-century writers mention the hemiola in the passepied,[27] and when it occurs, it is usually in this position in the phrase.[28] This hemiola is never a reflection of a dance step in the passepied, which always has a movement on the downbeat of the fifth measure. On the contrary, it seems to be a deliberate variation on the part of the composer, upon a constant element in the dance.

Despite the pas composés which the two dances have in common, "le Passepied" cannot be mistaken for a menuet. The tempo alone would distinguish "le Passepied" as a decidedly faster variant of the menuet, but it is the treatment of floor patterns as abstract geometrical entities and organizing elements for the Présence, as opposed to a dramatic sequence of events between the lady and gentleman, which finally distinguish "le Passepied" from the menuet.

Le Passepied

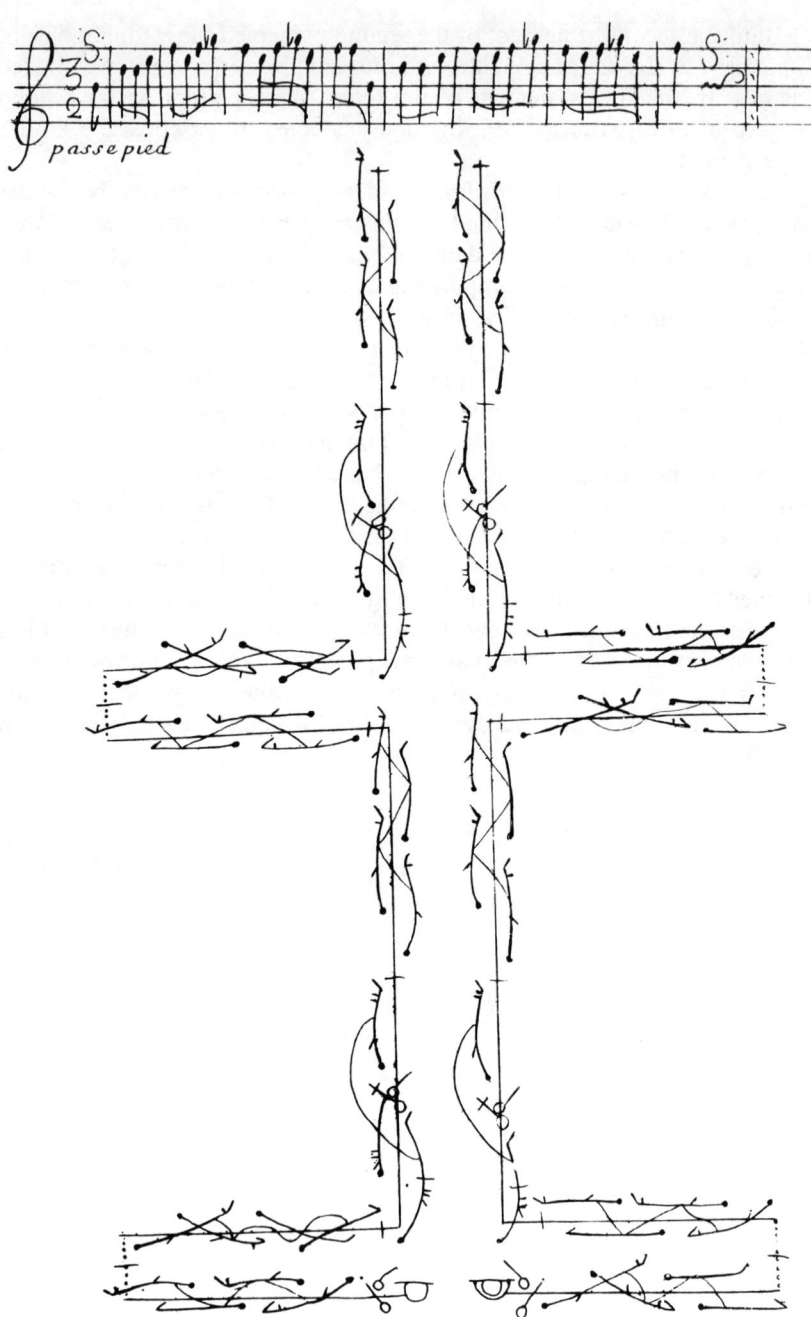

Le Passepied

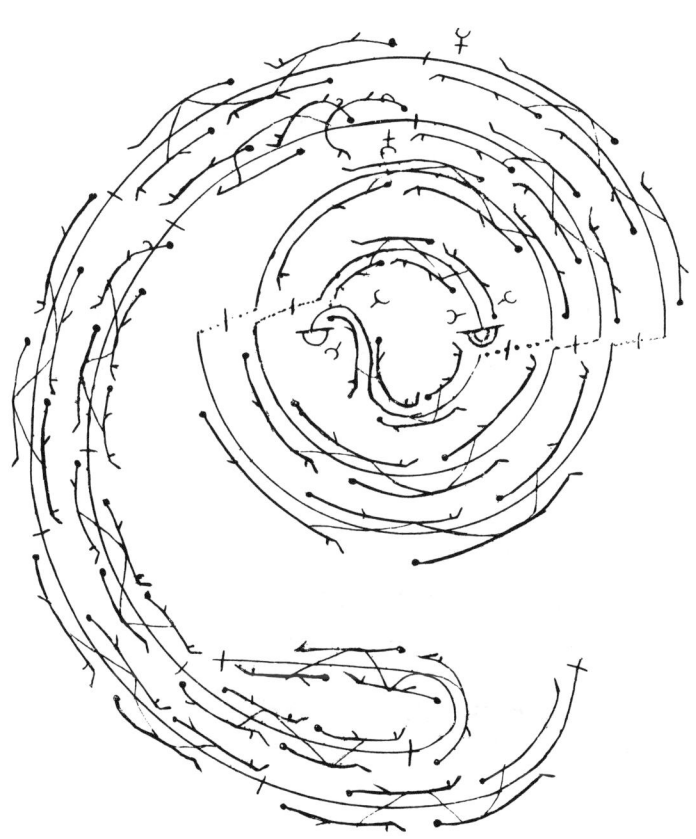

Le Passepied

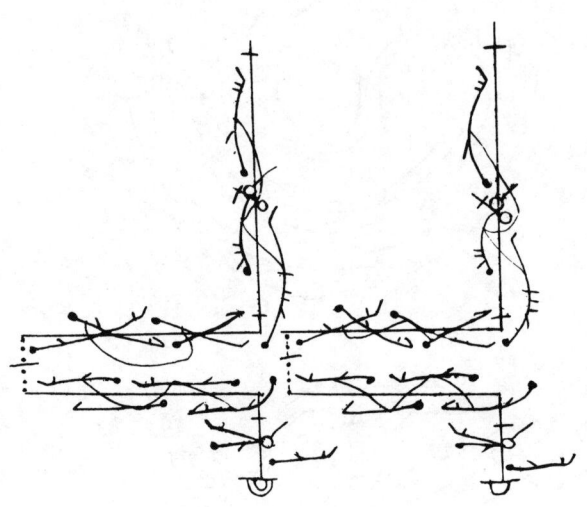

Le Passepied

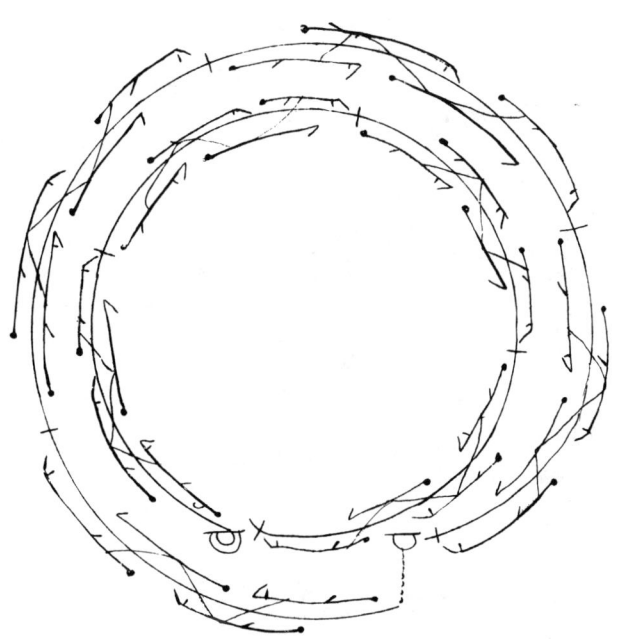

Le Passepied

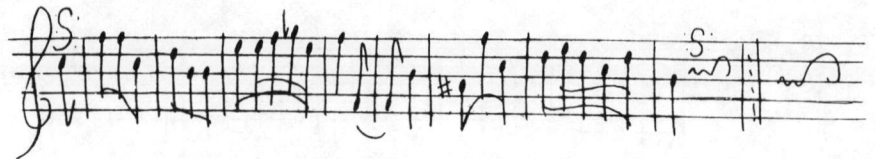

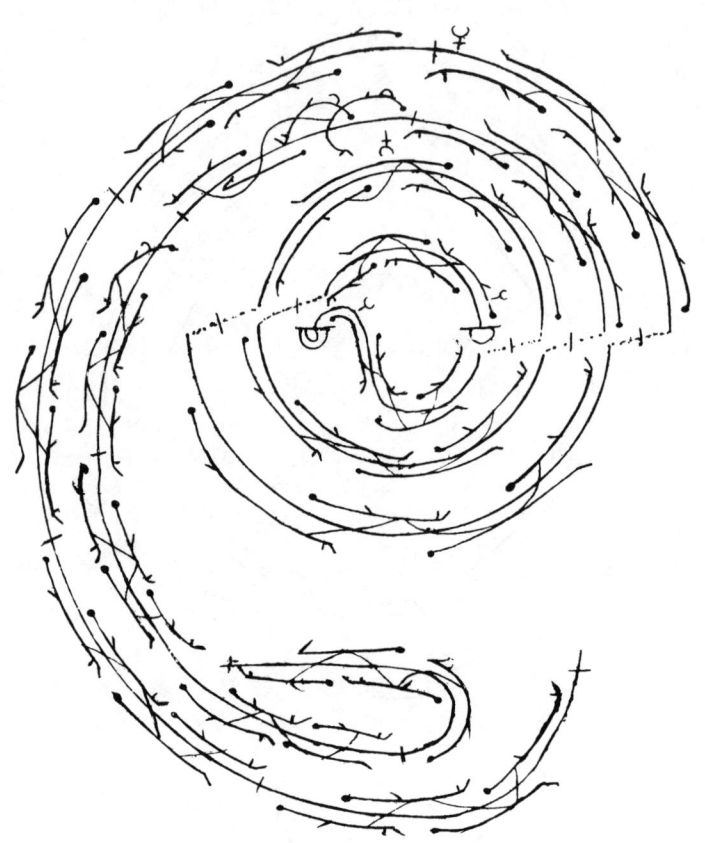

Le Passepied

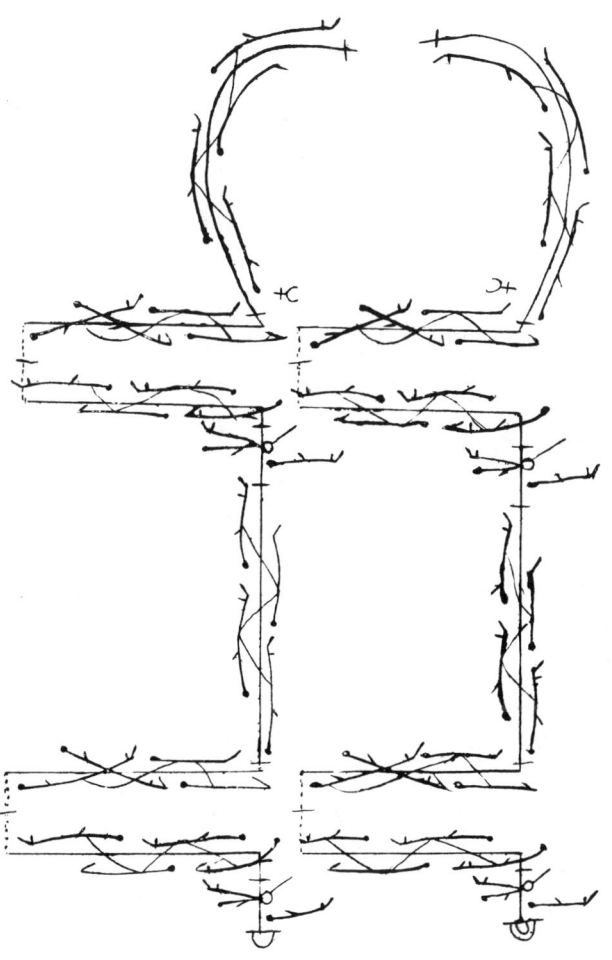

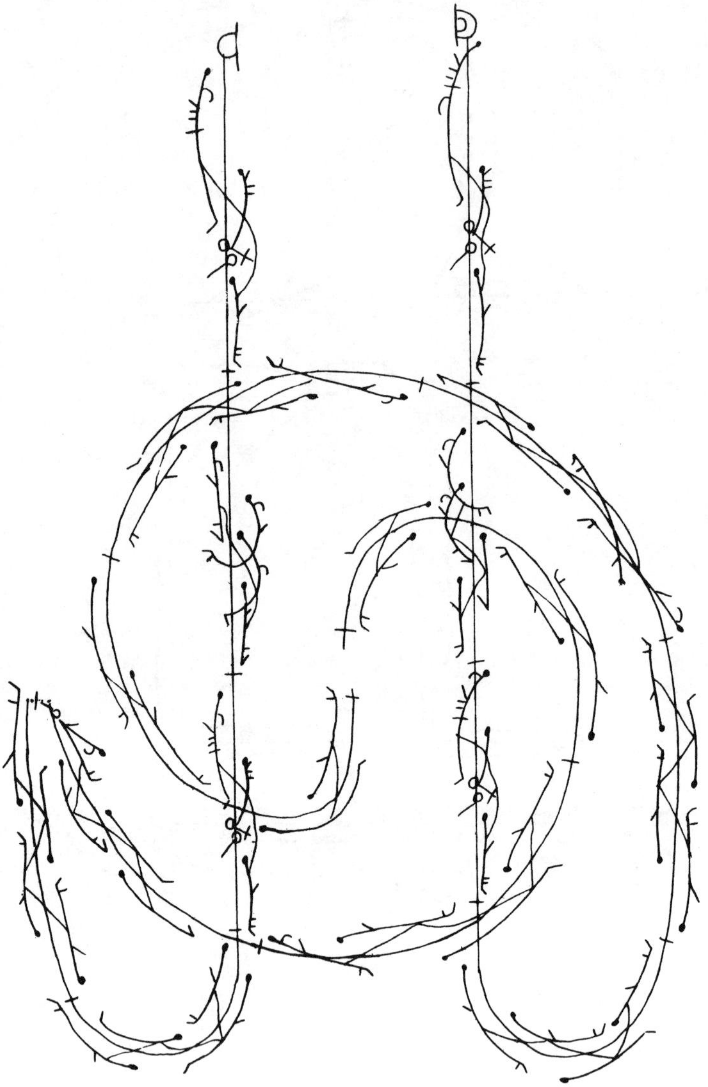

Le Passepied

Le Passepied

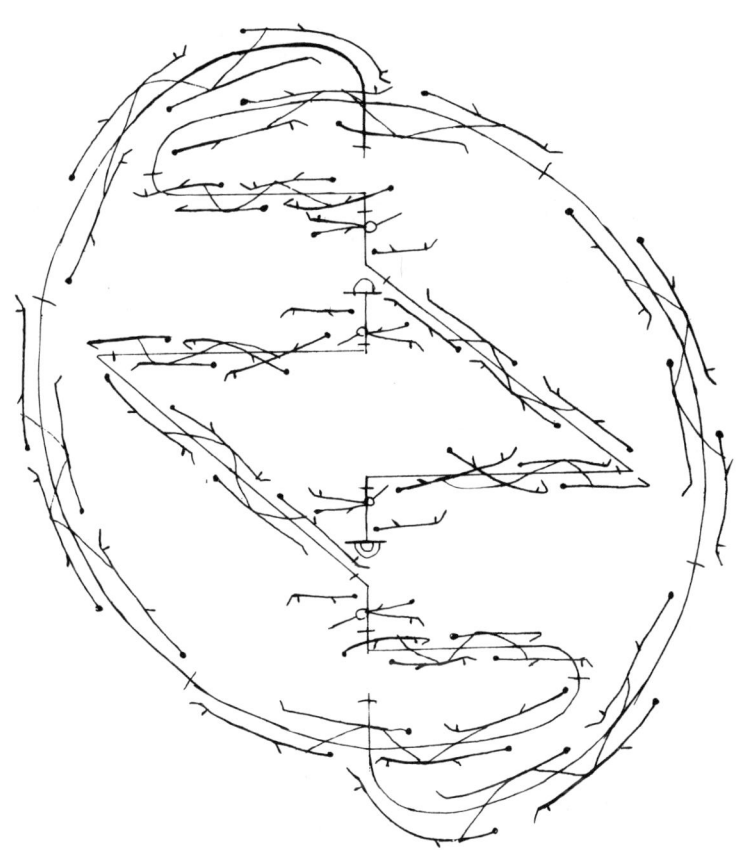

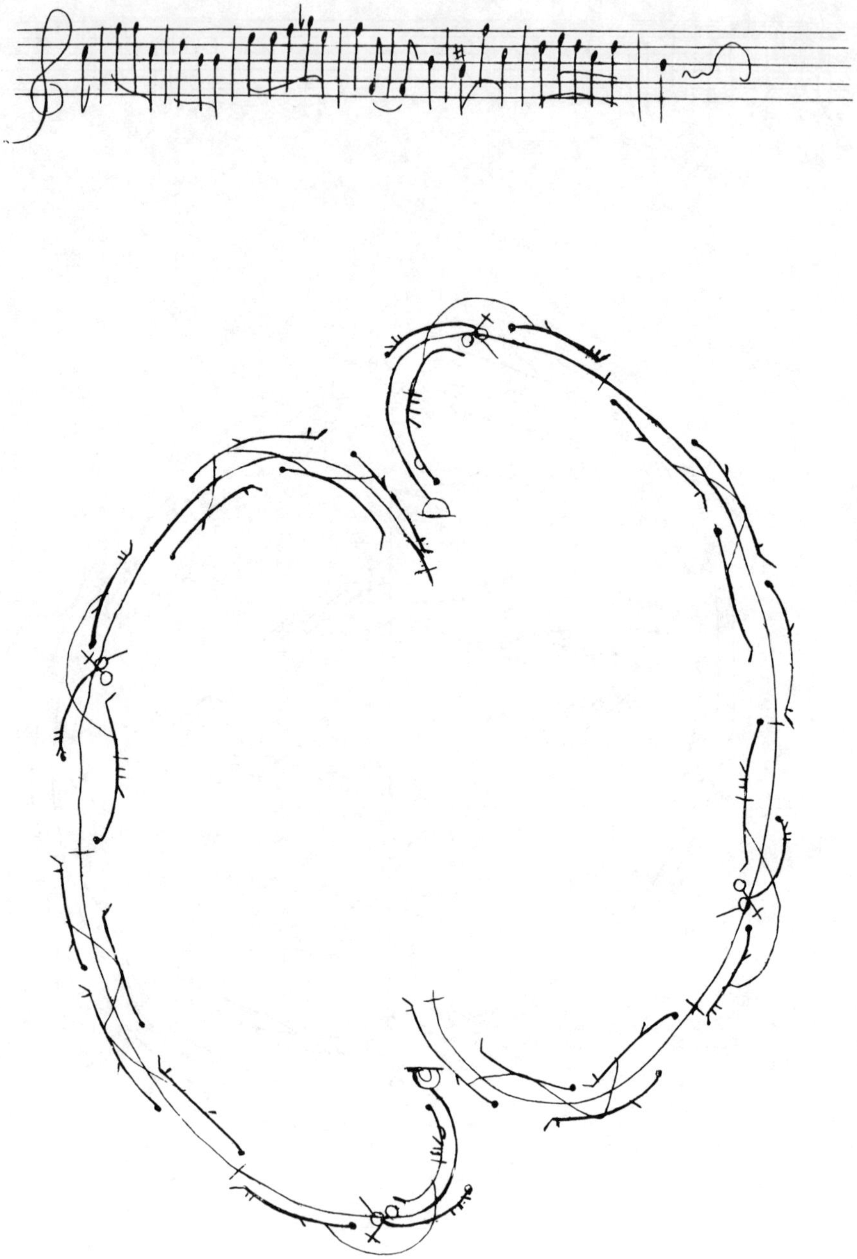

92 *Le Passepied*

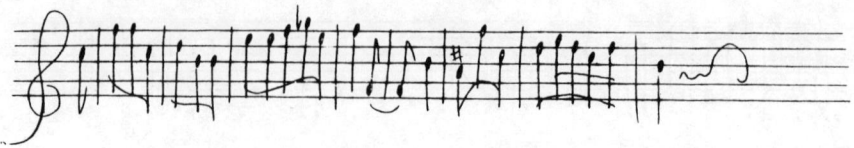

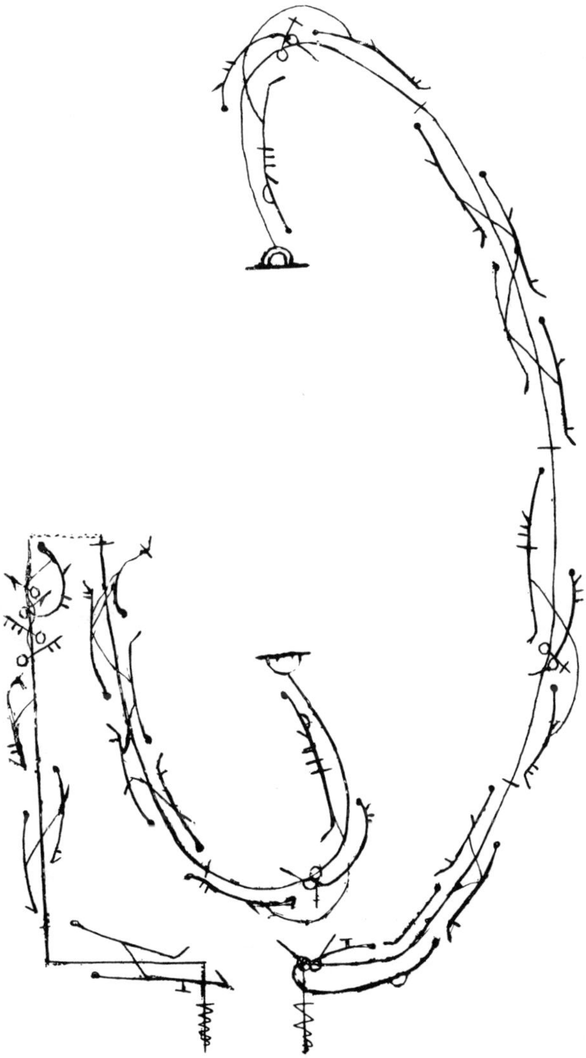

Le Passepied

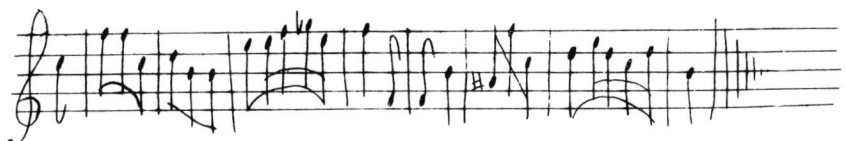

4

La Contredance

"La Contredance" (Gigue) reflects the growing popularity of the English country dance tradition among the younger members of the French court in a danse à deux by Louis Pécour, who, by 1700, was recognized as the principal choreographer of dances in the noble style of the court of Louis XIV.

The source of the tune is the first entrée of the ballet music which Lully composed to accompany a production of Cavalli's opera *Serse* in 1660. The original music, which accompanies one of a group of dances for an ensemble of Basques, is a straightforward ABACA rondo in 3/4 metre. It is called "2e AIR, Rondeau."

For use in his 1700 *Recueil,* Pécour sets the music in 6/4 metre (eliminating every other barline) and repeats the tune in its entirety with the resulting structure ABACAABACA. He titles his choreography "la Contredance" with the label "Gigue" under the music.

As a rule, in Pécour's published choreographies where the title at the top of the page differs from that under the music, the title under the music refers to the music, specifically, indicating either the source of the tune,[1] the dance type,[2] or the beginning of a new section of music.[3] The title at the top of each page is the name of the choreography by Pécour. The title "la Contredance" is intriguing because it is also a dance type.

From a musical standpoint, the contredanse and gigue are not mutually exclusive. Contredanse collections such as those published by Feuillet,[4] Dezais,[5] and later editors contain many 6/4 and 6/8 melodies with gigue rhythms to which contredanse figures have been choreographed. If Pécour's 1700 *Recueil* was a contredanse collection, one might reason that "Gigue" refers to the rhythm of the music alone.

The gigue and contredanse have contrasting implications as choreographies in France in this period. The gigue refers to a choreographed "danse à deux," danced by one couple before the King, which reached the height of its popularity during the reign of Louis XIV. The technique, steps, and style described by Rameau and the other dances in Pécour's 1700 *Recueil* exemplify this genre.

The contredanse was a fairly recent import from England, and whereas the French developed their own contredanse which could be distinguished from the English country dance,[6] it was definitely not a danse à deux. The contredanse was technically a much less demanding dance, performed by four or more dancers in which floor pattern far exceeded steps in importance, and no reference was made to the Présence. The popularity of the contredanse proved to be the downfall of the danses à deux at the French court, with the exception of the ceremonial menuet to open balls. Rameau found the new contredanses tasteless and chaotic because they employed none of the technique and style which he considered the pride of French dancing, and because they had no fixed steps.[7]

Is Pécour's "la Contredance" a gigue or a contredanse? I feel he has written a danse à deux which contains several references to the contredanse, not all of which are complimentary.

The most striking aspect of the dance is its cadence. For the first half of the choreography, the dancers' movements correspond to the four-measure musical phrases exactly; there is even a refrain of four pas composés which is danced at each return of the rondeau.

When the five-part rondeau music begins again, in measure 21, Pécour inserts a single pas marché. The rest of the dance is as regular as the first half, with four-measure phrases and a new refrain of four pas composés, but it is now one dotted half-note later than the music. This is not the clever shift of cadence that one finds in the 6/4 dances "la Forlana" and "la Conty;" it is an obvious device with the same oafish quality that one senses when the rondeau refrain is stated twice in a row, as the repetition of the music begins in measure 21.

Many of the elements of this choreography which seem to fall short of Pécour's most noble and subtle work are, in fact, deliberate references to the contredanse. The tune, although taken from a Lully ballet, is an ideal contredanse tune with uniform four-measure phrases.

The use of a single pas marché to mark a shift in cadence is a device used at the opening of contredanse gavottes such as "le Cotillon."[8] This choreography for four dancers is cited by Guilcher as a rare example of a contredanse in which all the pas composés are notated. If the pas composés employed in "le Cotillon" are typical of those employed in French contredanses, it is not surprising that editors didn't bother to write out the steps: "le Cotillon" uses only combinations of assemblé-pas marchés and contretemps de gavotte and series of demi-contretemps! It is not insignificant, however, that the pas composé refrain of the second half of Pécour's "la Contredance" is composed of contretemps and assemblé-pas marchés.

The neglect of the Présence in "la Contredance" is another reference to the contredanse, a dance for the enjoyment of the participants without regard for the spectators.

La Contredance 97

Yet Pécour's choreography does not fall within the tradition of the contredanse. The pas composés in the episodes are far too varied and intricate to be used by the exuberant contredanse enthusiasts who dance "as if they wore sabots."[9] The half-turns which Pécour inserts between the simpler pas composés of the refrains are not characteristic of contredanse practice, either, and require a great refinement of technique. I feel Pécour's "la Contredance" is best understood as a good-humoured caricature of the contredanse within a danse à deux which demands all the technical and stylistic refinement of the court of Louis XIV.

The cadence of "la Contredance" can be seen in the chart below. The pas composés are explained in detail in the following paragraphs.

la Contredance

A					B			
m.1	p db	p s	p d b	p s	ct dg	ct d g	j j	p d b

A							
m.9	p db	p s	p d b	p s	gl gl	c—oj	gl gl	c—oj

A				
m.17	p db	p s	p d b	p s

A					B			
m.21	p ct d	g a	pm ct d	g a	p db	p do	d ct a	

A							
m.29	pm ct d	g a	pm ct d	g a	pm p db	p db	j j a	

A			
m.37	pm ct d	g c —oj ct d	g c—

Pécour 1700, P. 32, Measures 1-4

step-units: pas de bourrée to the side before & before
pas de sissonne
pas de bourrée to the side before & before
pas de sissonne

"La Contredance" begins with a quarter-turn toward the partner and pas de bourrée to the side before and before; a half-turn in the direction of the Présence and pas de sissonne landing from the second saut with the weight on the foot which is behind; a pas de bourrée to the side before and before; and a half-turn in the direction of the Présence and pas de sissonne landing from the second saut with the weight on the front foot.

The first technical problem is that of the turning pas de sissonne. All the turning pas de sissonne in "la Contredance" are true pas de sissonne, in which the foot which is behind on the preceding step makes a half-circle in the air and cuts in to fifth (or third) position in front for the landing from the first saut. Thus, the turning pas de sissonne should be performed exactly as one would perform any pas de sissonne: in place with quick, precise movement of the foot which is brought in front. The momentum of the pas de bourrée to the side facilitates the half-turn in the same direction, and the head should be used to direct the turn.

Between the pas de sissonne in measure 2 and the pas de bourrée in measure 3, the place before the demi-coupé can be made directly from fifth position in front where the free foot rests in landing from the second saut.

Pécour 1700, P. 32 (cont.), Measures 5-8

step-units: contretemps de chaconne
contretemps de chaconne
jeté forward-jeté backward
pas de bourrée backward sans poser le corps/
coupé backward sans poser le corps

The choreography continues with a modified half-turn in the direction of the Présence and contretemps de chaconne (a contretemps de gavotte to the side with the last pas marché in fifth position), crossing into fifth position behind on the last pas marché; another contretemps de chaconne crossing into fifth position before; a half-turn away from the Présence and a pair of jetés forward and backward; followed by a pas de bourrée backward sans poser le corps (on the last pas marché) for the gentleman and a coupé backward sans poser le corps for the lady.

The pair of jetés in measure 7 has an internal ornament which probably amounts to a battement in practice, although it is not notated as one. It is noted as a spring forward landing on the downbeat with the free foot brought into third position en l'air behind, before the jeté backward. The double line of liaison between the jeté forward and the motion of the free foot into third indicates that these two events take place during the first dotted half-note of the measure, and the leap backward lands in the beginning of the second dotted half-note. In order to be this specific about the timing, Feuillet cannot use the customary means of notating a battement in which the beat is part of the second step:

In any case, observance of the precision with which Feuillet notates the position of the feet lends clarity to the last two measures of the phrase: a leap forward into fourth, a beat in third behind, a leap backward into fourth with the free foot brought into first on the plié, a place into fourth behind, a demi-coupé rising into first position, where the lady hesitates in order to emphasize the pointe in fourth position behind.

Pécour 1700, P. 33, Measures 9-12

step-units: pas de bourrée to the side before & before
                pas de sissonne
                pas de bourrée to the side before & before
                pas de sissonne

The refrain returns with a quarter-turn to the left and pas de bourrée to the side before and before; a half-turn in the direction of travel and a pas de sissonne landing from the second saut on the foot which is behind; and another pas de bourrée before and before. To end the phrase, the lady has a pas de sissonne without turn, landing from the second saut on the front foot, and the gentleman has a half-turn in the direction of travel to face the Présence and pas de sissonne, landing from the second saut on the foot which is behind.

The steps of this choreographed refrain are identical to those which were accompanied by the first statement of the rondeau in measures 1-4, with minor adjustments to prepare for the figure which follows.

Pécour 1700, P. 33 (cont.), Measures 13-16

step-units: glissades
                coupé to the side avec ouverture de jambe
                glissades
                coupé forward avec ouverture de jambe

Next, the dancers perform a pair of glissades crossing behind and before, and a coupé to the side avec ouverture de jambe; followed by a pair of glissades

100   La Contredance

behind and before in the opposite direction, and a quarter-turn toward the partner, and a coupé avec ouverture de jambe.

Pécour 1700, P. 33 (cont.), Measures 17-20

step-units: pas de bourrée forward
pas de sissonne
pas de bourrée backward
pas de sissonne

The return of the pas composés of measures 1-4 signals the final refrain of the first half of "la Contredance." This time the sequence is varied with a forward pas de bourrée, a pas de sissonne landing from the second saut on the foot which is behind, a pas de bourrée backward, and pas de sissonne backward, the lady landing from the second saut on the foot which is behind, the gentleman landing on the front foot.

Pécour 1700, P. 34, Measures 21-24

step-units: pas marché forward
contretemps de gavotte forward
pas de gaillard to the side (assemblé + pas)
contretemps de côté
assemblé

As the rondeau strain repeats to begin the second half of the dance, the dancers perform a pas marché and contretemps de gavotte forward, an assemblé and pas marché with the foot which the assemblé has brought in opening out into second position, a contretemps de côté crossing the first pas marché into fifth position before, a half-turn in the direction of travel to face the partner, and assemblé.

As a result of the insertion of a single pas marché at the beginning of this phrase, all of the pas composés which follow begin on the second dotted half-note of the measure. Thus, the pas composés extend across the barlines of both the choreographic notation and the music. Pécour's rebarring of the music in 6/4 (Lully's original was in 3/4) clarified this change.

The purpose of the assemblé-pas marché in this passage, which is the refrain for the second half of "la Contredance," is to transfer the dancer's weight to both feet in second position in order to take the contretemps de côté from two feet, as Rameau prefers it.[10] One wonders if Pécour considered this a pas de gaillarde, even though it does not prepare a pas tombé.[11] One might even speculate that such an introductory step might be another link between the contretemps de côté and tombé, which Pécour exploits in "la Conty."[12]

The assemblé-pas marche combination also characterizes the contredanse "le Cotillon." In "le Cotillon," however, the pas marché is performed either forward or backward to precede a contretemps de gavotte, a step which is not as difficult as the contretemps de côté and one which bears no resemblance to the pas tombé. By choreographing the assemblé-pas marché across the measure line to prepare a contretemps de côté, Pécour creates a refrain which combines a clear reference to the contredanse with the more subtle style and technique of the danse à deux.

Pécour 1700, P. 35, Measures 25-28

step-units: pas de bourrée ouvert
pas de bourrée ouvert
demi-contretemps backward
pas de gaillarde to the side (assemblé + pas)

After a half-measure rest, the dancers continue with a pair of pas de bourrée ouverts—the first toward and the second away from the Présence, a demi-contretemps backward, and an assemblé and pas marché opening to second position toward the Présence.

The half-measure rest which precedes the pas de bourrée ouverts occupies the position of the pas marché in other phrases. The pas de bourrée ouvert itself is a quick, precise, and fairly intricate step which can only be performed with insteps supple from training in the technique described by Rameau. The omission of a pas marché is a practical necessity for the dancers, who must begin the pas de bourrée ouvert from a closed position (in this case, first position from the assemblé), but the rest also lends variety to the phrase and decision to the pas de bourrée ouverts.

The demi-contretemps has the vertical motion and cadence of the assemblé-pas marché without closing into an assemblé. The dancer's weight rests on the foot which is away from the Présence in third position behind at the end of the pas de bourrée ouverts. He makes a plié with both knees and rises into the air in a hop straightening both knees. The leg which is in front (and closest to the Présence) begins moving to the back while the dancer is in the air so that, when he lands from his hop in a plié on the leg away from the Présence, the free leg is half-way around. The free knee remains straight so that the dancer rebounds out of his plié to step gracefully into a pas marché onto the free leg, which has finished its pas ouvert, moving to fourth position behind.

The dancer transfers all his weight on the pas marché back, leaves the other foot in front, and makes the plié with the back leg only. He brings the front leg into first position on the assemblé, which lands in a plié on both feet. The dancer must transfer all his weight upon landing, so that he can make his pas marché into second position toward the Présence.

102   La Contredance

Pécour 1700, P. 35 (cont.), Measures 29-32

step-units: contretemps de côté
      assemblé-pas marché to the side
      contretemps de côté
      assemblé-pas marché forward

  The dance refrain of the second half of "la Contredance" returns with a contretemps de côté turning away from the partner, a half-turn in the same direction to face the partner and an assemblé and pas marché into second position away from the Présence, a second contretemps de côté turning away from the partner, and a half-turn in the same direction to face the Présence and assemblé and pas marché forward with the outside foot transferring all the weight to the front foot.

  Rameau explains that the turning contretemps de côté may be used to accomplish a half or three-quarter turn.[13] In the first contretemps de côté of this refrain, the dancer performs the saut without turn and turns on the pas marchés so that he and his partner are back to back at the end of the second pas marché. On the second contretemps de côté, only a quarter-turn is necessary, and it should be performed on the second pas marché.

Pécour 1700, P. 36, Measures 33-36

step-units: pas de bourrée forward
      pas de bourrée forward
      jeté forward-jeté backward
      assemblé-pas marché backward

  Next, the dancers perform a pair of pas de bourrée forward, a quarter-turn toward the partner and a pair of jetés, and an assemblé and pas marché backward with the foot which is away from the Présence.

  The jetés in measures 35-36 are identical to those in measure 7 and should be performed in the same manner. However, because the jetés in this phrase are followed by an assemblé, the dancer may leave the free foot in front on the jeté back and bring it into first position on the assemblé. All the weight should be transferred on the pas marché backward which follows, leaving the free foot in fourth position in front en l'air.

Pécour 1700, P. 36 (cont.), Measures 37-40

step-units: contretemps de gavotte forward
      coupé forward avec ouverture de jambe
      contretemps de gavotte forward
      closing coupé soutenue

For the final refrain, the dancers perform a half-turn in the direction of the Présence to face the partner and a coupé avec ouverture de jambe, a modified quarter-turn away from the Présence and contretemps de gavotte forward, and a modified half-turn in the direction of the partner to face the Présence for the closing coupé.

The plié before each contretemps should be made in first position to clarify the pas composés and facilitate the turns.

The distinction between the ball dance for participants and the theater dance for spectators is also reflected in the floor pattern. Danses à deux are ball dances with a combined focus. The dancers wear no masks and take advantage of opportunities in the choreography to exchange discreet glances, yet they always move in patterns which are pleasing to the Présence seated at the head of the room, to whom the choreography pays homage.

The contredanses demand no such division of the dancer's attention. He turns his back on the Présence to dance a contredanse with his circle of friends. This removes the pressure of performance from the participants and effectively demotes those not dancing from recipients of a choreographed honor to wallflowers.

In "la Contredance," Pécour has not yet abandoned the Présence. He observes the convention of beginning and ending the dance at the foot of the room facing the Présence, which may be seen as an extension of the Réverence. During the course of the dance, the glissades and ouvertures de jambe to the side in measures 13-15 are also directed to the Présence: a step sequence and design never found in contredanses of the period.

Yet, while creating a floor pattern which offers the monarch aesthetic enjoyment, Pécour has minimized direct references to the Présence. The opening is just a pose before a quarter-turn to face the partner on the downbeat. With the exception of the glissades, every pattern depends upon the relationship between the dancers, who turn or pass and turn again in order to face each other. Before the final refrain, the dancers even advance toward the Présence in order to turn and face each other at the top of the room.

Only a few aspects of the choreographed floor pattern need clarification. Some of the turn signs should not be taken literally. The half-turns in the refrain in measures 1-4, 9-12, and 29-32 are correct and should be performed accurately. However, the half-turn in measure 5 is less than a half-turn so that the dancers angle away from each other in that measure before performing the contretemps de gavotte directly down the room in measure 6. Likewise, the quarter-turn sign in measure 39 indicates little more than an eighth-turn, so that the dancers angle in toward each other to finish the dance next to each other.

The steps in the refrain in measures 9-12 should be performed at a slight angle (the lady toward the front of the room, the gentleman toward the back), so that the glissades which follow can be executed on a line perpendicular to the view of the Présence. The dancers should be face to face on the pas de sissonne in measure 10, and the glissades in measure 13 should cover no more distance than the pas de bourrée in measure 11.

On the pas marché which begins the second half of the dance, the dancers must strike an angle which allows them to pass in that pas and a contretemps de gavotte forward which takes them the distance of one contretemps de côté from meeting face to face in the assemblé in measure 24.

The floor pattern determines the position of the dancer's head and direction of his gaze. Rameau provides specific instructions concerning the contretemps de côté:

> As for the head, when you rise, it should turn slightly toward the side to which you travel, though this is not a fixed rule; for if you dance with someone and make these *contretemps* while passing in front of each other, you must look at each other.[14]

In each instance of the contretemps de côté in "la Contredance," the turn of the head in the direction of travel can be used to facilitate the dancers' turns once they have passed each other.

The dancer's arm movements are subject to more than one interpretation, but in the interest of clarity the arm movements for the refrains should reflect the similarity of the step patterns. Rameau discusses no arm movements to accompany the pas de bourrée to the side before and before which is found in the first refrain. I use no opposition on this step, but employ the conventional opposition to the pas de sissonne, opposing the front foot on the first saut. Because each refrain is followed by a leapt step, bringing the arms down from the opposition to the pas de sissonne with the landing of the initial saut of the first pas composé of the following phrase emphasizes the simple cadence in the first section and the abrupt change which occurs at the opening of the second section.

The possibility of opening the arms out to facilitate a turn[15] can be used to the dancer's advantage before the contretemps in measure 5 and also in the turning contretemps de côté figures which constitute the refrain of the second half of the dance.

La Contredance 105

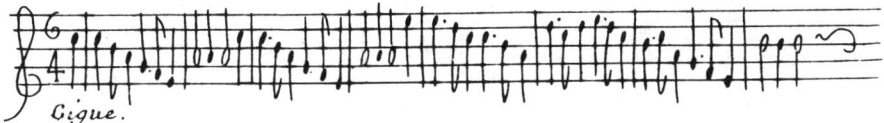

Gigue.

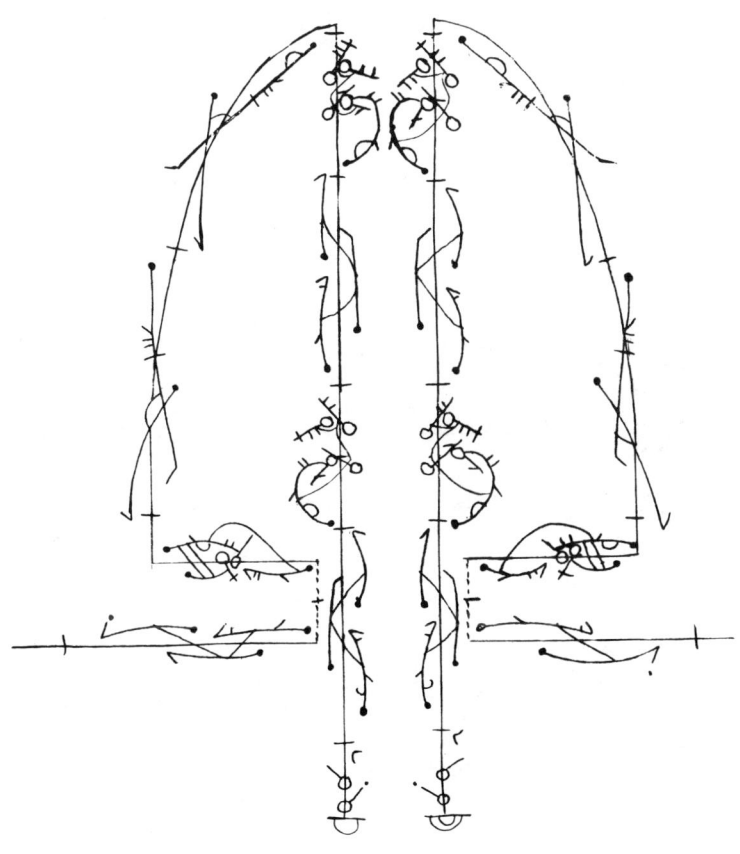

La Contredance

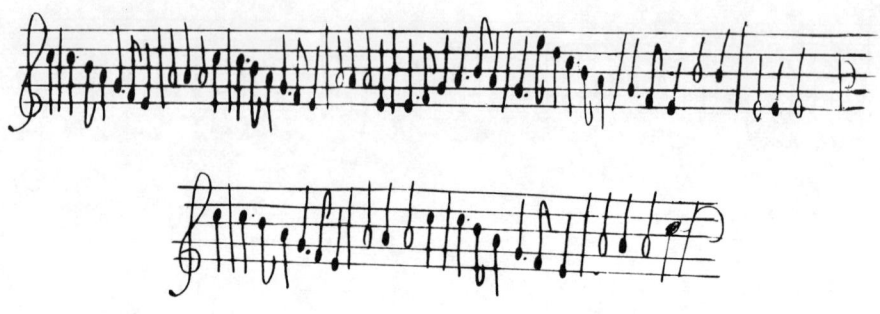

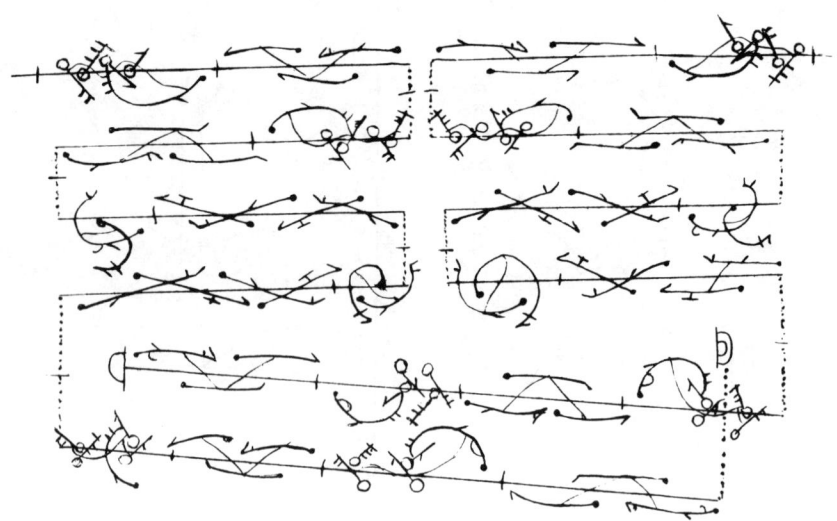

La Contredance

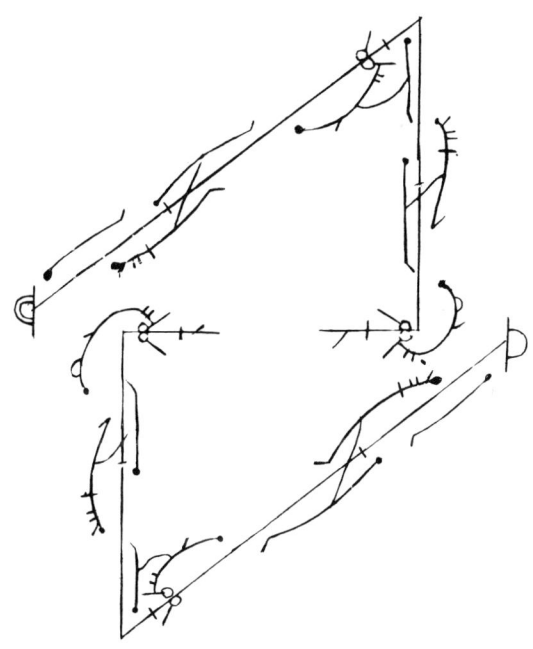

La Contredance

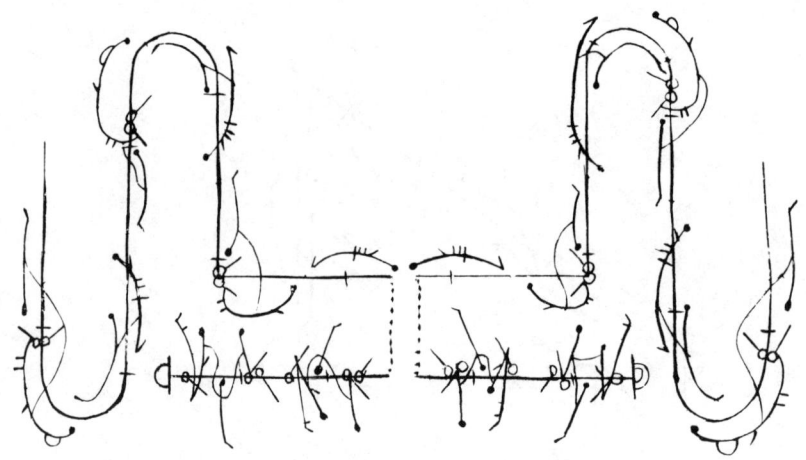

La Contredance 109

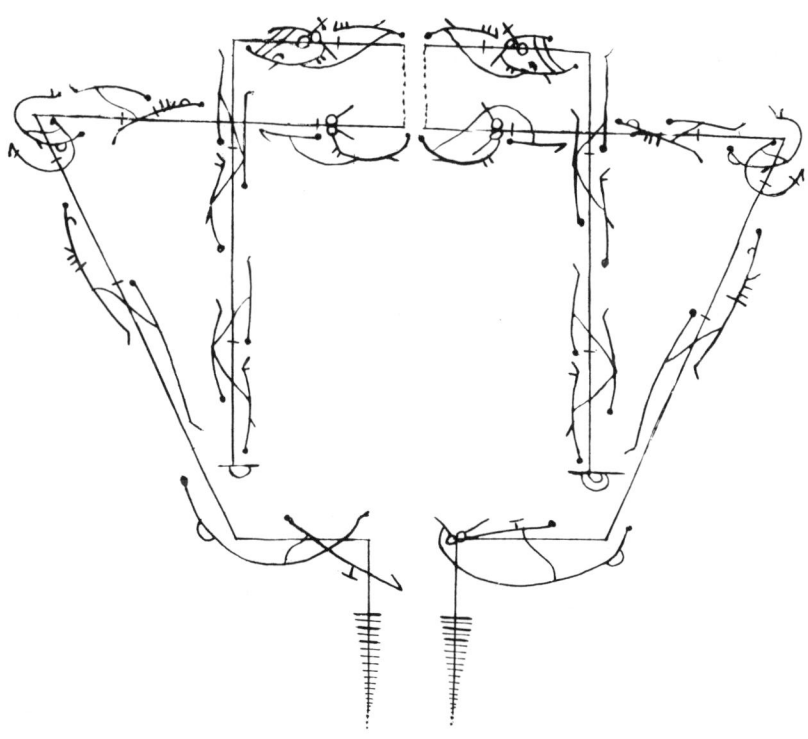

5

Le Rigaudon

Rigaudon I

A	♩♩ ♩	♩. ♩♩♩♩	♩♩♩♩	♩♩♩♩	♩♩♩♩	♩ ♩	♩
m.1	b	l	pd b	ct b	j j	p s	pd e

A rpt

m.9	ct dg	c--oj	ct dg	c--oj	j j	p d b	p s	pd e c...(

B	♩♩ ♩.♫	♩. ♩	♩♩♩♩	♩♩♩♩	♩ ♩	♩.		
m.17	ct dg	ct dg	p s	pd e	ct dg	c--(		

	♩♩ ♩.♫	♩. ♩	♩♩♩♩	♩♩♩♩	♩ ♩	♩.	
m.23	ct dg	ct dg	p d b	p d b	p s	pd e	

B rpt

m.29	pir	pir	ct dg	ct dg	pdb	—tc	

m.35	p d b	p d b	p d b	c—(	ct b	p d b	

Rigaudon II

A	♩ ♩ ♩	♩. ♩	♩♩♩♫	♩ ♩ ♩	♩♩♩♩	♩♫♫	♩♩♩♩	♩
m.41	p d b	c—(	p d r	d	gl gl	c–pt	gl gl	c—(

A rpt

m.49	pir s	pir s	ct b	p d b	ct b	p d b	pdb	—tc

B	♩ ♩♩♩♩	♩♩♩♩	♩.♪♫♫	♩♩♩♩	♩♫♫	♩♩♩♩	♩.	
m.57	c m	c m	p d b	ct d g	c--(	gl gl	c—(	

112   Le Rigaudon

```
          ♫  │♩♫♩♫│♩♫♩♫│♩♩♩♩│♩. ♪♩. ♪│♩.
   m.64  p d b  │p d o │ct b │p d b │ ─ t c
   Brpt
   m.69  p d b  │p d b │p d b│p d b │c -- |

   m.74  ct b   │p d b │ct b │p d b │ct b │p d b │c ─|
```

Pécour 1700, P. 37, Measures 1-8

step-units: balancé to the side
               pas de bourrée to the side
               contretemps ballonnée forward
               2 jetés forward
               pas de bourrée forward
               pas de sissonne forward
               pas de bourrée emboîté

To begin the "Rigaudon des Vaisseaux," the dancers address the Présence with a balance de côté; a pas de bourrée to the side behind and behind away from the partner; and a contretemps ballonnée forward. The phrase continues with a pair of jetés and a pas de bourrée forward; a pas de sissonne forward, landing from the second saut on the foot which is behind; and a pas de bourrée emboîté.

     The dancers' starting position is with the weight on the outside foot, the inside foot pointed in fourth position behind. The free foot is brought forward to first position to make the plié before placing it in second position for the demi-coupé.

Pécour 1700, P. 37 (cont.), Measures 9-16

step-units: contretemps de gavotte forward
               coupé avec ouverture de jambe
               contretemps de gavotte forward
               coupé avec ouverture de jambe
               2 jetés forward
               pas de bourrée forward
               pas de sissonne forward
               pas de bourrée emboîté/coupé simple
                  backward into 2nd

Le Rigaudon 113

As the first musical phrase is repeated, the dancers make a quarter-turn and a contretemps de gavotte forward toward each other; a half-turn in the direction of the Présence and a coupé avec ouverture de jambe; a contretemps de gavotte forward; and half-turn in the direction of the Présence and a coupé avec ouverture de jambe facing the partner. This is followed by a pair of jetés; a pas de bourrée forward; and a pas de sissonne forward landing from the second saut with the weight on the foot which is behind. To conclude the phrase, the gentleman makes a modified pas de bourrée emboîté with a demi-coupé to fourth position behind, a pas marché closing into third position behind, and a pas marché opening to second position with the weight on both feet. The lady makes a coupé with a demi-coupé to fourth position behind and a pas marché to second position with the weight on both feet.[1]

Pécour 1700, P. 38, Measures 17-28

step-units: contretemps de côté
contretemps de côté
pas de sissonne forward
pas de bourrée emboîté
contretemps de gavotte forward
coupé simple forward

contretemps de côté
contretemps de côté
pas de bourrée forward
pas de bourrée forward
pas de sissonne forward
pas de bourrée emboîté

The second phrase begins with a pair of contretemps de côté with plié on both feet, landing on the foot farthest from the partner, crossing the first pas marché in fifth position before and opening the second pas marché to second position with the weight on both feet. The second contretemps is performed in the same manner, except that all the weight is transferred on the last pas marché. This is followed by a pas de sissonne forward, landing from the second saut with the weight on the foot which is behind; and a pas de bourrée emboîté, a contretemps de gavotte, and coupé simple forward, ending with the weight on both feet.

The dancers continue the phrase with a pair of contretemps de côté identical to those in measures 9-10 described above, but traveling to the right; a quarter-turn in the direction of travel and a pair of pas de bourrée forward; a pas de sissonne forward, landing from the second saut with the weight on the foot which is behind; and a pas de bourrée emboîté.

114 Le Rigaudon

The contretemps de côté in measure 18 ends with a pas marché to second position. The pas de sissonne in measure 19 is notated as if the free foot is brought forward from fourth position behind. The dancer should bring the free foot in from second position on the plié before the pas de sissonne, so that he can bring it out to the side on the saut of the pas de sissonne. Perhaps the movement on the initial plié should be into third position behind rather than first position, so that the free foot travels from behind to cross in front.

In the coupé in measure 22, the pas marché should travel only to second position in preparation for the contretemps de côté which follows.

Pécour 1700, P. 39, Measures 29-40

step-units: pirouette
pirouette
contretemps de chaconne
contretemps de chaconne
pas de bourrée forward
temps de courante forward

pas de bourrée forward
pas de bourrée forward
pas de bourrée forward
coupé simple forward
modified contretemps ballonné forward
pas de bourrée forward

The repetition of the second reprise begins with a pair of pirouettes turning a half-turn to the right and back a half-turn to the left; another quarter-turn to the left and a pair of contretemps de chaconne closing the last pas marché into fifth position behind in the first contretemps and into fifth position before in the second contretemps; a quarter-turn to the right and a pas de bourrée; and temps de courante forward. The dancers continue with a quarter-turn to the right and three pas de bourrée forward, and a quarter-turn right and a coupé simple to first position; a quarter-turn toward the Présence and a modified contretemps ballonné with a quarter-turn on each saut, the first to face the Présence and the second away from the partner; and a pas de bourrée forward.

The pas in measure 39 appears in neither *Chorégraphie* nor *Abbrégé;* its performance is not described in any of the contemporary dance manuals, and, consequently, it has no name. In the 1700 *Recueil,* it occurs only in the "Rigaudon des Vaisseaux," where it is used several times, but Pécour also employs the pas frequently in the theatrical dances of the 1704 *Recueil.*

Based on the information provided in the notation, the dancers should make the initial plié on both feet in first position and execute a quarter-turn during the saut, landing on the outside foot with the inside foot en l'air in third position behind, as in a pas de sissonne. The next movement is a jeté forward. In this discussion, I will refer to this pas as a modified contretemps ballonné, because it might be considered a variation of a turning contretemps ballonné illustrated in *Abbrégé*.[2]

Pécour 1700, P. 40, Measures 41-48

step-units: pas de bourrée forward
                 coupé simple forward
                 pas de rigaudon
                 glissades
                 coupé soutenue to the side
                 glissades
                 coupé soutenue to the side

The dancers begin the second rigaudon tune with a half-turn in the direction of the Présence and a pas de bourrée forward; a coupé simple forward to first position toward each other; and a pas de rigaudon landing first on the foot nearest to the bottom of the room.

The dancers continue with a pair of glissades and a coupé soutenue to the side away from the partner, the gentleman traveling down the room and the lady up the room. The glissades are performed with demi-jetés[3] to second position closing with a glissé first into fifth position behind and then into fifth position before. The coupé is composed of a demi-coupé to second position and a glissé with no transfer of weight into fifth position behind. This is followed by another pair of glissades crossing behind and before; and a coupé crossing behind traveling toward the partner. Although it is not notated, the lady transfers no weight on the glissé of the last coupé, so that she can execute the following pirouette.

Pécour 1700, P. 41, Measures 49-56

step-units: pirouette avec saut
                 pirouette avec saut
                 modified contretemps ballonné forward
                 pas de bourrée forward
                 modified contretemps ballonné forward
                 pas de bourrée forward
                 pas de bourrée forward
                 temps de courante forward

On the repeat of the first reprise, the dancers execute a pair of pirouettes with quarter-turn and saut, the first to face the Présence, the second to face the partner. From the first position following the second pirouette, the dancers make a quarter-turn to face the Présence and a modified contretemps ballonné forward, landing from the first saut on the inside foot with the outside foot brought back into third position en l'air behind followed by a jeté forward; and a pas de bourrée forward; another modified contretemps ballonné forward, the free foot closing forward from fourth to third position en l'air behind followed by a jeté forward; and two pas de bourrée; and a temps de courante forward.

In my opinion, the position upon landing from the first saut is identical in the contretemps in measures 51 and 53. The difference in notation reflects the fact that, in measure 51, the free foot moves from first position back into third position behind during the saut. In measure 53, it moves from fourth position behind up into third position behind.

The placement of the signs at the beginning of the step symbol in measure 53 is evidence to support transferring only half the weight on the last pas marché of the pas de bourrée in measure 52. In that event, the plié is made on two feet in fourth position and the free foot moves into third position behind upon landing on the downbeat of measure 53, as in the second saut of the contretemps de menuet.

Pécour 1700, P. 41 (cont.), Measures 57-68

step-units: coupé de mouvement to the side
coupé de mouvement to the side
pas de bourrée forward
contretemps de gavotte forward
coupé soutenue forward
glissades
coupé soutenue to the side

pas de bourrée ouvert
pas de bourrée ouvert
modified contretemps ballonné forward
pas de bourrée forward
temps de courante forward

The second reprise of the second rigaudon begins with a pair of coupés de mouvement to the side with a demi-coupé in fifth position in front and a demi-jeté into second position; a pas de bourrée and contretemps de gavotte forward; and a coupé forward closing the pas marché into third position behind with no transfer of weight; a pair of glissades away from the partner, the first closing into fifth position behind and the second into fifth before; and a coupé to the side, placing the demi-coupé in second position and closing the glissé into fifth position behind.

The dancers continue with a pair of pas de bourrée ouverts, the first opening out away from the partner, the second toward the partner; followed by a modified contretemps ballonné forward; a pas de bourrée; and temps de courante forward.

The contretemps ballonné in measure 66 lands from the first saut on the inside foot with the free foot in third position before en l'air followed by a jeté forward. This is the only modified contretemps ballonné in this choreography which does not land from the first saut with the free foot in third position behind. The pas de bourrée ouvert which precedes it ends with the weight on both feet in third position, where the plié is made. During the saut, both knees are straight, and the outside leg, which was in third position in front, is extended to fourth position in front so that it can closed again into third position en l'air in front upon landing.

Pécour 1700, P. 42, Measures 69-80

step-units: pas de bourrée forward
pas de bourrée forward
pas de bourrée forward
pas de bourrée forward
coupé simple forward

modified contretemps ballonné forward
pas de bourrée forward
modified contretemps ballonné forward
pas de bourrée forward
modified contretemps ballonné forward
pas de bourrée forward
closing coupé soutenue

On the repeat of the second reprise, the gentleman has a half-turn in the direction of the partner, and both dancers have four pas de bourrée forward; then a coupé forward, closing the pas marché into first position.

The dancers continue with a modified contretemps ballonné with a quarter-turn on each saut, identical to that in measure 39; a pas de bourrée forward away from the partner; another modified contretemps ballonné with quarter-turns on each saut, the first to face the Présence, the second to face the partner; a pas de bourrée forward toward the partner; a third modified contretemps ballonné with a quarter-turn only on the first saut to face down the room; followed by a pas de bourrée forward; and half-turn in the direction of the partner and closing coupé soutenue facing the Présence.

In each modified contretemps ballonné in the final phrase, the dancer lands from the first saut with the free foot in third position en l'air behind. An orthodox reading of the placement of the signs on the first saut indicates that the initial plié for each contretemps is taken with the weight on both feet, whether in first position, at the end of the coupé in measure 73, or in fourth position, at the end of the pas de bourrée in measures 75 and 77.

In a few passages, the execution of the floor pattern demands careful examination. The dancers should begin the dance farther apart than usual to allow room for the first balancé and also for measures 13-15, in which the dancers make two jetés, a pas de bourrée, and pas de sissonne toward each other after having made only the pas de bourrée behind and behind in measure 3 away from the starting position.

The second pair of contretemps de côté in measures 23-24 begins the curved path of the figure culminating in the pas de sissonne and pas de bourrée emboîté face-to-face.

At the beginning of the second rigaudon, the dancers are face to face until measure 44, but must be back to back in measure 48. Thus, the glissades and coupé should angle forward at the same time they travel to the side, so that in measure 46 the lady blocks the Présence's view of the gentleman. After making the same degree of angle forward in the glissades and coupé to the side in measures 47-48, the dancers should find themselves back to back in measure 48 with enough room to perform the pirouettes avec sauts in the following measures.

In the second coupé de mouvement in measure 58, the dancers should begin a curved path.

The arm movements which accompany the less familiar pas and transitions are discussed below.

If the dancers use the same arm movements in measures 13-16 that they used in measures 5-8, they will help to delineate the repetition of the sequence of pas composés in the first phrase. In measure 16, however, both arms should be raised in double opposition at the end of the pas de bourrée emboîté to prepare for the contretemps de côté which follows.[4]

Rameau's arm movements from the shoulder should accompany all the contretemps de côté in measures 17-18 and 23-24. In the first pair, the dancers should look back at each other over the lower arm, the second fall of the arm leading into the opposition to the pas de sissonne. In anticipation of the second pair of contretemps de côté, the arms should be raised in double opposition at the end of the coupé forward to second position in measure 22. In the following contretemps de côté, the dancer should turn the head in the direction of travel as Rameau suggests.[5]

The arm movements for the pirouette also demand preparation at the end of the preceding pas. The position with the arm in opposition at the end of the pas de bourrée emboîté in measure 28 is the corrrect arm position to begin the following pirouette. After the élevé on the downbeat, the dancer extends this arm, opening out and down and turning both wrists from above downward during the turn. As part of the same movement while turning, the dancer brings up the other arm to oppose the foot which is in front at the end of the turn in anticipation of the following pirouette.

The arm movements for the second pirouette are the same, but because it is not followed by another pirouette, the arms only open out and down during the turn. I feel that because the second pirouette is followed by a quarter-turn in the same direction, the dancer might finish the pirouette with palms up, waiting until the next downbeat to make the final turn of the wrists from above downward upon landing from the saut of the contretemps.

Rameau indicates that the head leads the turn in the pirouette. In this case, the dancers turn the head first to face the Présence and then to face the partner. It is also effective if the dancers continue to look at each other, turning the head over the right shoulder during the contretemps back to back.

According to Rameau, the arm movements for the pirouettes with a spring are similar to those for the pirouette on the ground, "except that they imitate the legs a little in their movement by rising more quickly during the spring and extending with more vivacity...."[6] Thus, the arm movements for the pirouettes sauts in measures 49-50 should be the same as those which accompany the pirouettes on the ground in measures 29-30, varying the style as Rameau proposes. At the end of the coupé to the side in measure 48, the dancer should bring the arms into the position of opposition, raising the arm nearest to the Présence in preparation for the pirouette.

No arm movements are given for the modified contretemps ballonné. In the "Rigaudon des Vaisseaux," I find it sufficient to drop the arms and turn the wrists from above downward on the downbeat, as in a contretemps de gavotte. Leading with the head facilitates the turns and the precision of the dancer's position and focus upon landing.

The "Rigaudon des Vaisseaux" impresses the dancer, initially, as an exuberant potpourri of relatively unusual pas composés. I imagine it would be a favorite with dancers who have recently mastered these pas and are eager to display them all in one choreography.

The opening is a striking departure from convention. Pécour salutes the Présence with a balancé, yet keeps him waiting for the dancers to advance.[7] In the course of the dance, Pécour does not rely heavily upon pas de bourrée to cover ground, but employs instead pairs of contretemps de gavotte, de côté, and de chaconne and coupés de mouvement.

He has also given the dancers a variety of pas in place, the pas de rigaudon, pirouette both on the ground and with a saut, and pas de bourrée ouverts. The modified contretemps ballonné, introduced in measure 39, is a pas of energy and near-theatrical detail, which characterizes this choreography.

For all the stunning profusion of pas composés, their dissemination does act as an organizing element in the "Rigaudon des Vaisseaux." In the first rigaudon, the first reprise and its repetition employ the same four-measure conclusion, however subtly it may be stated.[8] The first statement of the second reprise is divided into subphrases, each of which begins with a pair of contretemps de côté.

Measures 35-40, which conclude the first rigaudon, introduce an important motive of the second rigaudon. The modified contretemps ballonné-pas de bourrée combination in measures 39-40 appears again in the second rigaudon in measures 51-54, 66-67, and finally in the repetition of the second reprise, which is an expansion, to twelve measures, of the pas composés and floor pattern of measures 35-40.

The relationship of musical and choreographic phrasing is more complex in the "Rigaudon des Vaisseaux" than in any of the bourrées in the 1700 *Recueil*. The music admits more interpretations and Pécour treats it with a variety of dance phrasing which rivals the variety of pas composés.

The dance is choreographed to a pair of rigaudon tunes in two-reprise form.[9] Each tune has an eight-measure first reprise and a twelve-measure second reprise. Each tune is stated once with its repeats.

	‖: A :‖:	B :‖:	A'	:‖: B' :‖
music	8 4 + 4	12 6 + 6	8 4 + 4	12 7 + 5
dance statement	8	6 + 6 4+2	4 + 4	7 + 5
dance repeat	4 + 4	6 + 6 4+2	8	5 + 7

In the eight-measure reprises, Pécour concerns himself with the question of observing the musical subdivisions in the choreography. In the first rigaudon, the contretemps ballonné in measure 4 bounces on into the jetés in the following measure. It is not clear until the repetition of the reprise that the pair of jetés begin the enchainement two jetés-pas de bourrée-pas de sissonne-pas de bourrée emboîté, which is so important in "la Savoye."[10]

After the statement of the pas de rigaudon which opens the second rigaudon, the flurry of glissades seems like an afterthought, but it does divide the reprise in half. There is no such division in the repetition. After the pretty event of the pirouette avec sauts, any further break is muddled by a statement and repetition of the contretemps ballonné-pas de bourrée motive and further obscured by the addition of another pas de bourrée (which feels like the second of a pair of pas de bourrée) and a temps de courante.

The possibilities of a twelve-measure phrase are explored by the composer, who divides the second reprise of the first tune in half and that of the second tune into parts of seven and five measures. Pécour exploits the situation and varies the dance phrasing with each repetition, not always adhering to the musical subdivisions and adding, at times, further subdivisions of his own.

Pécour observes the six-measure musical breaks in the first rigaudon, but creates an internal phrasing of 4 + 2 measures in the first figure. The pas de sissonne and pas de bourrée emboîté which follow the initial pair of contretemps de côté have already been established as a cadential figure in the first reprise. The contretemps de gavotte and coupé forward which follow reinforce the division with a change of direction. The next six measures which begin with the second pair of contretemps de côté form an unbroken phrase culminating in a truly cadential pas de sissonne-pas de bourrée emboîté.

In the repetition of the reprise, the temps de courante in measure 34 interrupts the forward motion and divides the reprise in half. The first six measures appear to be an unbroken phrase, particularly because the contretemps continues the turn of the preceding pirouette.

The second six measures are divided into a group of four measures, closing with a coupé to first position, and the modified contretemps ballonné and pas de bourrée. These last two measures form a puzzling culmination to a tune.

The contretemps ballonné and pas de bourrée seem less puzzling in light of the end of the second rigaudon, but the pas de bourrée is not a strong cadential pas, in any event. In the "Passepied" before the beginning of the second tune and in "la Mariée" before the repetition of the tune, Pécour does not use a cadential combination of pas composés either, a technique which minimizes the musical change.

In the first statement of the twelve-measure reprise in the second rigaudon, Pécour follows the composer's division into unequal seven- and five-measure parts. The seven-measure section hesitates a bit at the coupé in its fifth measure, but the glissades and second coupé provide a more definite break after the seventh measure. After the pas de bourrée ouverts, a temps de courante adds finality to the modified contretemps and pas de bourrée phrase motive.

In the repetition, Pécour does not observe the musical divisions and breaks the choreography between the fifth and sixth measures. The four pas de bourrée and coupé which constitute the five-measure segment are an extension, by one pas de bourrée, of the four-measure subdivision of the final six measures of the first rigaudon (measures 35-38).

The seven-measure conclusion is an extension of the contretemps ballonné-pas de bourrée motive which ended the first rigaudon in measures 39-40. The additional five measures, composed of two more statements of the motive which take the dancers back to the center of the room and down the room and a closing pas turning to face the Présence, provide a floor pattern and closing pas which lend a sense of finality to the choreography.

Le Rigaudon   123

124   *Le Rigaudon*

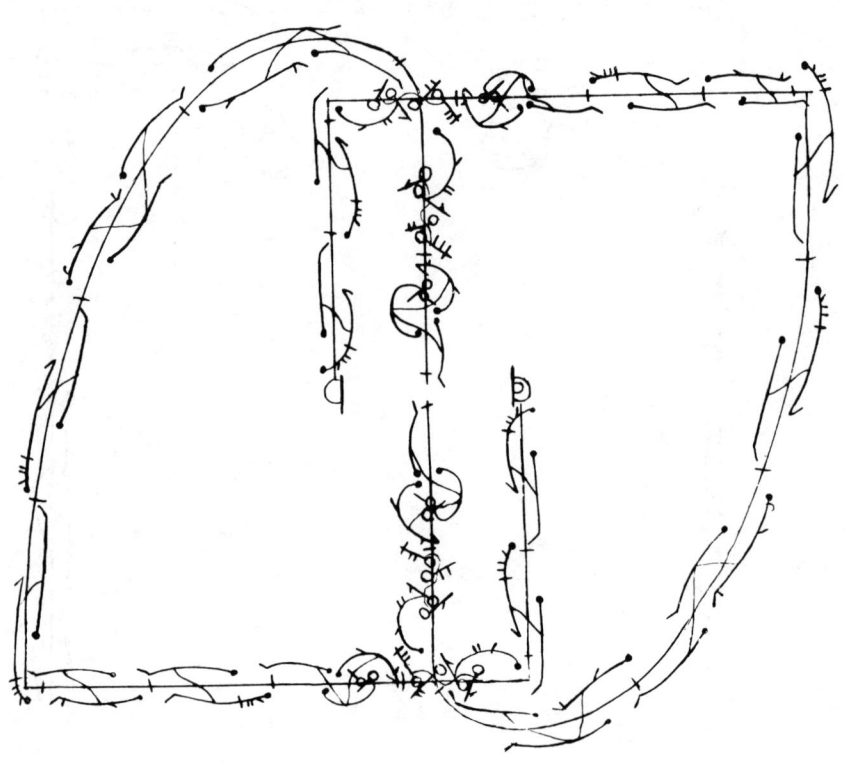

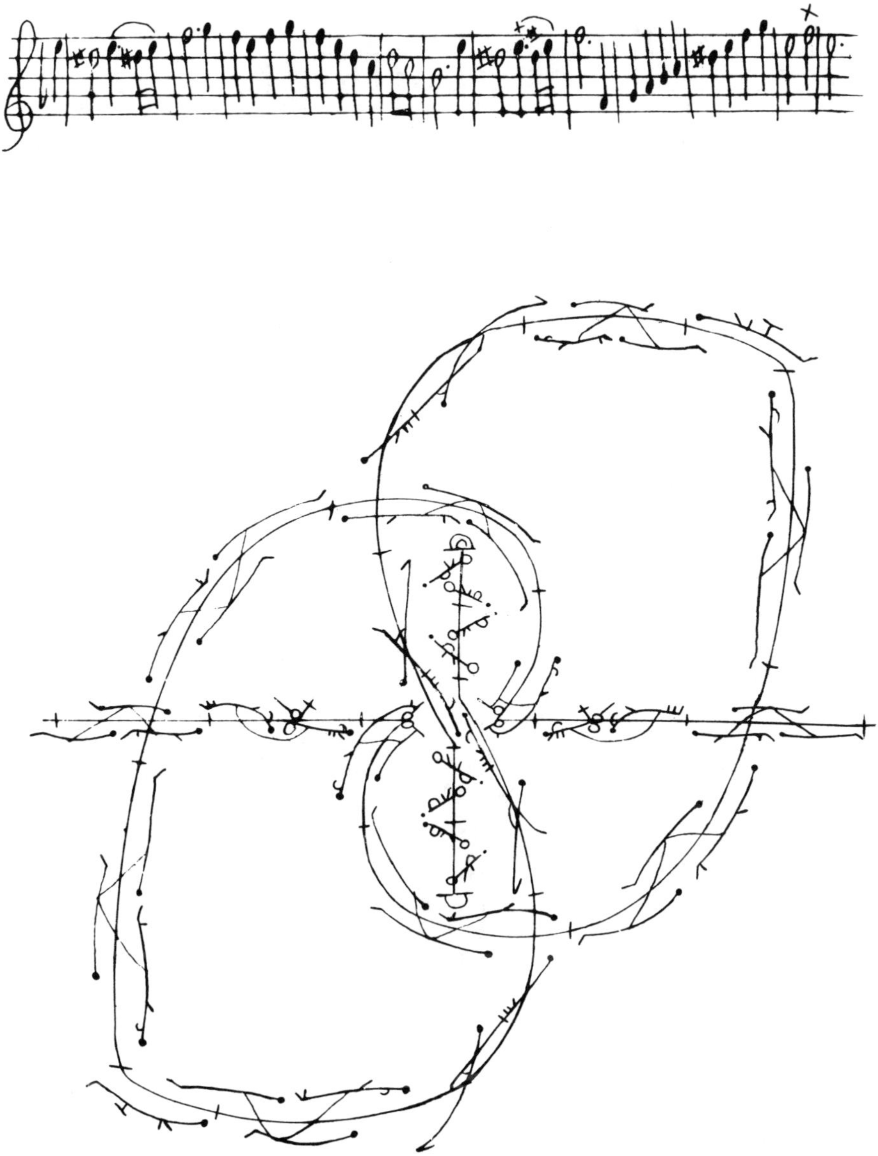

Le Rigaudon

Le Rigaudon

2.^e Rigaudon.

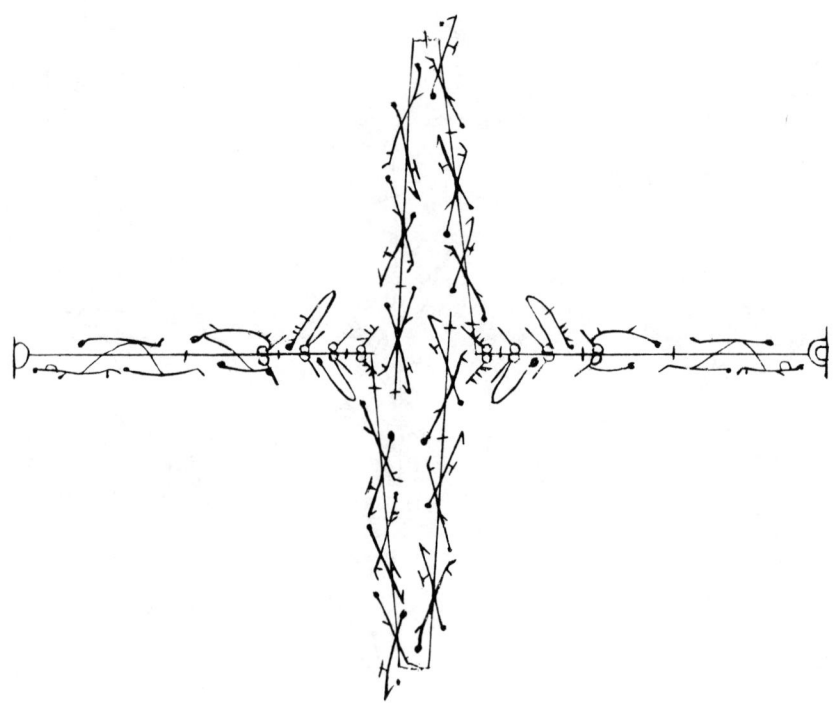

Le Rigaudon

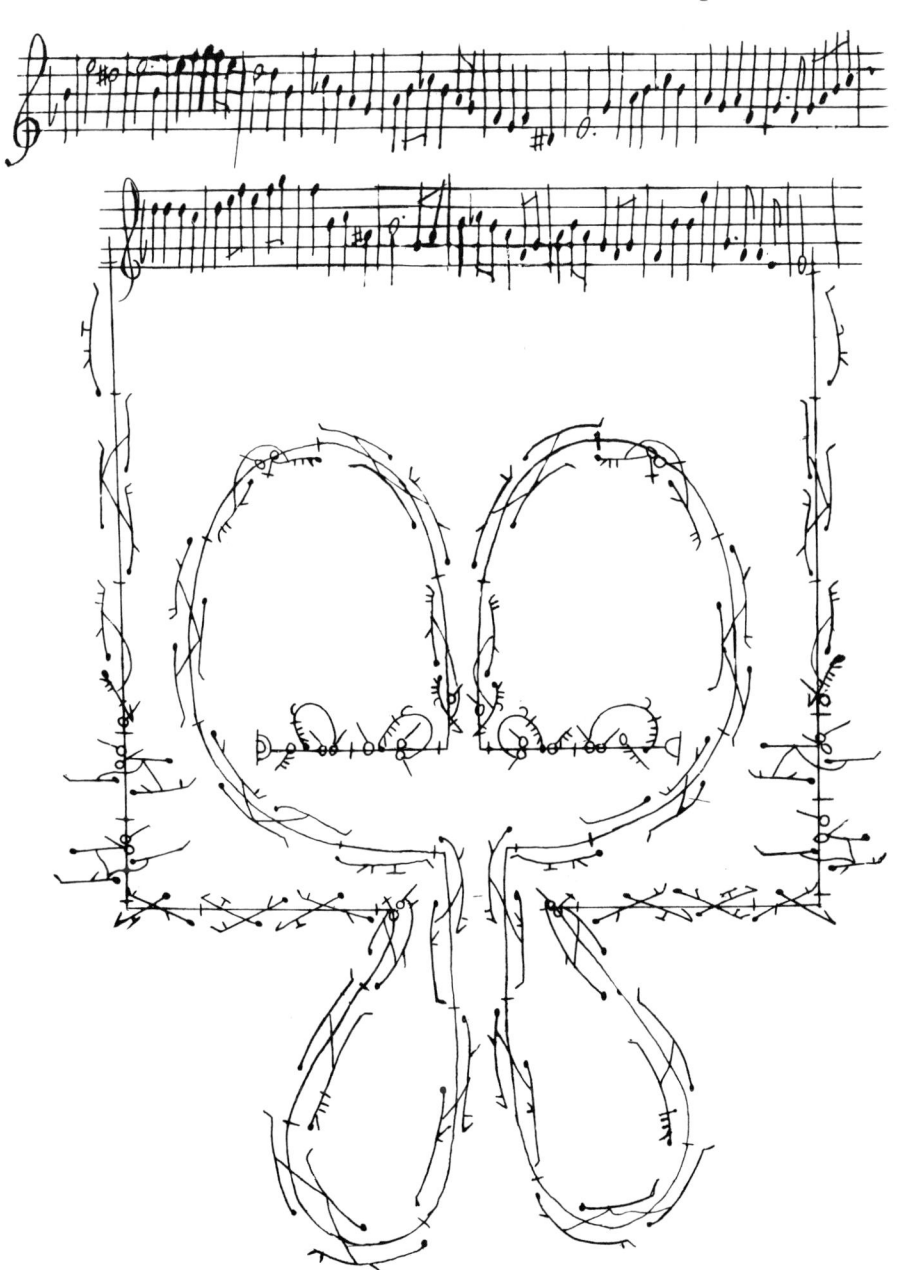

128 *Le Rigaudon*

6

La Bourgogne

courante A^c	♪|♩♫♩♩.♪|♩	♩♩.♪|♩.♪	♩♩♩♩|♩.	♩♩♪|♩♩♩.♫|o					
m.1	⊢tc dj	c⊣ dj	dc c--ı	c⊣ dj	c⊣ dj	⊢tc dj			
A^c rpt									
m.7	p d b	⊢tc dj	c⊣ dj	c⊣dj	c⊣ dj	pd e			
bourrée A^b	♫|♩♩♩.♪	♩♩ ♫	♩.♫♩♪	♩. ♫|♩.♩♩	♩.♩♩♩	♫♫|♩♩.			
m.13	j j	p d b	j j	p d b	b	1	p d b	⊢tc	
A'^b	♫|♩♩♩.♪	♩♩ ♫	♩.♫♩♪	♩. ♫|♩.♩♩	♩.♩♩♩	♩.♫♩♪			
m.21	j j	p d b	j j	c---ı p d b	b	1	p d b	⊢tc	
sarabande A^s	♩♩|♩♩♩	♩♩♩	♩♩♩	♩					
m.29	pir	c--oj	pir	⊢tc					
A^s rpt									
m.33	c⊣	⊢tc	c⊣	⊢tc					
B^s	♩.♪♩♩ ♩.♪|♩	♪♪|♪♪♪.♪|♩							
m.37	ct dg	c--oj	ct dg	c--pt					
B^s rpt									
m.41	pt	pt	c--ı j	p d b					

130   La Bourgogne

passepied

A^p								
m.45	m	3	m	3	m	3	m m	2 3
A^p rpt								
m.53	m	3	m	3	m	3	m m	3 2
B^p								
m.61	m	3	m	2	ct	m	ct	m
B'^{p}								
m.69	m	3	m	2	m	3	ct	m
B^p rpt								
m.77	m	3	m	3	ct	m	ct	m
B'^{p} rpt								
m.85	m	3	m	3	ct	m	c + c m	2+c1

Pécour 1700, P. 43, Measures 1-6

step-units: temps de courante forward
demi-jeté forward
coupé soutenue forward
demi-jeté
demi-coupé backward
coupé simple backward
coupé soutenue forward
demi-jeté forward
coupé soutenue forward
demi-jeté forward
temps de courante forward
demi-jeté forward

The dancers begin "la Bourgogne" with the weight on the outside foot and the inside foot in fourth position behind. They open the dance with a temps de courante and a demi-jeté forward; a coupé soutenue forward and a demi-jeté into fifth position in front, turning a quarter-turn in the air to face the partner; a demi-coupé backward and a coupé simple backward with the pas marché in fifth position behind.

The dancers continue with a quarter-turn to face the Présence and a coupé soutenue and a demi-jeté forward; a coupé soutenue forward, tracing a half-circle toward the partner finishing side by side facing down the room; and a demi-jeté forward. The dancers conclude the first phrase with a temps de courante forward and a demi-jeté forward.

In the courante, Feuillet notates the single pas at the end of a measure (measures 1, 2, 4-6, 8-11) as a demi-coupé, while Rameau notates this step as a demi-jeté.[1] Because Feuillet had no sign in his system of notation for the demi-jeté, and because the courante had a configuration of steps as peculiar to that dance as the pas de menuet is to the menuet and the passepied, it is not unreasonable to assume that the demi-jeté is just as authentic to a reconstruction of a performance of "la Bourgogne," circa 1700, as it is to a reconstruction of its performance circa 1725.

In any event, my solution to this question of execution, bolstered by Pécour's approbation of the notation of his dances in *Abbrégé,* is analogous to the solution to the question of the demi-jeté in the pas de menuet of three movements:[2] if such a step-unit was notated at all in 1700, the demi-jeté was taken for granted by the performer. The involved question of the existence of a step-unit called a "pas de courante" will be discussed in detail later in this chapter.

Pécour 1700, P. 44, Measures 7-12

step-units: pas de bourrée to the side before and behind
temps de courante to the side
demi-jeté forward
coupé soutenue forward
demi-jeté forward
coupé soutenue forward
demi-jeté forward
coupé soutenue forward
demi-jeté forward
modified pas de bourrée emboîté/
pas de bourrée emboîté

To begin the courante's second phrase, the dancers turn a quarter-turn to face each other and perform a pas de bourrée to the side before and behind up the room; a temps de courante to the side, opening out to second position, and a quarter-turn and a demi-jeté forward; a coupé soutenue forward and a demi-jeté forward; a second coupé soutenue forward and demi-jeté forward; a third coupé soutenue forward and demi-jeté forward. Then the lady makes a pas de bourrée emboîté as the gentleman makes a modified pas de bourrée emboîté.

132 *La Bourgogne*

The temps de courante to the side in measure 8 is a good example of this step-unit as it is described by Rameau.[3] Because this step characteristically follows a pas de bourrée to the side before and behind, as it does in "la Bourgogne," Rameau explains that the initial plié of the temps de courante to the side should be made with both knees as usual but with the weight on both feet, with the feet remaining in *third* position, in which the pas de bourrée closed. This exception to the rule of making the plié in first position draws attention both to the contrast between the pas de bourrée's opening in order to close again and the temps de courante's slow opening to second position, and to the connection between these two step-units as part of one line of movement. This temps de courante completes one line, and another pattern begins with the demi-jeté which follows. For these reasons, I would follow Rameau's instructions to plié in third position.

This temps de courante provides another striking moment in that, in opening to second position, the dancer does not follow a path directly up the room. With this glissé, he begins his circle away from the partner so that the pair of dancers completes the temps de courante in a position in which their gaze toward each other includes the Présence.

In measure 12, the gentleman's part begins with the beaten demi-coupé backward and pas marché closing into third position behind of the conventional pas de bourrée emboîté. Instead of continuing with a pas marché forward, however, the gentleman makes his next pas marché backward in Feuillet's notation of "la Bourgogne." Rameau notates a conventional pas de bourrée emboîté in *Abbrégé*.[4] Neither notator indicates that the final pas marché of this step-unit should be made sans poser le corps, as it must be in order to begin the bourrée on the correct foot.

Pécour 1700, P. 45, Measures 13-20

step-units: 2 jetés forward
pas de bourrée forward
2 jetés forward
pas de bourrée forward
balancé to the side
pas de bourrée forward
temps de courante forward

Pécour 1700, P. 46, Measures 21-28

step-units: 2 jetés forward
pas de bourrée forward
2 jetés forward

coupé simple forward/pas de
   bourrée forward
balancé to the side
pas de bourrée forward
temps de courante forward

"La Bourgogne's" bourrée begins with a pair of jetés forward, a pas de bourrée forward, a second pair of jetés forward, and a pas de bourrée forward. The dancers continue with a balancé, a pas de bourrée forward, and a temps de courante forward.

The dancers begin the bourrée's second page with a pair of jetés forward, a pas de bourrée forward, a pair of jetés forward, and a pas de bourrée forward for the lady, while the gentleman makes a coupé simple forward in order to make an adjustment for the symmetry of the following step-units. The dancers complete the bourrée with a balancé facing the Présence, a quarter-turn and a pas de bourrée forward toward the partner; and a temps de courante forward.

Whereas the execution of the step-units of the bourrée is absolutely straightforward, at least two adjustments are necessary to preserve the symmetry of the floor pattern. The dancers' paths in measures 21-24 must be worked out so that the woman does not get farther up the room than the man in her last pas de bourrée before the balancé, and so that, after the balancé, the dancers have enough room to make their steps toward each other and meet at the center of the room. It is a passage which allows little margin for error.

At the end of the first page of the bourrée, in both Rameau's and Feuillet's notations, the dancers appear to have passed each other by the end of the temps de courante, yet in both versions the next page begins with the dancers shoulder to shoulder. The exact solution may be left to the couple, but I do feel the indication not to meet head-on in the temps de courante is clear.

The final temps de courante of the bourrée, in measure 28, is another example of a closing step in which, if a complete transfer of weight were to be made (and neither Feuillet nor Rameau indicates that it should not be made), it would be impossible to begin the next dance on the proper foot. In the case of this temps de courante, I prefer the solution of transferring part of the weight to the foot which has just moved forward, finishing the bourrée with the weight on both feet.

Pécour 1700, P. 47, Measures 29-36

step-units: pirouette
                coupé forward avec ouverture de jambe
                pirouette
                temps de courante forward

coupé soutenue forward
temps de courante forward
coupé soutenue forward
temps de courante forward

Pécour 1700, P. 48, Measures 37-44

step-units: contretemps de gavotte forward
coupé forward avec ouverture de jambe
contretemps de gavotte forward
coupé simple forward sans poser le corps
temps forward
temps backward
coupé + jeté forward
pas de bourrée forward/coupé
soutenue forward

The dancers open the sarabande with a half-turn pirouette away from the partner in the direction of the Présence; a coupé forward avec ouverture de jambe; a half-turn pirouette turning in the direction of the Présence back to face the partner; and a temps de courante forward, passing left shoulders.

The dancers continue circling to meet each other with a coupé soutenue forward, a temps de courante forward, a coupé soutenue forward, and a temps de courante forward.

To begin the sarabande's second strain, the dancers perform a half-turn in the air in the direction of the Présence and a contretemps de gavotte forward away from the partner; a coupé forward avec ouverture de jambe, turning a half-turn in the direction of the Présence back to face the partner; a contretemps de gavotte forward toward the partner; a quarter-turn to face the Présence, and a modified coupé simple sans poser le corps.

The dancers continue with a temps or point forward, a temps or point backward, and a coupé simple to first position and a jeté forward. Finally, the gentleman performs a pas de bourrée forward as the lady makes a coupé soutenue forward so that both dancers can begin the passepied on the right foot.

In measure 36, the temps de courante forward should not transfer all of the weight. In this instance, Rameau has notated a temps de courante forward sans poser le corps.[5]

The coupé simple sans poser le corps in measure 40 is made with a quarter-turn and demi-coupé forward, bringing the free foot into first position on the rise, followed by a pas marché sans poser le corps into fourth position behind, with the free foot.

The first step in the lady's part in measure 43 should not have a sign to leap, but only an élevé. The step is notated correctly in the gentleman's part by Feuillet, and in both parts by Rameau.[6]

Feuillet's use of the double line of liaison for the coupé in this measure indicates that he wishes to allow half as much time for the coupé as he does for the jeté. Thus, the élevé of the coupé would occur on beat 1 and the dancer would land from the jeté on beat 3. Rameau does not use the double line of liaison in his notation of this measure.[7]

Pécour 1700, P. 49, Measures 45-60

step-units: pas de menuet of 3 mouvements forward
pas de menuet of 3 mouvements forward
pas de menuet of 3 mouvements forward
pas de menuet of 2 mouvements to the
   left/of 3 mouvements forward
pas de menuet of 3 mouvements forward
pas de menuet of 3 mouvements forward
pas de menuet of 3 mouvements forward
pas de menuet of 3 mouvements forward/
   of 2 mouvements to the right

Pécour 1700, P. 50-51, Measures 61-76

step-units: pas de menuet of 3 mouvements to the left
pas de menuet of 2 mouvements to the right
contretemps de menuet forward
contretemps de menuet forward
pas de menuet of 3 mouvements forward

pas de menuet of 2 mouvements to the right
pas de menuet of 3 mouvements to the left
contretemps de menuet forward

To begin the passepied, the dancers take hands and perform three pas de menuet of three movements forward, tracing a half-circle; the gentleman makes a pas de menuet of two movements before and before to the left, as the lady makes one more pas de menuet of three movements forward so that the couple completes the fourth pas facing the Présence.

Then the dancers perform three pas de menuet of three movements forward, tracing a half-circle; and the lady makes a pas de menuet of two movements before and before to the right as the gentleman makes a pas de menuet of three movements forward so that the couple completes this reversed-S figure facing the Présence.

La Bourgogne

To begin the passepied's second strain, the dancers perform a pas de menuet of three movements behind and behind to the left and a pas de menuet of two movements behind and before to the right. Letting go hands, the dancers make two contretemps de menuet forward; and a pas de menuet of three movements forward, tracing circles away from the partner and back to meet the partner at the end of the pas de menuet.

Taking hands once again, the dancers perform a pas de menuet of two movements behind and behind to the right, a pas de menuet of three movements behind and behind to the left, and a contretemps de menuet forward.

Pécour 1700, P. 52, Measures 77-84

step-units: pas de menuet of 3 mouvements backward/forward
pas de menuet of 3 mouvements backward/forward
contretemps de menuet forward
contretemps de menuet forward

Pécour 1700, P. 53, Measures 85-92

step-units: pas de menuet of 3 mouvements forward
pas de menuet of 3 mouvements forward
contretemps de menuet backward/forward
coupé soutenue backward + coupé
   soutenue to the side/pas de menuet
   of 2 mouvements forward + close

To begin the repetition of the passepied's second strain, the gentleman makes two pas de menuet of three movements backward down the room, dropping hands at the end of the second pas, as the lady makes two pas de menuet of three movements forward, crossing in front of the gentleman and following him down the room. Taking left hands, the couple performs a contretemps de menuet forward, dropping hands at the end of the pas. Taking right hands, the dancers perform another contretemps de menuet to complete their individual circles.

The couple continues with two pas de menuet of three movements forward, tracing a half-circle with the gentleman facing the Présence and the lady facing down the room at its completion. Then the gentleman makes a contretemps de menuet backward, as the lady makes a contretemps de menuet forward. To close, the gentleman makes a coupé soutenue backward and a coupé soutenue to the right, as the lady makes a modified pas de menuet of two movements turning to face the Présence.

In the second pas de menuet backward for the gentleman (measures 79-80), Rameau[8] writes a simple backward pas, while Feuillet indicates a modification of the last movement of the pas—an eighth-turn to the right (indicated not by a turn sign, but by the path and the angle of the foot at the end of the demi-jeté), so that this demi-jeté begins the circle which the contretemps continue. This is a minor decision for the gentleman, but Feuillet's notation indicates a need, whether or not the gentleman elects to make the early turn, for more room between the dancers when they take left hands, in measure 81, than was possible when the gentleman's right hand guided the lady on his left, in measures 77-80.

Feuillet gives more detailed indications of the exchange of hands in this passage than does Rameau.[9] It is possible that, because the lady does not change the hand given to her partner between measures 80 and 81, the signs to drop hands and take hands again are omitted at this point in her part, even by Feuillet.

The closing step-unit of "la Bourgogne," identical to that of "le Passepied," is the standard closing for passepieds: two coupés backward for the gentleman, the second moving in toward the lady while the lady makes a pas de menuet of two movements forward with a half-turn in the direction of the partner to face the Présence on the final pas marché, and a close into first position. In order to make her half-turn, the lady must drop hands, although this sign does not appear in the notation.

Like "la Bourrée d'Achille," "la Bourgogne" is a mixed dance-type choreography, several other examples of which are found among the notated ball dances of this period. These dances are not analogous to the musical suite of dances nor to Couperin's ordres, which are collections of relatively short, complete pieces in the same key. In the performance of a musical suite, neither the order of these pieces nor including all of the movements is necessarily essential.

"La Bourgogne" is one dance which employs different dance types within the course of its choreography to reflect changes of mood in the contrast of tempo, metre, quality of movement, and structure of the courante, bourrée, sarabande, and passepied. None of its sections could be performed as an independent piece, and the order of the sections could not be changed.

The courante section of "la Bourgogne" has been analyzed in articles in two recent musical journals.[10] The number of musical courantes from this period and the complexity of these pieces have contributed to many musicians' curiosity about this dance, in particular. Unfortunately, the danced courante was on the wane by the time Beauchamp-Feuillet's system came into general use, and only five choreographies have been preserved. Of these, the courante in Pécour's "la Bourgogne" is the best known.

The courante of this period is a dance with a limited number of step-units and an elliptical floor pattern. "La Bourgogne's" reference to the ellipse is clear.

138   La Bourgogne

The steps which Pécour employs (the temps de courante, the demi-jeté, the coupé, and the pas de bourrée) are all among those associated with the courante. In "la Bourgogne," these step-units divide the musical measure either into two unequal parts, each marked by a movement,

$$\begin{array}{cc} o & d \\ c \text{———} & dj \\ \text{or } \vdash \text{———} tc & dj \end{array}$$

or into three equal part with one movement on the downbeat,

$$\begin{array}{ccc} d & d & d \\ p & d & b \end{array}$$

The first division of the musical measure was the more common of the two.

In *Le Maître,* Part I, Chapter 26, "Of the Courante in General," Rameau mentions a step-unit called the pas de courante. It consists of a demi-jeté followed by a coupé. After the opening temps de courante, the dancers employ a series of pas de courante to travel the path of their ellipse.

Rameau's lines of liaison in his notation of the courante in "la Bourgogne"[11] make it clear that this notator considered measures 8-11, at least, to be pas de courante. The distinction between viewing these measures as pas de courante or as Feuillet's combination of one and one-half step units is purely a matter of theory and does not affect the performance of the steps.

In the bourrée, placement of Pécour's sequences of step-units reflects the musical phrases exactly, repeating an eight-measure sequence of step-units when the music repeats. Within the sequence, the pattern of step-units also reflects the pattern of rhythmic repetitions of the musical measures.

bourrée

A^b

m. 13   j j   p d b   j j   p d b   b   1   p d b   ⊢tc

A'^b

m. 21   j j   p d b   j j   p d b   b   1   p d b   ⊢tc

I have always appreciated "la Bourgogne's" sarabande as a dance which, for all its tenderness, never deteriorates into sentimentality. A sensitive and fairly intricate relationship of music and dance is responsible for some of the dance's strength.

The music is composed of two repeated four-measure phrases, each beginning on the second beat of the measure. Although the melody of each phrase is diatonic, with leaps only to begin each phrase or repetition, the dotted rhythms and hemiola of the second phrase provide a contrast to the even line of the first.

In the first phrase, Pécour has chosen step-units whose second beat may be considered not only a continuation but an expansion of the élevé on each downbeat: the turn of the pirouette, the ouverture de jambe of the coupé, the glissé of the temps de courante. In the second phrase, he introduces step-units with quite a different internal character: the contretemps de gavotte, with its leap on the downbeat and unaccented pas marché, and the point and the pas in measure 43, with no movement on the second beat. These new step-units are exploited to provide rhythmic contrast to the musical hemiola.

The passepied which concludes "la Bourgogne" exhibits many of the characteristics of these exclusive step-unit dance types discussed earlier in this work in the chapters on "la Bourrée d'Achille" (its menuet) and "le Passepied." One observes the conventional use of pas de menuet of three movements to the left and two movements to the right in the repeated pattern on pages 50-51. Pécour lets another pattern overrule strict adherence to this convention in the gentleman's pas de meneut of two movements to the left in measures 51-52.

The choice between Feuillet's pas de menuet of three movements forward and Rameau's simpler pas of two movements forward must be made in this section of "la Bourgogne," as in "la Bourrée d'Achille" and "le Passepied." Feuillet's use of the pas de menuet of three movements backward in measures 77-80 is unusual, but obviously it was not considered an unreasonable demand to make of a gentleman accommodating a lady's pas forward in 1700. By 1725, the lady made her pas forward with two movements and the gentleman was spared this challenge.

It is difficult to avoid discussion of the relationship of music and dance in "la Bourgogne." To me, the most intriguing aspect of Pécour's "la Bourgogne" is the encouragement it gives the scholar to see this relationship as a variable element, influenced first by the choreographer and also, to a certain extent, by the performers.

Those dance types which had characteristic step-units, each with a standard timing or cadence,[12] left the choreographer with fewer choices. Precisely because of those fixed elements, he could choose to alter the coincidence of patterns in music and dance with great impact. A striking example is found in the second figure of the passepied (measures 61-76). The music is divided equally into 8 + 8 measures, but the repetition of dance step-units follows a pattern of 5 + 3.[13] This division is clarified by Feuillet's notation of the figure on two pages.

Pécour could easily have choreographed a symmetrical dance pattern here by using only the two contretemps de menuet to make his circle in measures 65-68, beginning the pas de menuet of two movements to the right in measure 69, and adding a second contretemps de menuet forward to complete the phrase.

La Bourgogne   *141*

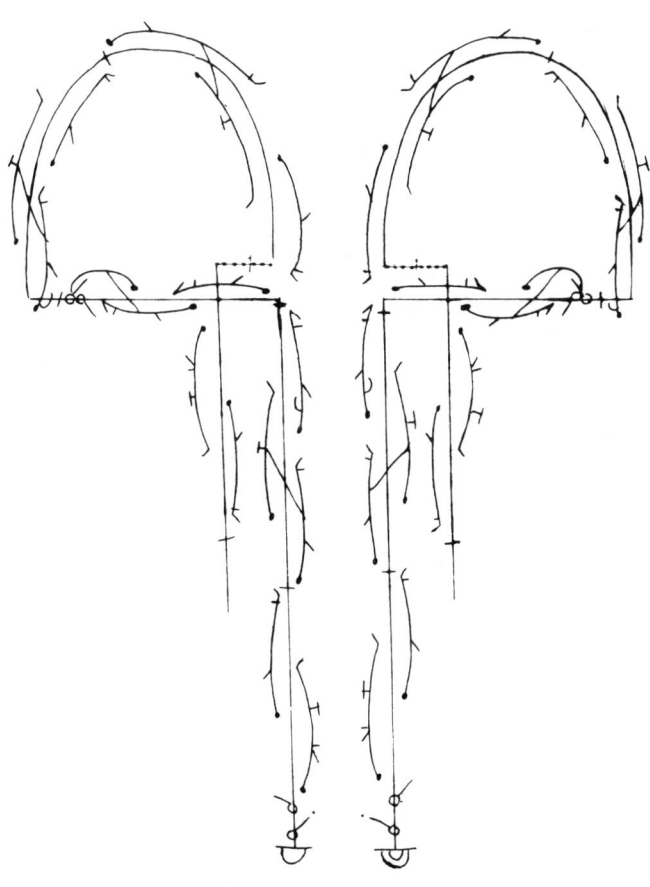

142 La Bourgogne

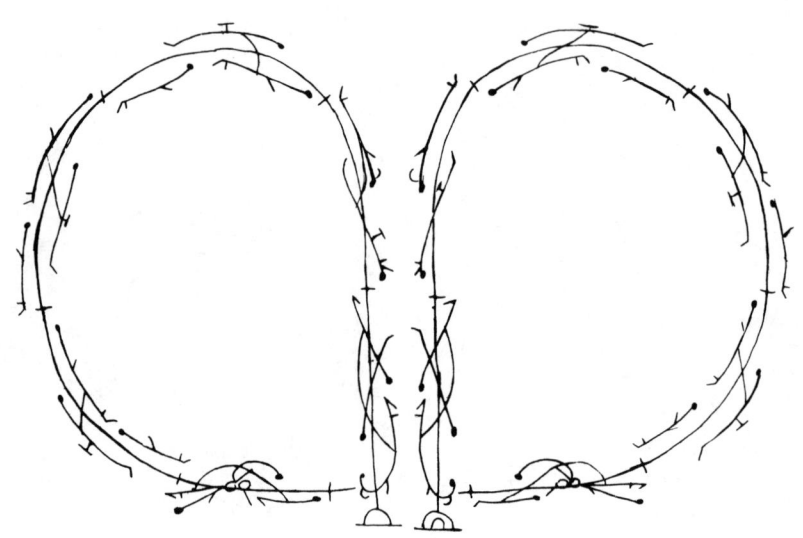

La Bourgogne

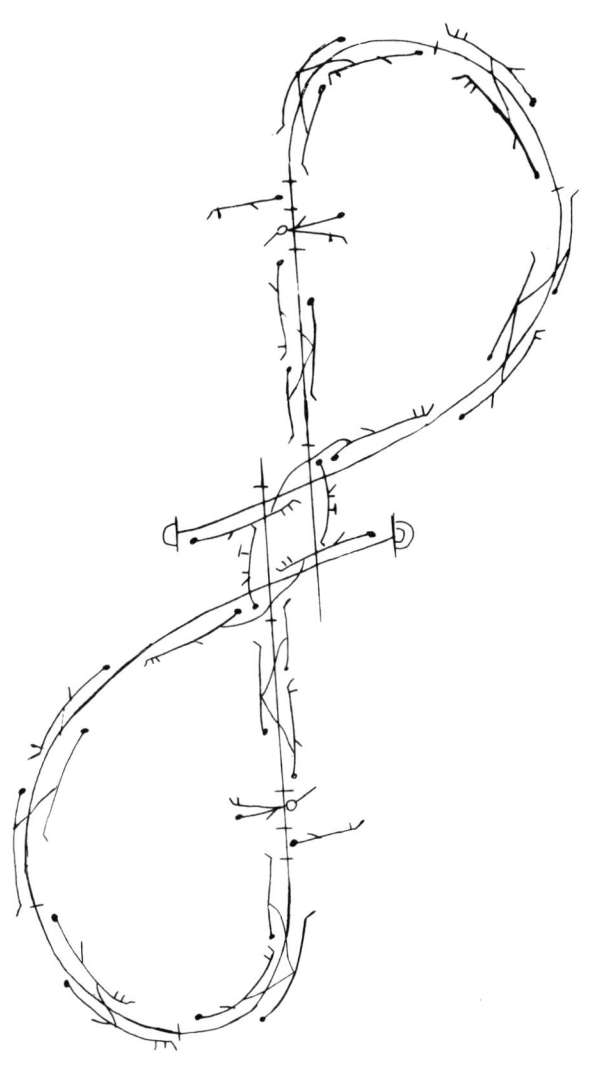

144 La Bourgogne

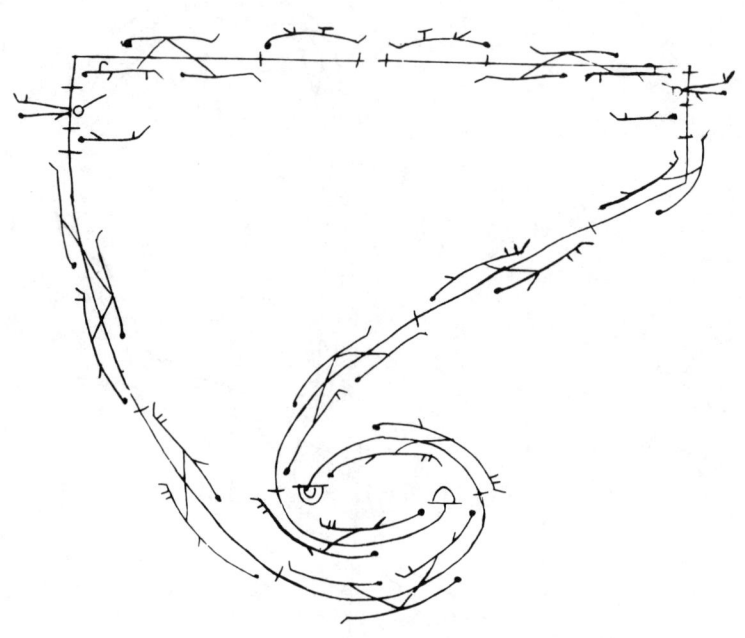

La Bourgogne   145

Sarabande

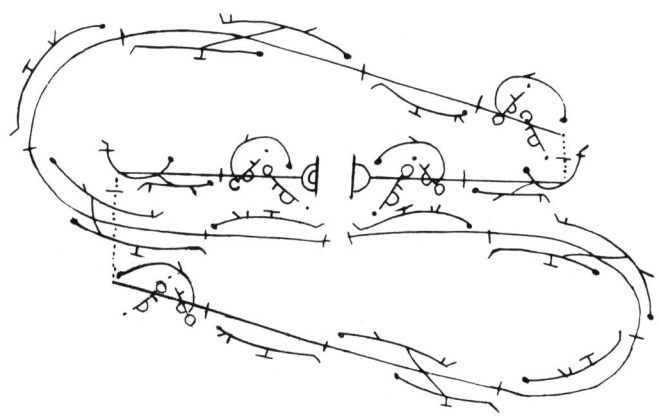

146 La Bourgogne

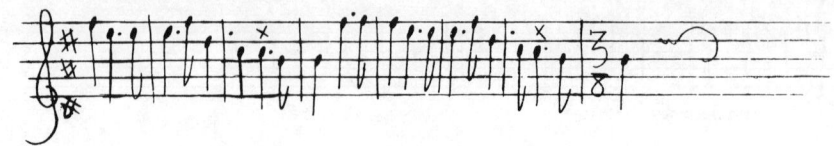

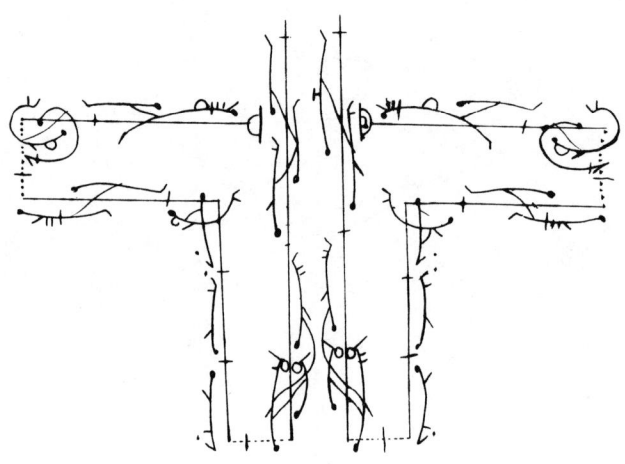

Passe Pied.

La Bourgogne

148 La Bourgogne

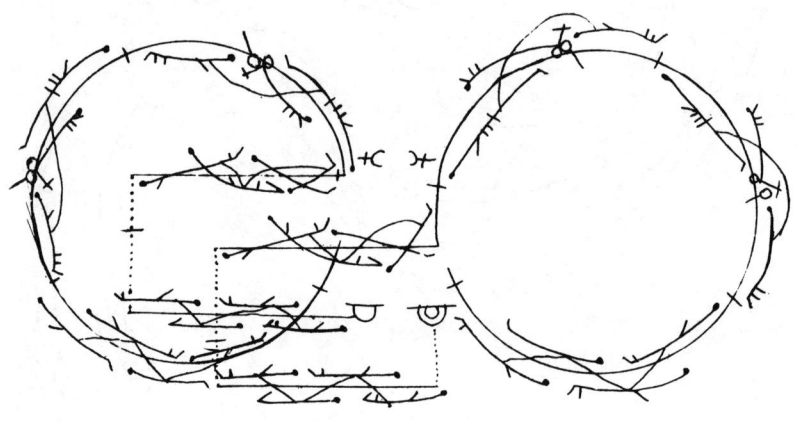

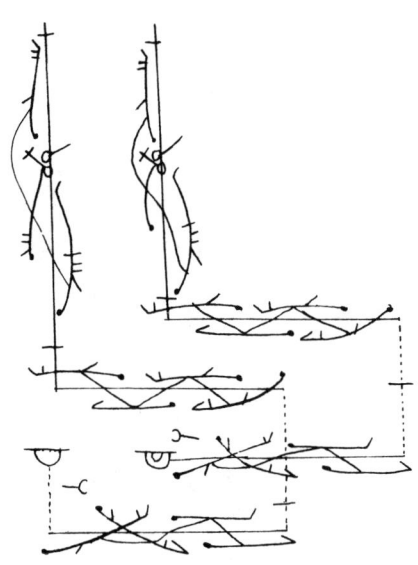

La Bourgogne

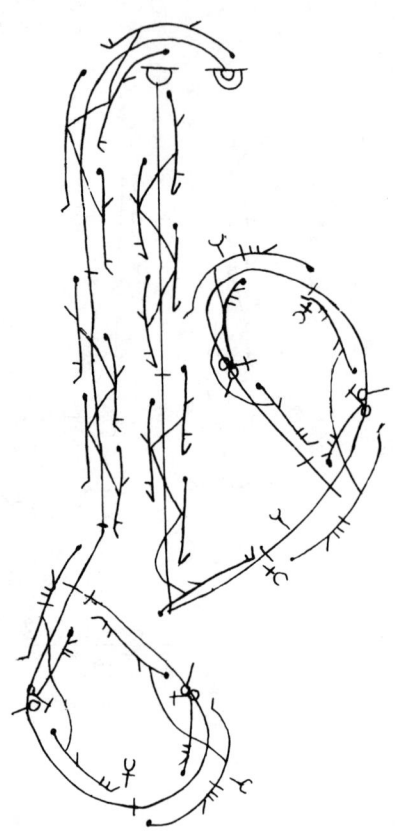

La Bourgogne 151

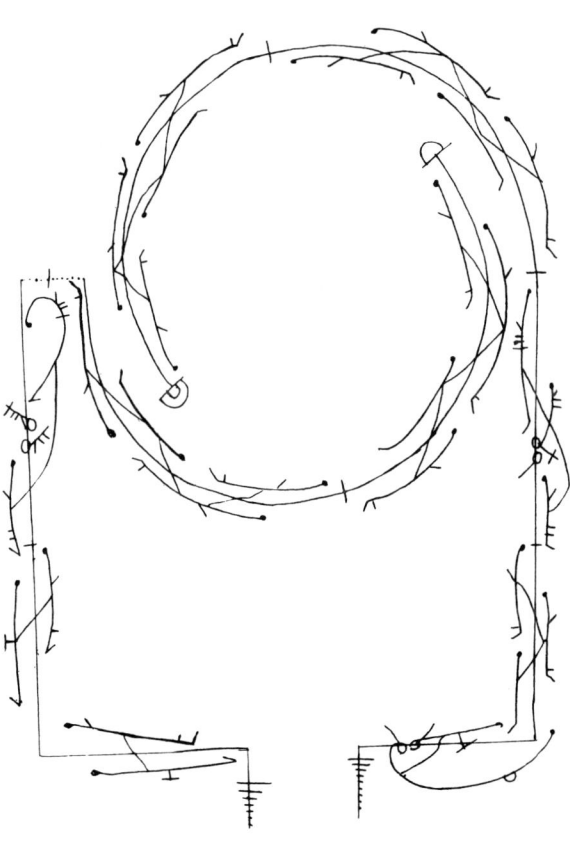

7

La Savoye

Eighteenth-century composers and musical theorists created a number of musical games in which a dance tune could be composed by the players, who tossed dice to select measures supplied by the compiler.[1] To my knowledge, no accompanying volumes have been designed to choreograph the dance itself, although it would not have been difficult for Pécour to construct such a game. The vocabulary of pas composés used in the danses à deux is limited; certain pas move felicitously into others and came to be used together in choreographies, and the movement of the pas composés further links them to a particular sort of floor pattern and a position in the dance phrase.

In the bourrée "la Savoye," Pécour exploits these conventions of the French danse à deux so that it appears that he has choreographed it with dice until he introduces an unexpected turn of phrase to delight the courtiers and assure them that he has not. Some of "la Savoye's" two-measure formulae which the Court would have recognized are listed below accompanied by one of the many possible instances of their analogous use in other dances from Pécour's 1700 *Recueil*.

	Phrase beginning	Phrase ending
Forward:	1. pdb pdb (Bourée d'Achille, m. 1-2) 2. j j pdb (Rigaudon 5-6)	6. pdb c--l (Conty 15-16)
To the side:	3. pdb c b (Mariée 53-54)	7. pdb pt (Mariée 22-23) 8. gl gl c-oj (Contredance 15-16) 9. pdb c--l (Forlana 23-24)
In place:	4. pir pir (Rigaudon 29-30) 5. pde pde (Forlana 45-46)	10. p s pde (Rigaudon 7-8)

154   La Savoye

It is obvious from the combinations of two-measure formulae used in "la Savoye" diagrammed below that taste and experience governed Pécour's choices just as they did those of the compiler of a musical game. Pécour has established, within his own works, a grammar and syntax of choreographic composition, a norm from which he could deviate with striking effect.[2]

FIGURE 1:   Music   Formulae

A	1	8	1	8
B	2	2	10	0
C	2	10	2	(10)
C	3	7	3	10
A	4	7	3	(1)
B	0	0	10	0
C	1	9	1	6
C	5	1	1	(10)

Pécour scrupulously observes "la Savoye's" musical form in his application of choreographic "ars combinatoria." The tune, which is stated twice, is composed of three eight-measure phrases with the third phrase repeated. The first and third phrases are divided into parallel four-measure segments.

$$\|: \underset{a^1 a^2}{A} \quad \underset{}{B} \quad \underset{c^1 c^2}{C} \quad \underset{c^1 c^2}{C} \ :\|$$

As one observes in Figure 1, Pécour confines his departures from stereotypical step progressions to the B phrase, which does not have parallel subphrases.

The pas composés of "la Savoye" and their cadence may be seen in the chart below, followed by an explanation of their performance. At the close of this chapter, I have included a discussion of the relationship of the sequences of pas composés and floor patterns to the musical phrasing and the effect this might have upon the performance of the movements of the arms and head.

La Savoye

La Savoye 155

Pécour 1700, P. 54, Measures 1-8

step-units: pas de bourrée forward
 pas de bourrée forward
 glissades
 coupé to the side avec ouverture de jambe
 pas de bourrée forward
 pas de bourrée forward
 glissades
 coupé forward avec ouverture de jambe

156   La Savoye

"La Savoye" begins with a pair of pas de bourrée forward, the first beginning on the outside foot; a pair of glissades and a coupé avec ouverture de jambe to the side; a second pair of pas de bourrée forward to meet the partner at the top of the room; a pair of glissades to the side down the room and a quarter-turn to face the Présence, and coupé forward avec ouverture de jambe.

Pécour 1700, P. 55, Measures 9-14

step-units: two jetés forward
              pas de bourrée forward
              two jetés forward
              pas de bourrée forward
              pas de sissonne forward
              coupé simple backward to 2nd/
                  pas de bourrée emboîté

The dancers continue with a pair of jetés and a pas de bourrée forward; a second pair of jetés and pas de bourrée forward; followed by a pas de sissonne forward landing from the second saut with the weight on the foot which is behind. The purpose of the final step in this dance phrase is to transfer the dancer's weight to both feet in second position in preparation for the contretemps de côté, which begins the next phrase in such a way that the step which opens to second position indicates the direction of the contretemps. The gentleman executes a coupé, composed of a demi-coupé into fourth position behind and a pas marché opening into second position. The lady performs a modified pas de bourrée emboîté, composed of a demi-coupé into fourth position behind, a pas marché into third position behind, and a second pas marché opening the front foot out into second position.

Two details of execution merit explanation. First, the progression from a pas de bourrée to a pas de sissonne forward is an example of a step with an initial plié which is not taken in first position. Rameau says only that in the pas de sissonne the free foot opens out to the side during the plié and crosses into third position in front during the hop.[3] Tomlinson's description and plate of the starting position clearly show the plié beginning in the third position with the knee of the free foot a little bent so that the ankle of the free foot rests against the heel of the foot which is supporting the weight.[4]

Although Tomlinson's pas de sissonne may open out to the side later than Rameau's and pass farther in front for the landing, I think it is still possible to take advantage of the plié beginning in third position as a result of the transfer of weight on the last pas marché of the pas de bourrée in the preceding measure. In any event, there is no question of a plié in first position in a step whose purpose is to take the foot from behind and cross it in front.

The second question is the timing of the step-unit which the lady performs in measure 14. Although, strictly speaking, it is not the same pas de bourrée emboîté described by Rameau[5] and illustrated by Feuillet,[6] the single difference is the direction of the last pas marché. In measure 14, it is taken to second position in preparation for the following contretemps de côté. The step-unit does feature the same initial emboîté movement (crossing the first pas marché into third position behind), and it occupies the same position in the dance phrase which is characteristic of the pas de bourrée emboîté (end of a dance phrase, immediately following a pas de sissonne). For these reasons, I feel this pas composé serves the purpose of the pas de bourrée emboîté and should employ its cadence, closing into third position before the second quarter-note beat and waiting a little before moving to the second pas marché on the third quarter-note beat.[7]

Pécour 1700, P. 56, Measures 15-24

step-units: contretemps de côté
                pas de bourrée forward
                two jetés forward
                pas de bourrée forward
                pas de sissonne forward
                pas de bourrée emboîté

                two jetés forward
                pas de bourrée forward
                pas de sissonne forward
                coupé simple backward to 2nd

The dancers begin the next floor pattern with a contretemps de côté, making the plié on both feet in second position landing from the saut on the foot farthest from the partner, crossing the first pas marché into fifth position in front and opening the second pas marché to second position. Then both dancers make a quarter-turn in the direction of travel and a pas de bourrée forward. This is followed by a pair of jetés and a pas de bourrée forward; and a pas de sissonne forward landing from the second saut on the foot which is behind and a pas de bourrée emboîté.

The dancers continue the pattern with a pair of jetés forward and a pas de bourrée forward in which the dancers make a half-turn to the right during the course of the pas marché; a pas de sissonne forward landing from the second saut with the weight on the foot which is behind and a coupé simple backward which is composed of a demi-coupé into fourth position behind and a point opening out to second position which marks the second half-note of the measure, but receives no weight.

158   La Savoye

In measure 16, a turn sign has been omitted from the lady's part: on the demi-coupé, the sign for the plié should be preceded by a sign indicating a quarter-turn to the right.

Pécour 1700, P. 57, Measures 25-32

step-units: pas de bourrée to the side
contretemps ballonné to the side
pas de bourrée to the side
temps to the side
pas de bourrée to the side

The 1700 *Recueil* contains only three pairs of pirouettes, all of which lead into steps to the side. The pirouettes which begin this phrase of "la Savoye" differ from those in "le Rigaudon," measures 29-30, by finishing the second pirouette not on two feet but on one, with the free foot pointed in second position. In this respect, it resembles the pair of pirouettes in "la Mariée," although the pirouette with point in "la Mariée" does not include an extra quarter-turn.

There is no evidence to indicate that the cadence of the pirouette on one foot with a point should differ from that of the pirouette on two feet. In my opinion, the élevé should occur on the downbeat and the point should mark the end of the turn at the beginning of the second half-note of the measure.

Pécour 1700, P. 59, Measures 41-47

step-units: coupé simple to the side
pas tombé to the side
pas de sissonne forward
coupé simple to the side
pas tombé to the side
pas de sissonne forward
pas de bourrée emboîté

The dancers begin the second B phrase with a half-turn and coupé to the side, placing the demi-coupé in fifth position before and opening the pas marché into second. The coupé prepares the following tombé, falling into fifth position behind and demi-jeté to second, followed by a pas de sissonne landing from the second saut on the foot which is behind. The dancers continue with coupé to the side, placing the demi-coupé in fifth position behind and opening the pas marché to second to prepare a tombé into fifth position behind and its demi-jeté into second, followed by another pas de sissonne, landing from the second saut on the foot which is behind, and a pas de bourrée emboîté. The performance of the pas composés is straightforward, although the dancers should finish the demi-jetés in a plié in first position in order that the same free foot may be brought out clearly in the next pas de sissonne.

Pécour 1700, P. 59 (cont.)-60, Measures 48-56

step-units: contretemps de gavotte forward
              pas de bourrée forward
              pas de bourrée forward
              pas de bourrée before and behind to the side
              coupé simple to the side
              pas de bourrée forward
              pas de bourrée forward
              pas de bourrée forward
              coupé simple forward

The contretemps de gavotte forward in measure 48 begins the next floor pattern and the arc is continued with a pair of pas de bourrée forward. This is followed by a half-turn to the left and pas de bourrée to the side before and behind, facing the partner, and a coupé to the side, placing the demi-coupé in fifth position before and opening the pas marché to second. The dancers continue with a quarter-turn to the right, three pas de bourrée forward, and a coupé simple forward.

Pécour 1700, P. 61, Measures 57-64

step-units: pas de bourrée emboîté
              pas de bourrée emboîté
              pas de bourrée forward
              pas de bourrée forward
              pas de bourrée forward
              pas de bourrée forward
              pas de sissonne forward
              coupé soutenue

In the final phrase, the dancers perform a pair of pas de bourrée emboîtés, four pas de bourrée forward, a quarter-turn to face the Présence, and a pas de sissonne and closing coupé. The gentleman lands from the second saut of the pas de sissonne with the weight on the foot which is behind, followed by a coupé into fourth position behind; the lady finishes the pas de sissonne with the weight on the front foot and her coupé closes in first position.

160   La Savoye

Upon close examination, "la Savoye" rises discreetly out of the ranks of dice-game choreography through Pécour's adroit superimposition of sequences of step-units, floor patterns, and musical phrasing.

Music	A	$\dfrac{8}{4+4}$	B	8	C	$\dfrac{8}{4+4}$	C	$\dfrac{8}{4+4}$
Dance		$\dfrac{8}{4+4}$		$\dfrac{6}{2+4}$		$\dfrac{10}{6+4}$		$\dfrac{8}{4+4}$

Music	A	$\dfrac{8}{4+4}$	B	8	C	$\dfrac{8}{4+4}$	C	$\dfrac{8}{4+4}$
Dance		$\dfrac{8}{4+4}$		$\dfrac{7}{3+3}$, $\dfrac{2+1+1}{2}$		$\dfrac{9}{5+4}$, $\dfrac{}{3+2}$		$\dfrac{8}{2+4+2}$

Pécour's dance patterns mirror the parallel substructure of the first musical strain perfectly in the first statement of the tune, and reflect the equal subdivision in the second statement. After this predictable opening, Pécour focuses his wit upon the second musical strain, which is the only strain without parallel subphrases, where he makes a major aberration out of what would seem to be only a minor inconsistency in the musical structure.

The dance phrase which begins with the second musical strain is never eight measures long: in the first statement it is six, and in the second, seven, measures long. The pas composés performed during the remaining measures of the second musical phrase form the beginning of the floor pattern which continues through the first statement of the third musical phrase, thereby destroying the possibility of exactly mirroring the parallel subphrases of this strain as well. In the repetition of the third musical strain, Pécour observes the parallel substructure in the first statement of the tune, but in the second statement of the tune he sets a four-measure irregular figure which overlaps the division of the musical subphrases for a more exhilarating conclusion.

In the passage which accompanies the first statement of the second and third musical strains, six- and ten-measure dance sequences divide the eight-measure musical phrases into unequal parts which, nevertheless, reflect the parallelism of the third musical strain. The key to the organization of these sixteen measures is the sequence of step-units: two jetés, pas de bourrée, pas de sissonne, pas de bourrée emboîté. This combination of two two-measure formulae occurs three times in these sixteen measures (measures 11-14, 17-20, and 21-24).

The first statement of this sequence which is introduced by a two-pas segment concludes the six-measure floor pattern. The second statement, which is introduced by another two-pas segment, creates only a caesura in the forward motion of the floor pattern. The third statement follows the second statement and concludes the ten-measure floor pattern. Thus, the last eight measures of the ten-measure dance phrase are two statements of one progression of four pas composés, which reflect the parallel subphrases of the third musical phrase, even though the floor pattern does not.

When these strains appear again in the repetition of the tune, Pécour provides an even more remarkable example of choreographic defiance of the musical phrase. The dancers perform a three-measure pas tombé sequence, coupé-tombé-pas de sissonne. Characteristically, the tombé is employed as the second step in a two-measure segment, although a three-measure sequence similar to that in "la Savoye" in which a leapt step continues the momentum of the fall (coupé-tombé-contretemps ballonné) is employed in "la Mariée," measures 1-6.

Pécour's use of the pas de sissonne as the third element of the three-measure tombé sequence in "la Savoye" is particularly clever, because he has established the pas de sissonne-pas de bourrée emboîté as his strongest choreographic cadential formula. When the second coupé-tombé-pas de sissonne figure is followed by a pas de bourrée emboîté, whatever regularity has been achieved by balancing two irregular three-measure segments is obscured by a dance phrase which closes on the seventh measure of an eight-measure musical phrase. Thus, in a musically straightforward bourrée, Pécour creates parallel subphrases where there are none in the music, sets a dance figure of 3 + 4 measures to a musical phrase of 4 + 4 measures, and confuses the end of the danced repetition with a standard choreographed cadential formula.

Beginnings of floor patterns in "la Savoye" are clear, reinforcing the distinction observed in the pas composés between dance phrases which correspond to the accompanying musical phrase (those beginning in measures 1, 9, 25, 33, 41, and 57) and those which do not reflect the musical phrasing (those dance phrases beginning in measures 15 and 48). Beginnings of parallel musical subphrases reflected in the pas composés are further emphasized by changes of direction in the figure in measures 5, 29, 37, and 53.

The parallelism in the phrase in measures 33-40 seems to demand adjustment in the size of the dancers' steps. Here the dancers perform two pas de bourrée and a contretemps ballonné to the side traveling away from each other, and in the parallel four measures they have only one pas de bourrée and a contretemps ballonné to return to the starting position.

Dancers familiar with the most famous Pécour ball dances will recognize the opening figure of the "Bourrée d'Achille" in "la Savoye's" first figure.

162   La Savoye

Similarly, the figure in measures 48-52 of "la Savoye" is identical to that in measures 21-24 of "la Forlana." This seems to be an indication of the possibility of standardization in this genre, not only of two- or four-measure combinations of step-units, but also of certain of these combinations appearing characteristically in certain floor patterns. It is a potential which Pécour certainly does not pursue to the point of boredom in his choreographies, but I feel the passages cited are examples of this aspect of the predictability of French court dances, rather than instances of Pécour's deliberately quoting passages from other choreographies.

By contrast, the final figure of "la Savoye" is quite unusual. A standard ball dance final phrase includes the dancers' return to pas composés on opposite feet and their focus on the Présence, marked perhaps by a pair of pas de bourrée emboîtés facing the Présence,[8] followed by a symmetrical pattern creating a smooth transition into the symmetrical honours after dancing.

In the final phrase of "la Savoye," however, the dancers do not return to pas on opposite feet until the second saut of the pas de sissonne in the penultimate measure. The phrase does begin with a pair of pas de bourrée emboîtés, but not on opposite feet, and facing the partner instead of the Présence, who has a view of the lady's back.

The pattern which follows is one which Feuillet calls "irrégulière,"[9] an unbalanced figure in which both dancers follow an arc on the same side of the room. In this case, the gentleman leads and the couple completes the arc in the center of the foot of the room with a quarter-turn to face the Présence and a pas de sissonne. After an irregular figure and pas composés which sweep across the balanced division of the musical phrase, the pas de sissonne and closing coupé make a sudden return to symmetry at the last possible moment.

The simplest solutions to questions concerning the head and arms are most successful in "la Savoye." The focus of the dancer's gaze is clearly on his partner from the beginning of the second figure until the penultimate measure. In addition to creating a pleasant, friendly mood, the focus on the partner seems particularly essential in measures 25-28 and in the final irregular figure to reinforce the centripetal force of the dance which these figures seem to challenge.

Consistent use of Rameau's arm movements clarifies the formulaic use of pas composés in "la Savoye." The opposition to the demi-coupé of the coupés avec ouverture de jambe is displayed to great advantage in the opening figure. The possibility of opening the left arm out can facilitate the turn backward between the pas de bourrée in measure 40 and the following coupé to the side.

Bourée

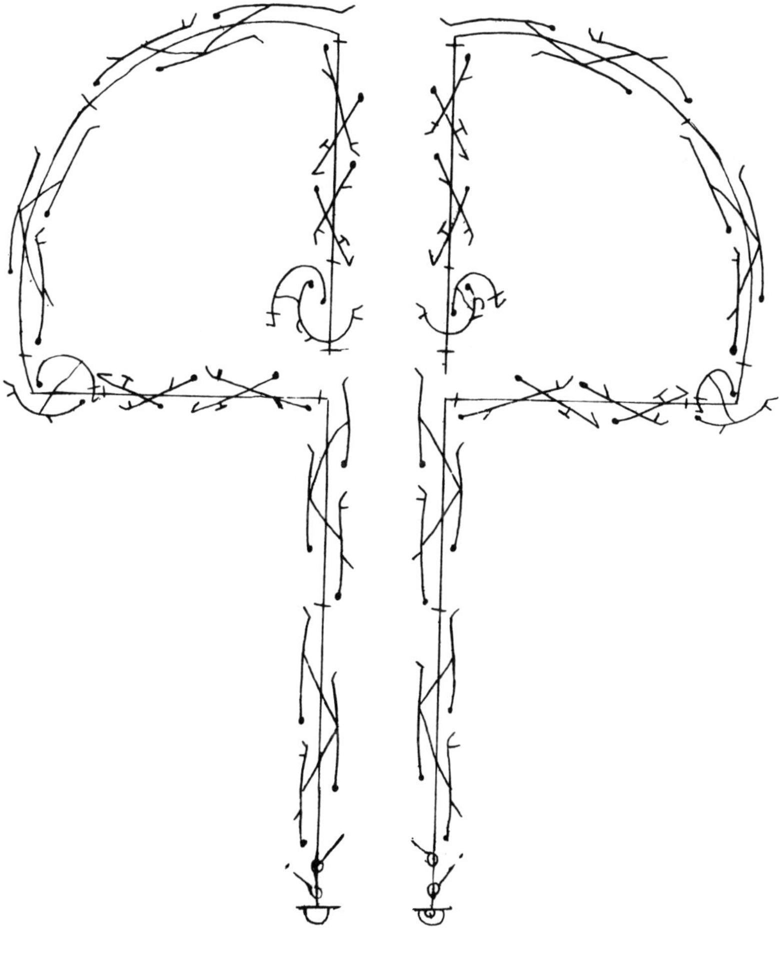

164 La Savoye

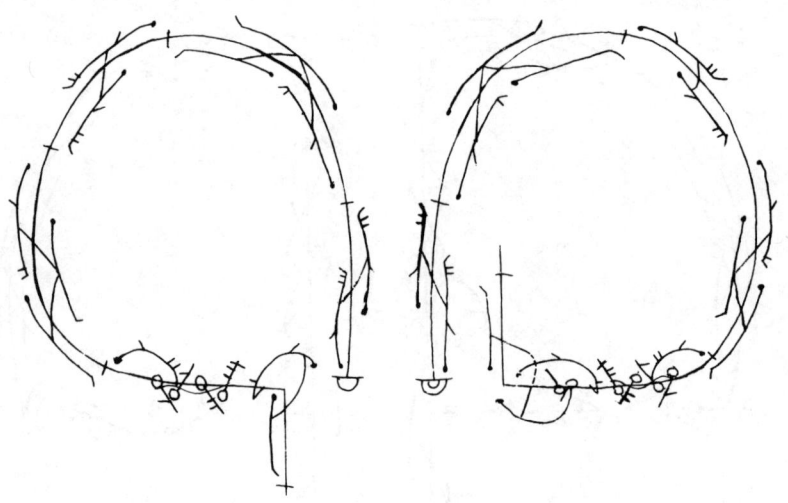

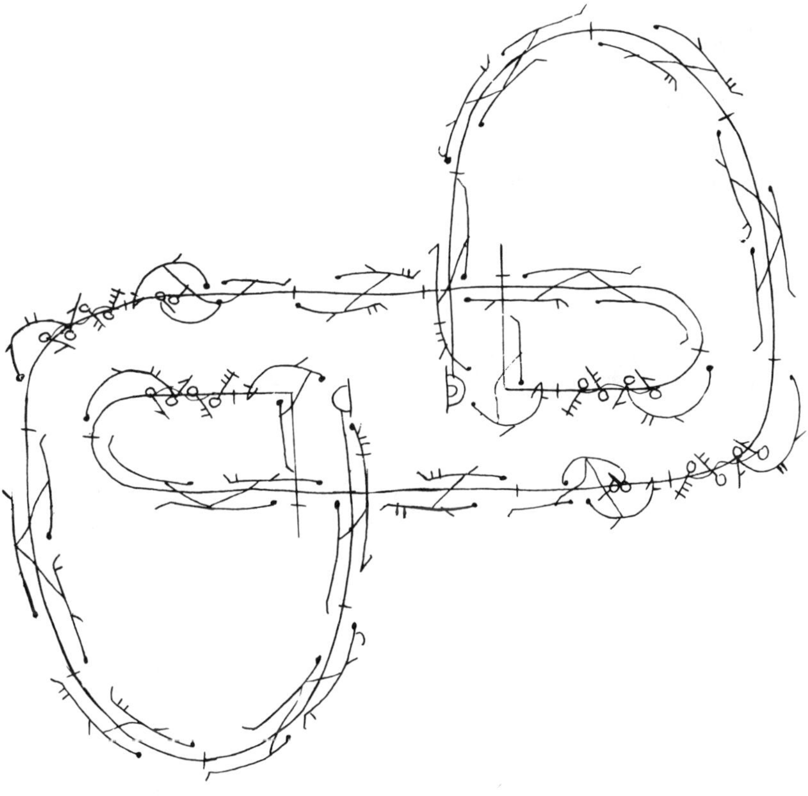

La Savoye

166 La Savoye

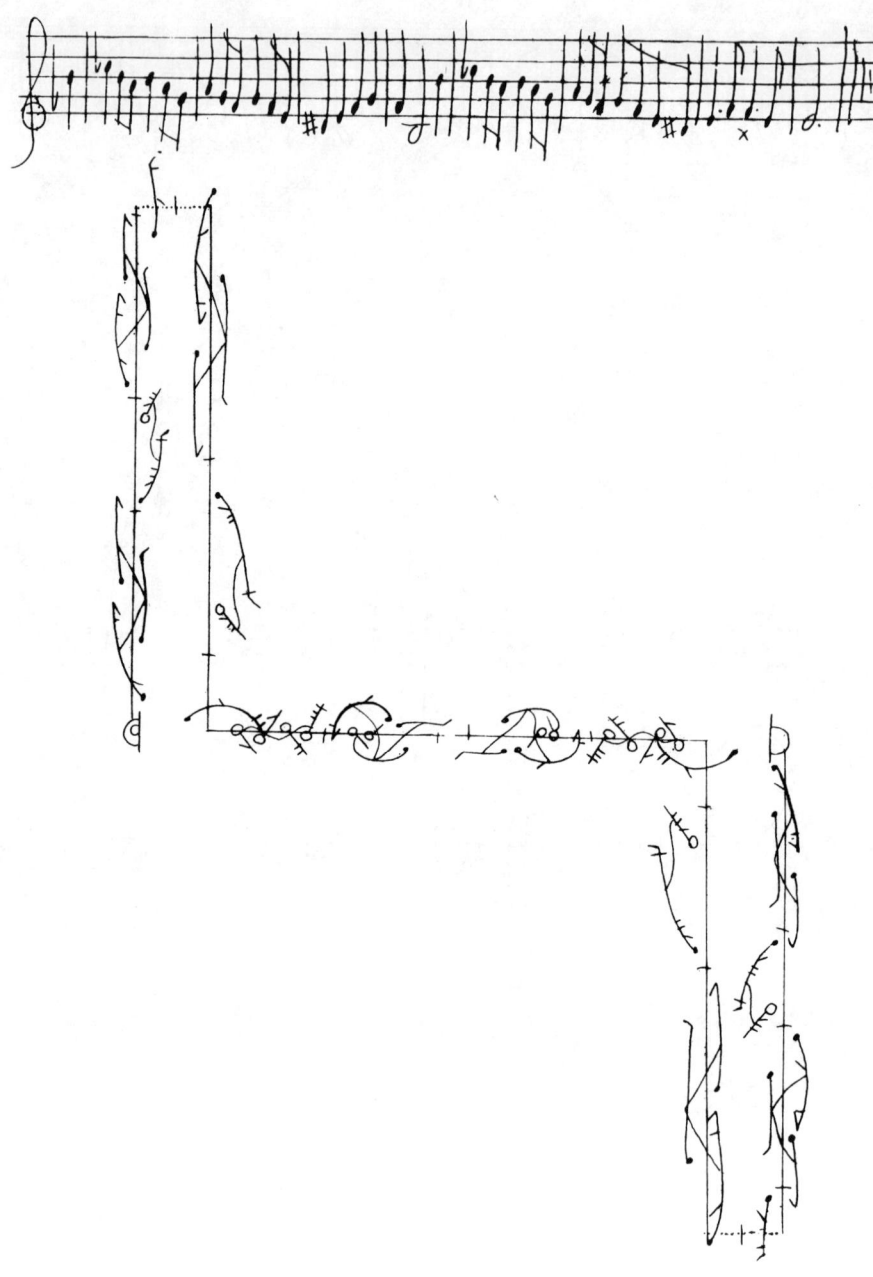

La Savoye 167

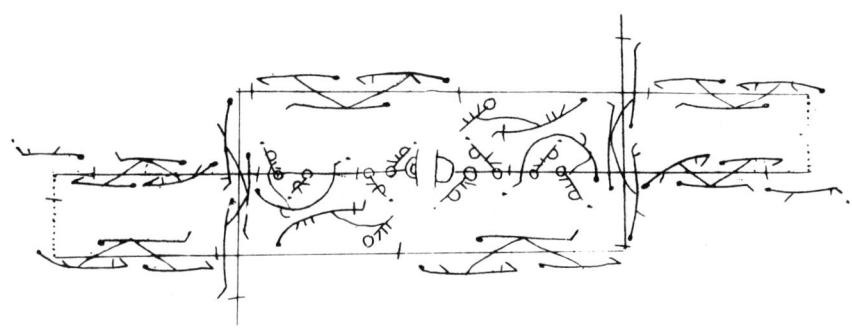

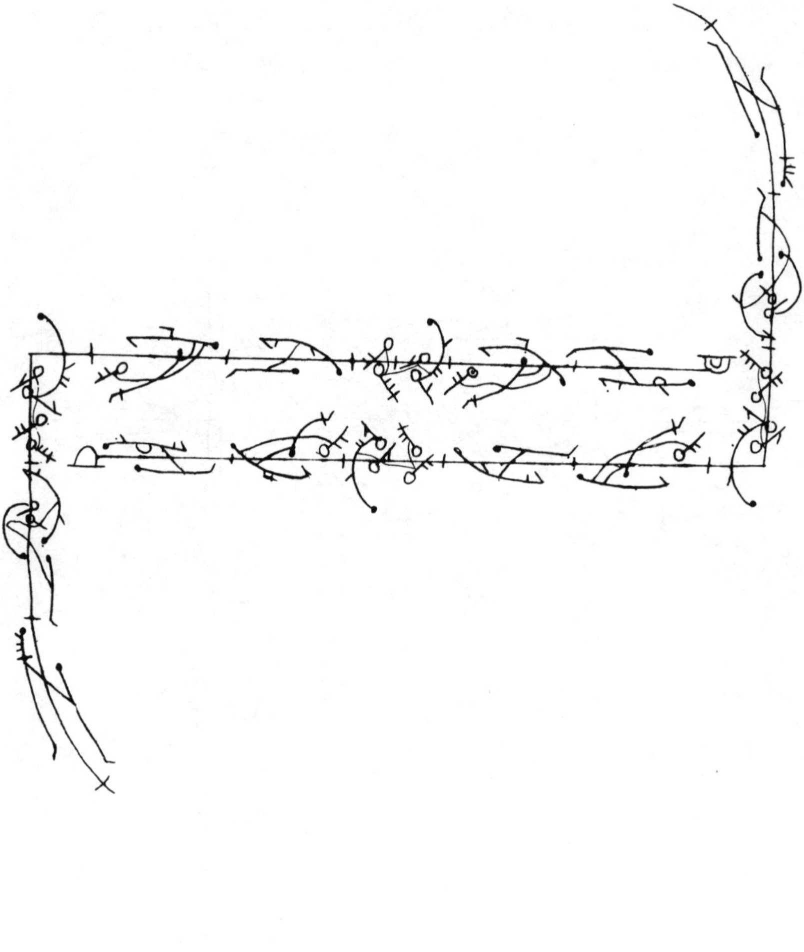

168 *La Savoye*

La Savoye

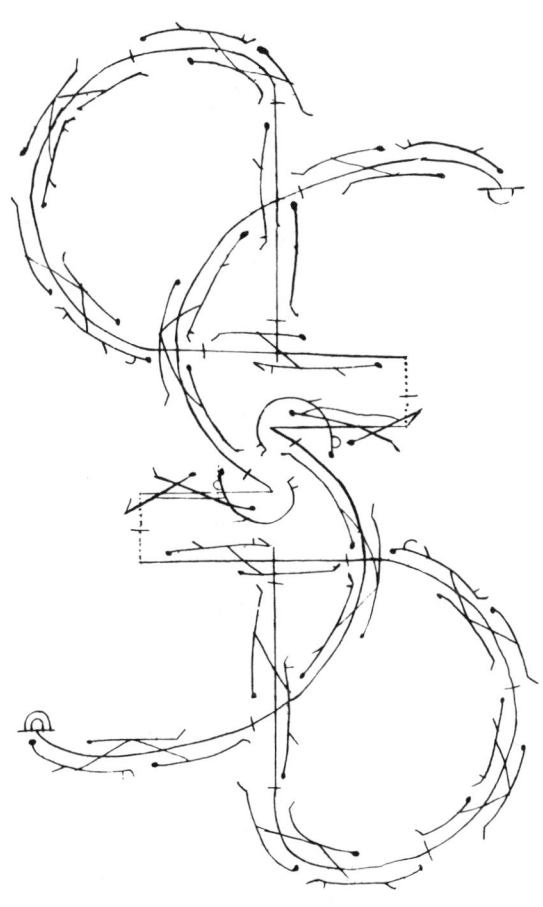

La Savoye

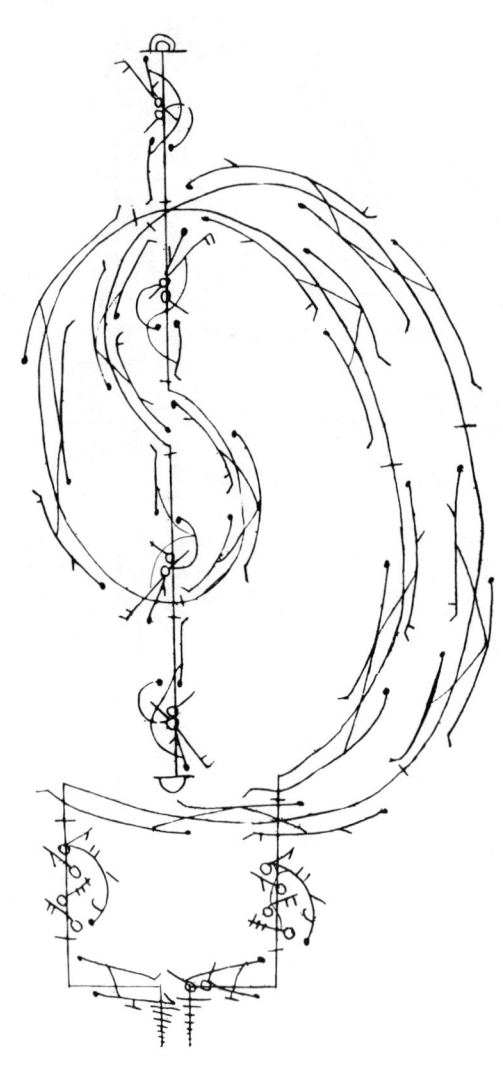

8

La Forlana

The music for the forlana, "la Forlana," is taken from the second scene of the third entrée of André Campra's ballet *l'Europe Galante* (1699). Like most forlanas, this melody is not in two-reprise form, but is composed of two-measure segments which are repeated and varied by the occasional repetition of a one-measure segment. A diagram of the melodic structure and cadences of La Forlana is found on page 172 of the following chapter.

The harmonic rhythm of the two-measure groups is either

| ♩· ♩· | 𝅗𝅥· | or | 𝅗𝅥· | 𝅗𝅥· |

The melodic line has a pastoral quality, with skips of a fifth and repeated notes which suggest a horn. The repetition of short phrases whose harmonic rhythm reaches a standstill is the antithesis of the "drive to the cadence." The combined effect of the pastoral melody and its harmonic rhythm is one of cheerful optimism that the piece will end on the tonic, which is reinforced by the absence of unsettling modulations.

While the choreography provides a certain gaiety of movement for the dancing couple, it also introduces an intricacy of structure which the music, alone, does not suggest. Pécour passes from four-measure dance phrases which follow the music exactly to a section in which a two-measure pas composé extends across the last measure of one two-measure segment and the first measure of the following phrase. When the choreography links musical phrases in this manner, Pécour uses a pas de gaillarde so that the dancers execute the rise and shift before the tombé at the moment when there is no motion in the musical harmony.

M. 15-18

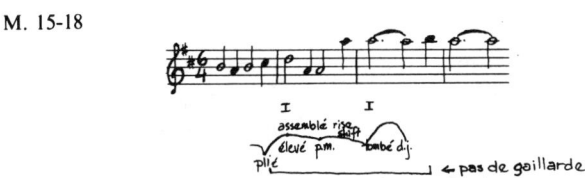

172   La Forlana

The shifts in dance phrasing upon the musical phrases can be seen in the chart below. The steps are explained in the paragraphs which follow.

```
A  ♪|♩ ♪♪♪♪|♩ ♪♪♪|♩  ♪♪♪♪|♩ ♪♪♩ |♩.♪♪ ♩ ♪|♩♪♪♪|♩♪♪♩ ♪♪|♩ ♪♪

m.1   ct d g  c*⏋  ct d g   s    p d r   d     gl gl    c⏋
                                 gl     gl c⏋  p dr     d

B  ♩|♩ ♪♪♩|♩ ♪♪♩|♩♩ ♩♩|♩ ♪♪♪|♩ ♪♪♪♩|♩♪♪♩|♩ ♩♩ ♩|♩ ♩♩
9      p d b   p db    p — g   t j    p  s    p sp db   p - g

♩|♩. ♩ ♩|♩ ♩♩|♩. ♪♪♩. ♪♩|♩ ♪♪♩|♩.♪♪♩ ♪♪|♩♪♪♪|♩.♪♪♪♪|♩ ♩♩
17     t j     p db    pd e    pd e  j    j    pdb  p d b    c⏋

♩|♩.♪♪♩ ♩|♩ ♩♩ ♩|♩♪♪♩ ♩|♩ ♪♪♩|♩.♪♪♪♪|♩♪♪♩|♩ ♪♪♪♪|♩ ♩♩.
25     t j    p db    c⏋    t j  ct dg   a    c  m    c  m

♪♪|♩ ♩♩.♪♪|♩♩♩.♪♪|♩ ♩♩♩|♩♩♩♩|♩. ♩♩|♩♩♩ ♩|♩.♪♪♪♪|♩♩ ♩
33     j j    p db    j j     p db   pir    pir pir   p d b
                                     p d b  pdb p d b p d b

A  ♩|♩ ♩♩♪♪|♩♩♩ ♩|♩ ♩♩. ♪♪|♩♩♩ ♩|♩.♪♪♪♪|♩♩♩|♩.♪♪♩ ♪♪|♩ ♩♩
41     d ct   t j    d ct    t j   pd e   pde  p d b   p d b
```
*coupé battu

Pécour 1700, P. 62, Measures 1-8

step-units: contretemps de gavotte forward
            coupé battu
            contretemps de gavotte backward
            saut
            pas de rigaudon/glissades
              (cont.)   /coupé soutenue to the
                               side to 1st
            glissades   /pas de riguadon
            coupé soutenue /   (cont.)
              to the side
              to 5th

"La Forlana" begins with a contretemps de gavotte forward, a quarter-turn and beaten coupé facing one's partner, a contretemps de gavotte backward with the last pas marché closing in first position, and a jump in place.

In the next four measures, the lady performs a pair of glissades and a coupé soutenue to the side opening to second position and closing into first, followed by a pas de rigaudon. The gentleman begins this phrase with a pas de rigaudon followed by a pair of glissades and coupé soutenue to the side, opening to second and closing into fifth position in front.

According to Rameau,[1] a battement between the demi-coupé and pas marché of a coupé should be performed with a straight knee. There is a theoretical option to take the plié before the following contretemps de gavotte backward in the first position, bringing the free foot in and bending both knees in first on the plié, then returning the free foot to fourth position in front en l'air with a straight knee on the landing from the saut. I feel that this creates an undesirable fidget in the dancer's line and prefer to leave the free foot in fourth position in front throughout the saut, bringing it directly through first and bending the knee after the landing as part of the movement to fourth position behind for the first pas marché.

The dancer should exercise particular control in the insteps, when landing from the jump in measure four. It is the only movement in the measure and the end of a phrase. If care is not taken to complete the four-measure line gracefully, the dancer appears to collapse under his own weight.

The sequence in measures 5-8 is the first example in this collection of the simultaneous performance of different pas composés governed neither by the exigencies of changing feet nor by the characteristic use of certain menuet steps for traveling in different directions. Here, and in comparable passages in other collections, one dancer appears to perform for the amusement of his partner, who either rests or performs a step in place (the pas de rigaudon, in this case), followed by an immediate reversal of roles in a sort of echo. Pécour employs this device for its dramatic and geometric effect rather than to introduce counter-rhythms between pas composés. The pas de rigaudon and glissade-coupé group, which have the same rhythm, accompany a two-measure musical segment and its repetition.

Pécour 1700, P. 61 (cont.)-62, Measures 9-16

step-units: pas de bourrée forward
pas de bourrée forward
pas de gaillarde
pas tombé to the side
pas de sissonne forward
pas de sissonne forward
pas de bourrée forward
pas de gaillarde

174 La Forlana

The second musical phrase begins with a pair of pas de bourrée forward; a half-turn and assemblé without leap and a pas marché into second position for a tombé and demi-jeté; a pair of pas de sissonne; a pair of pas de bourrée forward, and another assemblé without leap and pas marché into second.

The step in measure 11 which introduces the pas tombé merits some discussion. During the preparatory plié, the free foot makes a small semi-circle in the air, reaching first position at the depth of the plié, as in an assemblé, whereupon the dancer immediately begins an elevé, as in a temps de courante, followed by a pas marché without glissé to second position. For a diagram of the vertical motion, see page 171 above. The dancer creates the impression that he has been drawn up into the elevé and will have as little to do with the ground as possible until the recovery from the tombé.

Although the performance of this pas is clear, naming it is a problem because Pécour's contemporaries have handed it down in a state of theoretically confused terminology. They did not agree upon the definition of the term "pas de gaillarde" (i.e., whether the step in measure 11 constitutes an entire pas de gaillarde or only its first half), and they were divided in their opinion of the classification of the step in measure 11 as an assemblé or a temps de courante.

The notation of the pas is found in Feuillet's *Chorégraphie* among the temps de courante, where it is called a "pas de gaillarde" and notated either as an assemblé without leap and pas marché or a temps de courante without glissé, which is the notation used by Feuillet in "la Forlana."

Feuillet, *Chorégraphie*, p. 48 "Table des tems de Courante"

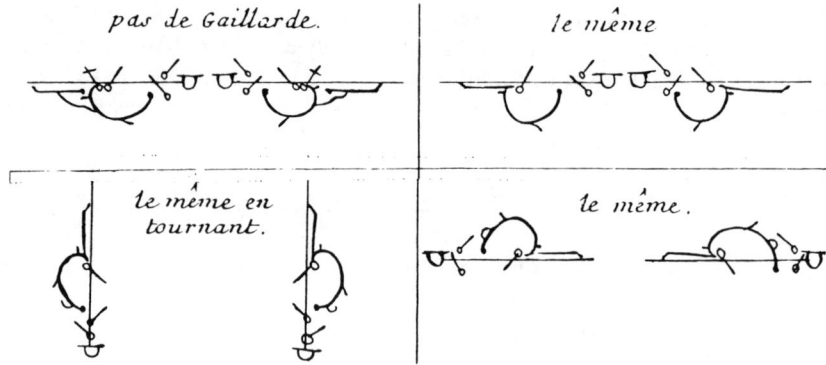

Rameau uses the term to denote a two-measure pas composé composed of an assemblé, a pas marché, and a pas tombé with its demi-jeté.[2] In *Abbrégé,* he explains two methods of executing the assemblé; the first, "en pliant & en se relevant lorsque les deux pieds sont pres l'un de l'autre"[3] adds the element of the beginning of a temps de courante to bringing the free foot into first position in an assemblé. According to Rameau, his own "pas de gaillarde" may begin either with this assemblé without leap or with the leapt variety.

Tomlinson uses the term "*Galliard* Step" to mean an assemblé from one foot to one foot with or without leap, followed by a pas marché. He explains that this step is inseparable from the tombé in performance, "tho' they are two distinct steps in themselves."[4]

The variety of definitions of the term "pas de gallarde" is an instructive reminder of the caution which must be observed when reading different authors, even two Frenchmen associated with Pécour. The use of the terms "assemblé" and "tems de courante" (steps whose differences are as significant as their similarities) to refer to the same pas reflects the striking effect of this step.

The first pas de sissonne is that which Feuillet calls "en avant et la jambe de devant s'ouvre en arrière."[5] After bringing the free foot into fifth position in front to land with the weight on both feet, the dancer will land from the second saut on the foot which is behind on the first landing. However, instead of merely lifting the free foot in the fifth position in front, the dancer brings it around to fourth position behind en l'air.

The second pas de sissonne is the most common variety, bringing the free foot into fifth position in front for the first landing on both feet, and landing for the second time on the front foot with the back foot raised off the ground in fifth position behind.

Feuillet, *Chorégraphie*, p. 81

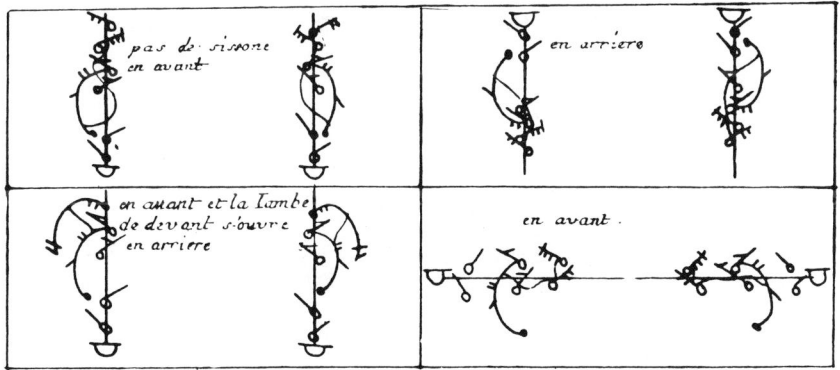

176   La Forlana

Pécour 1700, P. 63 (cont.)-64, Measures 17-24

step-units: pas tombé to the side
pas de bourrée forward
pas de bourrée emboîté
pas de bourrée emboîté
2 jetés
pas de bourrée forward
pas de bourrée to the side
coupé simple to the side

The third musical phrase begins with a tombé and demi-jeté, which have been introduced by the assemblé without leap and pas marché in the cadential measure of the preceding musical phrase, and a pas de bourrée forward; a pair of pas de bourrée emboîtés with a beat in fifth position behind before each demi-coupé; a pair of jetés and a pas de bourrée forward; followed by a half-turn and pas de bourrée to the side, crossing the last pas marché into fifth position behind and a coupé simple to the side placing in fifth position in front and opening to second position.

From Feuillet's notation of "la Forlana," alone, it is difficult to determine the placement of the demi-coupé in the pas de bourrée to the side in measure 23. It is clear that the first pas marché opens to second position and the last pas marché closes into fifth position behind, but it seems that the élevé of the demi-coupé which follows a half-turn during the plié might rise either in second position or in fifth position before, to make a genuine pas de bourrée before and behind.

I have reproduced Feuillet's illustrations of two similar step-units from the "Table des Pas de Bourrée" in *Chorégraphie:* the first with the demi-coupé into second position, the second with the demi-coupé into fifth position before.

Feuillet, *Chorégraphie,* P. 69

Feuillet, *Chorégraphie*, P. 70

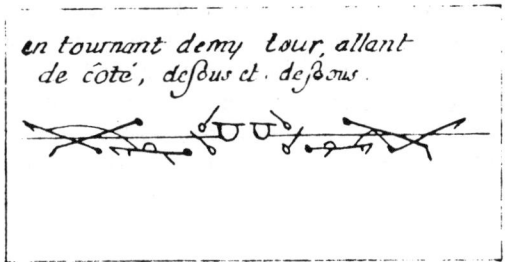

From these and other examples in this "Table," it appears that the final foot position of the demi-coupé does not necessarily have to cross over the head of the following pas marché symbol for Feuillet to indicate a pas crossing in fifth position. The curve of the step symbol is a more reliable indication with those demi-coupés which cross all curving one half-circle and then, continuing farther, closing in.

Also, in the "Table," the only pas de bourrée which begin with a demi-coupé to second position followed by a pas marché to second position are examples of the pas de bourrée ouvert, closing the last pas marché into third position behind, instead of fifth position, found in the example from "la Forlana."

In Rameau's notation of this passage, reproduced below, the demi-coupé clearly crosses in fifth position before in a standard pas de bourrée before and behind. By 1725, this seems to have been Pécour's intention.

Rameau, *Abbrégé*, Part II, P. 36

Pécour 1700, P. 64 (cont.)-65,, Measures 25-32

step-units: pas tombé to the side
                 pas de bourrée forward
                 coupé simple to the side
                 pas tombé to the side
                 contretemps de gavotte forward
                 assemblé
                 coupé de mouvement to the side
                 coupé de mouvement to the side

178 La Forlana

The fourth phrase begins with a tombé and demi-jeté to the side which have been prepared by the coupé to the side in the last measure of the third phrase. The fourth phrase continues with a quarter-turn and pas de bourrée forward; a coupé to the side with a three-quarter turn (half-turn on the demi-coupé and quarter-turn in the same direction on the pas marché) followed by a tombé and demi-jeté to the side; a contretemps de gavotte forward and assemblé; and a pair of coupés de mouvement to the side crossing the demi-coupé of the first in fifth position before and that of the second in fifth position behind.

Pécour 1700, P. 65 (cont.)-66, Measures 33-40

step-units: 2 jetés forward
pas de bourrée forward
2 jetés forward
pas de bourrée forward
pirouette/pas de bourrée forward
pirouette/pas de bourrée forward
pirouette/pas de bourrée forward
pas de bourrée to the side behind and before

The fifth musical phrase begins with a pair of jetés and a pas de bourrée forward and another pair of jetés and a pas de bourrée forward. In the second part of the phrase, the gentleman performs three one-quarter turn pirouettes to the right and a pas de bourrée behind and before with a quarter-turn to the right on the demi-coupé in order to face the Présence. The lady performs three pas de bourrée forward and a modified pas de bourrée behind and before with a half-turn to the right on the demi-coupé and a quarter-turn to the right on the first pas marché, so that she too finishes the phrase facing the Présence.

Pécour 1700, P. 67, Measures 41-48

step-units: demi-contretemps forward
pas tombé forward
demi-contretemps forward
pas tombé forward
pas de bourrée emboîté
pas de bourrée emboîté
pas de bourrée forward
pas de bourrée forward and close

In the final phrase, the dancers perform a demi-contretemps with a quarter-turn away from each other on the saut and a tombé and demi-jeté forward; a demi-contretemps with a half-turn in the direction of the Présence on the saut and a tombé and demi-jeté forward toward each other; a quarter-turn to the Présence and a pair of beaten pas de bourrée emboîtés; and a pair of pas de bourrée forward, the first traveling down the room with a half-turn in the direction of the partner on the demi-coupé, the second with a half-turn in the direction of the partner to face the Présence on the second pas marché. The gentleman closes in fourth position behind as the lady closes in first.

The changing relationship of musical phrasing and sequences of pas composés during the course of "la Forlana" contributes to the subtly seductive quality of the dance. In the first and last musical strains, the dancers' sequences mirror the four-measure phrases and balanced additive composition of the music. In the internal strains, however, Pécour abandons four-measure dance phrases as the clear correspondence of music and dance seems to fade out of focus for a while.

The first shift out of synchronization occurs with the pas de bourrée in measure 15 in the second musical strain. The entire third strain is colored by beginning at the midpoint of a two-measure pas composé (one of Rameau's pas de gaillarde), and continuing with the music one measure behind the dance.

In the fourth strain, Pécour increases the distance between dance and musical phrasing from one to two measures and employs a clear four-measure dance phrase for the first time since the end of the second musical phrase. The insertion of a single pas de bourrée in measure 26 places the next turning coupé-tombé group in a two-measure musical segment.

The contretemps de gavotte and assemblé which follow may be a reference to the end of the first four-measure phrase of the dance. In any case, the finality of the assemblé makes the turning coupé-tombé group appear, in retrospect, to have been the beginning of a four-measure dance phrase, which anticipates the beginning of the musical phrase by two measures. The pair of coupés de mouvement to the side appear to begin a new dance phrase in spite of the music, which is an echo of the segment which accompanied the contretemps de gavotte and assemblé.

By the final strain, four-measure phrases of music and choreography are synchronized once again. The pirouette sequence in the fifth musical strain is, in fact, a four-measure dance phrase which corresponds to its accompanying music. However, largely as a result of the floor patterns discussed below, this change is not obvious until the beginning of the last strain, in measure 41, with the pas tombés forward, the contrast in floor pattern, and the return to the first eight measures of music.

The floor patterns of "la Forlana" reflect the cadence of pas composés and musical phrasing. Where dance and music correspond, in the first and final phrases the dancers trace straight lines and have a clear point of reference, both facing either the Présence or each other. Where shifting rhythms prevail, the dancers circle each other. They meet directly only when passing through tombé sequences to the side and perform steps in place only in an ambiguous position side by side.

In two places in particular, it is necessary to gauge the circling figures so that the partners pass each other before making a half-turn followed by a pas performed facing the partner. This is true in the second phrase before the non-leapt assemblé, in measure 11, and before the pas de bourrée before and behind, in measure 23, which leads into a tombé sequence.

The phrasing and execution of the floor pattern between the assemblé, in measure 30, and the beginning of the final phrase also demand some consideration, because the recovery of synchronized four-measure phrases takes place in this passage almost imperceptibly. After the coupés de mouvement to the side, the dancers begin a circular figure which continues spiraling in through the pirouette sequence from which the dancers emerge to face the Présence in measure 40.

Although the change in direction between the coupés de mouvement and jetés is identical to that between the first and second musical phrases, the effect of an important change of phrase is negated here by the continuous movement of the pas and the absence of a strong musical cadence. The floor pattern has no break at all before the pirouette sequence; the step-units continue and the music lingers on so that the first clear sense of the musicians and dancers beginning a phrase together does not occur until measure 41.

It is also important to note that, in the pirouette sequence, the lady performs her pas de bourrée around the circle a little ahead of the gentleman. The dancers look at each other over their right shoulders, and the gentleman appears to be following the lady, an agreeable effect which makes the turn to face the Présence an even greater surprise.

The floor pattern supplies the most important clues to the position of the head as determined by the direction of the gaze which, from measure 2 until the final phrase, is concentrated upon the partner. The floor pattern takes precedence over pictorial evidence for the head position turned to look over the lower arm in all tombés, with the exception of that in measure 17, when the dancers are back to back.

When coming out of the pirouette figure, it is effective if both dancers fix their gaze on the Présence at the same moment during the pas de bourrée behind and before. This demands some adjustment on the part of the gentleman, who must look at the lady until she can face the Présence, usually at the first pas marché of the pas de bourrée behind and before.

The arm movements should be deployed with care in "la Forlana." If all the possible turns of wrist are used on the frequent leapt steps, the dance takes on a quality which is more nervous than lively. Judicious use of turns of the wrist may be used profitably in the central section of the dance to clarify the internal rhythms.

La Forlana

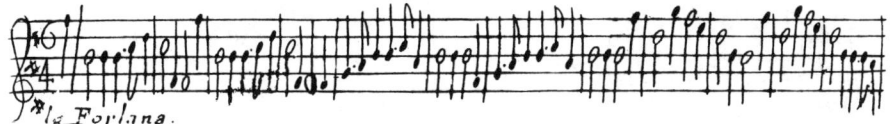

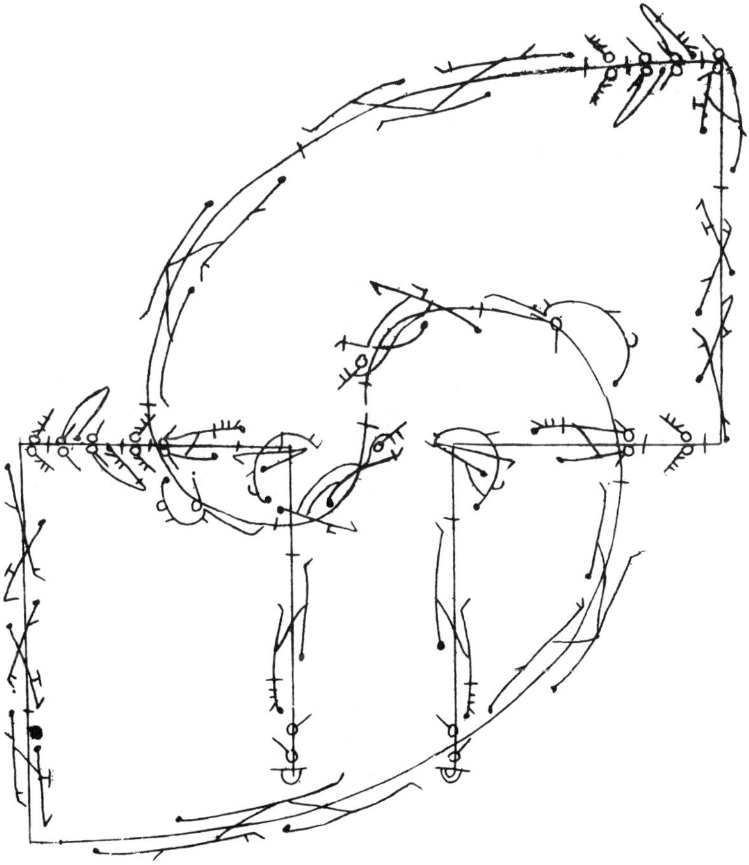

la Forlana.

182 La Forlana

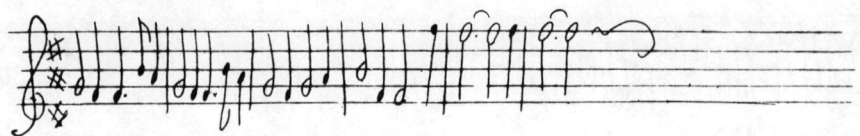

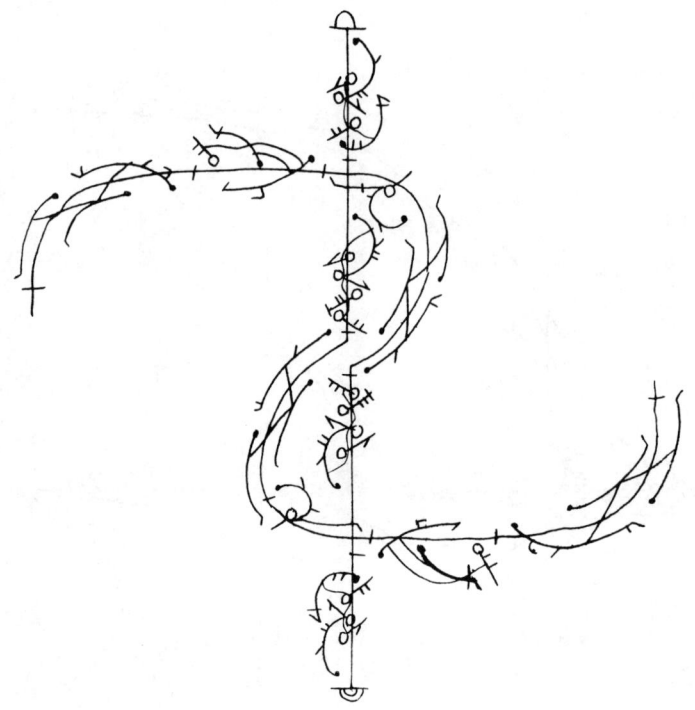

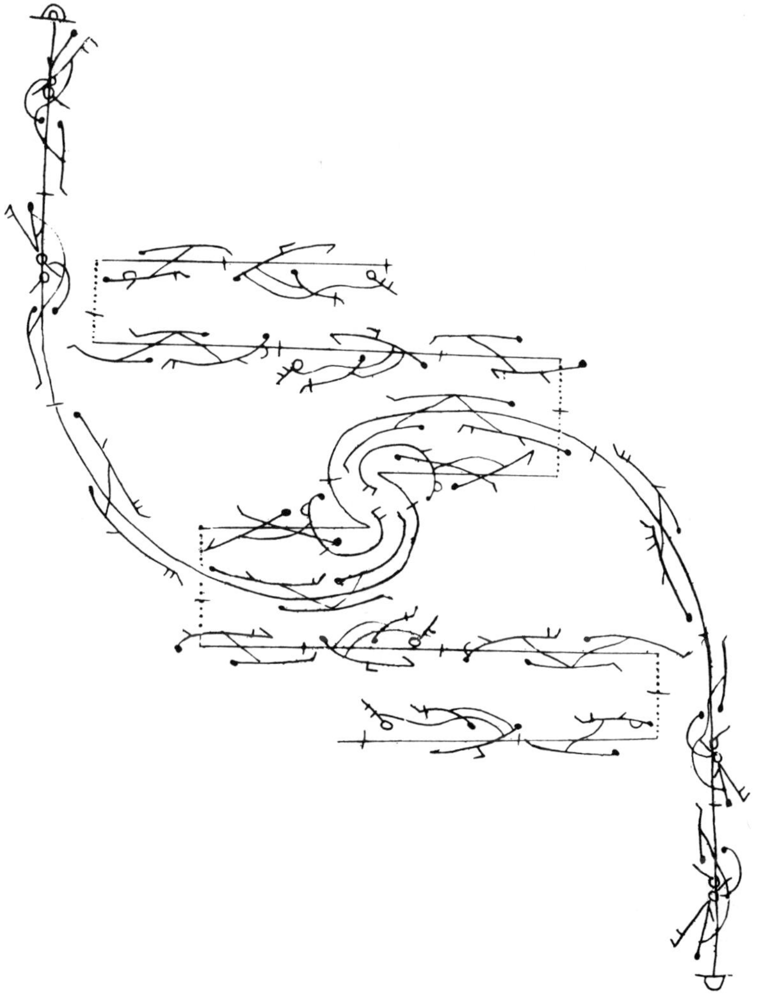

La Forlana

184 La Forlana

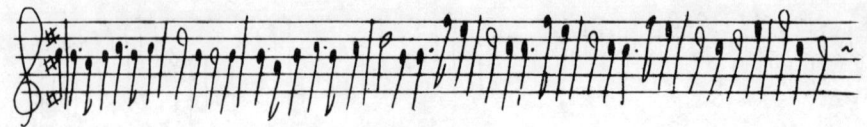

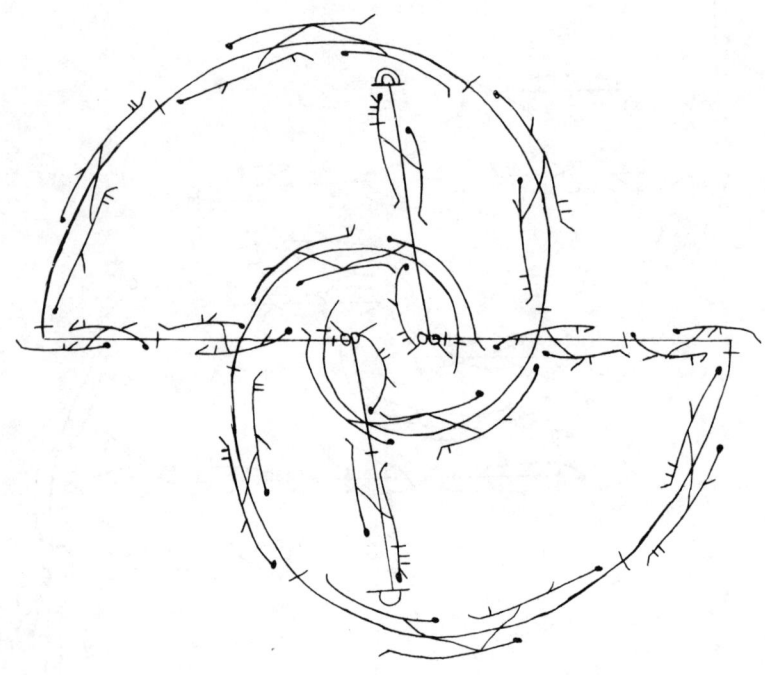

La Forlana

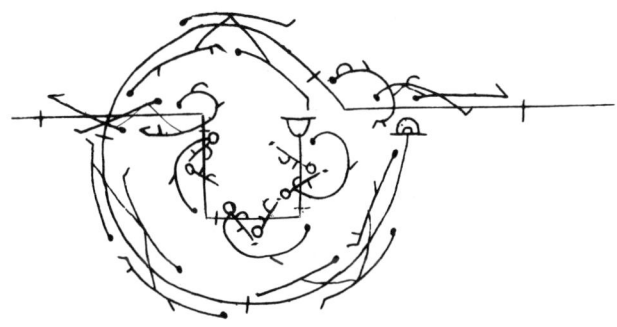

186   La Forlana

9

La Conty

The final dance in the 1700 *Recueil,* la Conty-Venitienne, is choreographed to music by André Campra, who calls this tune "la Venitienne" in Act I, Scene 4 of his ballet, *Le Carnaval de Venise* (1699). In the ballet, this tune opens a divertissement which also includes a villanelle, a second venitienne, and dance songs and choruses based upon similar melodic material.

The melodies of the venitiennes in this scene are composed of short repeated segments like a forlana, but each phrase straddles the barline in the manner of a gavotte. The forlana itself is described by Brossard (1703) as a Venetian dance, and Paul Nettl uses the melody of "la Conty" as a musical example for his article "Forlane" in *MGG*. An analysis of "la Conty" reveals that Pécour treats Campra's venitienne not as a simple forlana, but as a dance which combines some choreographic and musical elements of the forlana with the practice of beginning and ending a melody in mid-measure, which was the rule with the gavotte and also common in one of the faster dances of the same metric classification as the forlana, the contredanse.

The identification of the steps of "la Conty" will be explained in the paragraphs below; their timing or cadence is reconstructed in the following chart.

188   La Conty

```
C  ♩ ♩ ♩ |♩♩♩♩|♩ ♩♩.♪|♩.♪♩ ♩|♩ ♩♩.♪|♩ ♩♩.♪|♩ ♩ ♩|♩.♪♩ ♩|♩ ♩♩.♪|♩ ♩♩.♪| ♩
m.25      c  m    c  m    p d b   ct  b  p d b   ct  b    p db    a  p   ctdg    ct

A  ♩ ♩ ♩ |♩ ♩♩.♪|♩ ♩♩ ♩|♩ ♩♩.♪|♩♩♩ ♩|♩ ♩♩.♪|♩ ♩ ♩ |♩ ♩♩.♪|♩
m.35      p d b   p d b   p d b   pdb    pd  e    pd   e   p d b  c
  d g
```

*rest

———————————————

Pécour 1700, P. 68, Measures 1-8

step-units: demi-coupé-pas tombé to the side
demi-coupé to the side
demi-coupé-pas tombé to the side
demi-coupé to the side
temps de courante to the side
pas tombé to the side
temps de courante to the side
pas tombé to the side

The dance opens with a demi-coupé with the outside foot to second position, a pas tombé to the side falling into fifth position behind and a rebound into a demi-coupé in second, where the dancers balance. This sequence is then repeated in the opposite direction. The dancers continue with a quarter-turn to face the partner and a temps de courante to the side to second position, followed by a pas tombé to the side falling into fifth position behind and rising into a balance in second position. After a half-turn in the direction of the Présence, the dancers repeat this sequence back to back.

The initial demi-coupé is a more direct approach to the pas tombé than any suggested by Rameau in *Le Maître*. The second demi-coupé substitutes what is actually one-half a balancé for the usual demi-jeté. This demands more control than a demi-jeté because the dancer must place for a rise to a secure balance at a point when his momentum as a result of the fall to regain equilibrium could easily take him too far. The use of a grave temps de courante to introduce the pas tombé is a variation mentioned by Rameau in *Le Maître*, Part I, Chapter XXXI.

Pécour 1700, P. 68 (cont.)-69, Measures 9-16

step-units: pas de bourrée forward/coupé de
mouvement forward

> coupé soutenue forward/coupé de
>   mouvement forward
> pas de bourrée to the side before and behind
> coupé soutenue forward
> pas de sissonne forward
> pas de sissonne forward
> pas de bourrée to the side before and behind
> coupé soutenue forward

The next phrase is composed of a pair of coupés de mouvement; a pas de bourrée before and behind to the side and a coupé soutenue forward; a pair of pas de sissonne forward facing the partner; and another pas de bourrée before and behind and coupé soutenue forward. In place of the coupés de mouvement, the gentleman has a pas de bourrée and coupé forward, which enable him to begin the following figure on the proper foot.

> Pécour 1700, P. 70, Measures 17-24

> step-units: pas de gaillarde to the side (assemblé + pas)
>   pas tombé to the side
>   pas de gaillarde forward (assemblé + pas)
>   pas tombé forward
>   pas de gaillarde to the side (assemblé + pas)
>   pas tombé to the side
>   pas de bourrée forward
>   coupé soutenue forward

The third phrase of "la Conty" marks a return of the melodic refrain with a new treatment of the pas tombé, the pas de gaillarde. The dancers first execute a pas de gaillarde to the side with a quarter-turn and assemblé into third position, a pas marché opening the front foot out into second position, a pas tombé falling into fifth behind, and a demi-jeté into second. This is followed by a pas de gaillarde forward with assemblé into third in front, pas marché opening the front foot to fourth, tombé into fifth behind, and demi-jeté into fourth in front; a half-turn and pas de gaillarde to the side; and a quarter-turn to the right and pas de bourrée and coupé forward.

> Pécour 1700, P. 71, Measures 25-34

> step-units: coupé de mouvement forward
>   coupé de mouvement forward
>   pas de bourrée to the side behind and behind

>   contretemps ballonné to the side
>   pas de bourrée to the side behind and behind
>   contretemps ballonné to the side
>   pas de bourrée to the side behind and before
>   pas de gaillarde to the side (assemblé + pas)
>   contretemps de côté
>   contretemps de côté

The fourth phrase begins with a pair of coupés de mouvement; a quarter-turn and pas de bourrée to the side behind and behind, followed by a contretemps ballonné to the side; another pas de bourrée behind and behind and contretemps ballonné to the side; a pas de bourrée behind and before and a quarter-turn and assemblé to first position followed by a step to second position with the weight on both feet; and a pair of contretemps de côté, hopping onto the left, crossing the right into fifth before, and opening the left into second with the weight on both feet.

>   Pécour 1700, P. 72, Measures 35-42
>
>   step-units: pas de bourrée forward
>   pas de bourrée forward
>   pas de bourrée forward
>   coupé simple forward/pas de bourrée forward
>   pas de bourrée emboîté
>   pas de bourrée emboîté
>   pas de bourrée forward
>   closing coupé soutenue

The contretemps de côté gives the dancers no significant pause before the final return of the rondeau. The dancers continue with four pas de bourrée forward (the gentleman has three pas de bourrée and one coupé in order to change feet); a pair of pas de bourrée emboîtés; a half-turn in the direction of the partner and pas de bourrée forward down the room, and a half-turn and closing coupé facing the Présence.

"La Conty" may be considered a study of the pas tombé. The essential elements of the choreographed pas tombé are a step into an open position,[1] a rise on that foot followed by a shift of the weight of the body out of equilibrium, a fall into a closed position to regain equilibrium,[2] and a rebound (usually a demi-jeté), into an open position.

In addition to employing both the pas tombé to the side and the pas tombé forward, Pécour presents the tombé in three different sequences: that in which it is introduced by a demi-coupé, as in the opening of the dance, that in which it is introduced by a temps de courante, as in measures 5-8, and in a pas de gaillarde, as in measures 17-22. The dancer's line in each of these pas tombé sequences is illustrated below:

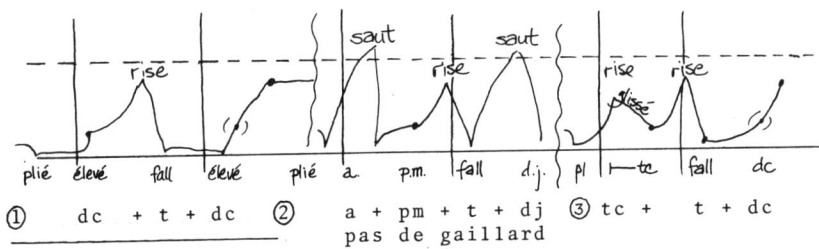

In the opening pas, the rising line from the initial plié to the rise onto demi-pointe before the shift and fall is punctuated but not broken by the first demi-coupé onto a flat foot. The plié at the base of the tombé must be sustained in order to execute a second smooth rise into a demi-coupé.

In a pas de gaillarde, the initial plié is executed more quickly and with greater energy in order to take the dancer into the air so that he lands in an assemblé in plié. As a result of this second plié, the subsequent pas marché appears to be a demi-coupé without placing the foot and the rise, shift, and fall continue in the same sequence as before. You will note, however, that now the step to open position and all following movements occur one dotted half-note, or one half-measure, later than in the opening pas. The plié at the base of this tombé must be performed with energy to take the dancer into the air a second time for the demi-jeté.

An understanding of the pas de gaillarde increases one's appreciation of Pécour's introduction of the temps de courante variation in the first phrase. In this step sequence, the line from the initial plié to the step into open position is broken, not by a leap, but by the most sustained slow rise onto demi-pointe and glissé out and down into the open position on a flat foot. The second rise to demi-pointe before the shift makes the tombé an even greater contrast, and it is easy to overlook the fact that the fall now occurs one dotted half-note later than it did in the opening pas composé.

The relationship of the step-units to the music is the principal element which distinguishes "la Conty" from a forlana. "La Conty's" musical similarity to "la Forlana" may be seen in the following diagram, which reflects the melodic structure and cadences of "la Conty" and the preceding "la Forlana" with no reference to musical or choreographic measure.

192 La Conty

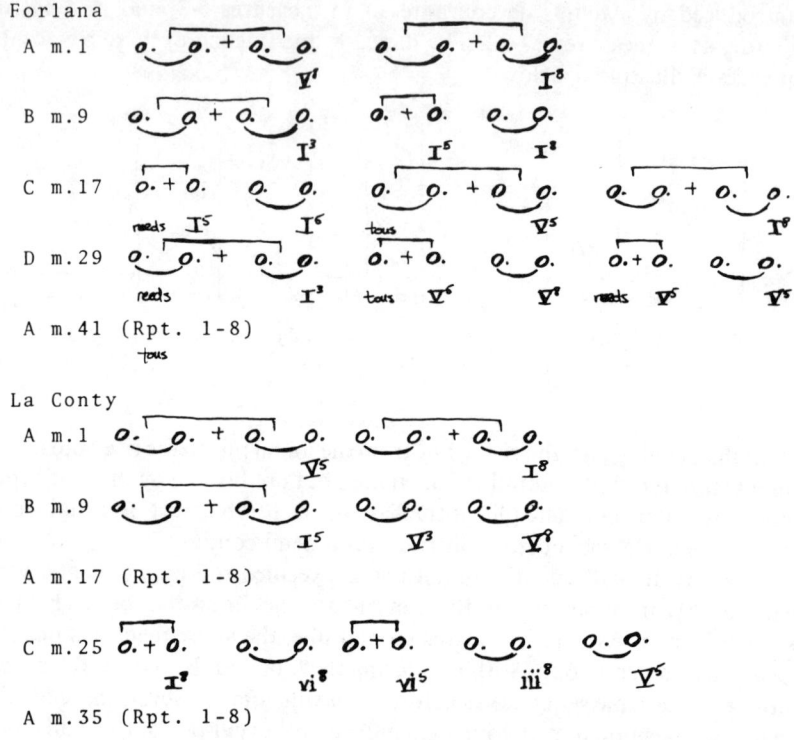

In each dance, the melody is composed of segments two dotted whole-notes long which are repeated exactly and of combinations of single dotted whole-note segments which are repeated and two dotted whole-note segments which are not. Each dance begins with the symmetrical phrase,

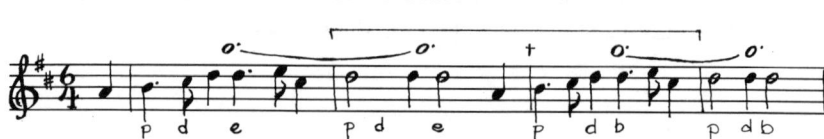

which returns as the final phrase of the piece. A greater variety of melodic structure, orchestration (in the original score), and harmonic digression is found in the intervening phrases. The penultimate phrase of each piece ends on a dominant chord with the fifth in the melody.

The essential differences between "la Conty" and "la Forlana" are evident in a comparison of the last four dotted whole-notes of each dance, in which the melodic structures and final pas composés are virtually identical.

"la Conty"

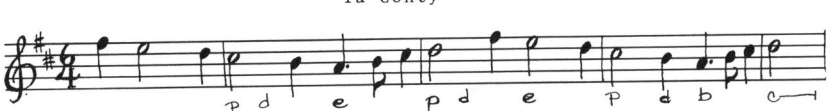

The melody of "la Conty" does not pause for a dotted whole-note on each cadence, but rests for only a dotted half-note, which contributes to the continuity of musical movement. The beginning of the tune is notated as a pickup to the middle of the measure. The dance phrase begins one dotted half-note later with the first complete musical measure. Each pas composé is at least one dotted whole-note long, so that the dancers, who appear to have entered a half-measure late, are completing a pas composé as the musicians begin a new phrase.

Feuillet's notation is quite clear on this point; his choreographic measure lines always correspond to musical ones[3] and he carefully indicates rests to account for the first incomplete musical measure. Thus, there is no question that the pas composés fall within the musical measure and that it is Pécour's and perhaps even Campra's intention that the music and dance should be delicately out of synchronization in "la Conty."

Two problems of cadence remain to be solved by the dancer. The first concerns the notation of the second rest in the dance. One would expect that because the demi-coupé which introduces the first pas tombé has its élevé on the first beat of the first complete measure of the dance, the demi-coupé which introduces the second pas tombé would have its élevé on the first beat of the third complete measure. However, Feuillet has placed a rest at the beginning of the third measure, followed by the demi-coupé and tombé.

If the rest were performed where it is written, the demi-coupé and tombé would be performed in the time of a dotted half-note, a unique telescoping of the preparation and fall into less than one measure. I doubt that the rest disturbs the customary execution of the élevé at the beginning of the measure, and its placement is probably an error, albeit one which is repeated by other notators.[4]

The second problem of cadence also involves the first four pas composés of the dance: how long is the plié before each one? In the first three pas tombé figures, the introductory plié might be either one quarter-note or one dotted half-note long. The plié which introduces the fourth figure must be performed in the time of a quarter-note, because the élevé of the demi-coupé rebound of the preceding pas composé occurs on the last dotted half-note beat of measure 6.

A variety of solutions to this particular question produces pleasing results, but the matter must be carefully considered by the dancers, because this decision determines the phrasing of the first figure of the dance.

The floor pattern of "la Conty" reflects Pécour's choice of steps because the pas tombé is always performed on a straight line. The first three figures present the pas tombé in striking tableaux; the last two figures form an uninterrupted swirl of circular figures spiraling in and opening out to a final straight line directed to the Présence.

The length of "la Conty's" floor patterns or figures corresponds to that of the musical phrases through the third phrase of the piece, although the floor patterns are performed one half-measure later. The dancers do not change direction nor alter their path between the third and fourth phrases and between the fourth and fifth phrases of music. This serves to blur the distinction between the third and fourth figures, which depends solely upon the coupé, and to eliminate effectively any sense of more than one choreographed figure during the fourth and fifth musical phrases.

The dancers meet face to face during the first temps de courante in the first phrase, at the pas de sissonne in the second phrase, during the pas de gaillarde in the third phrase, and at the first contretemps de côté in the fourth phrase. The pas de bourrée emboîtés are the first acknowledgment of the Présence following several phrases devoted to circling while watching one's partner.

The symmetrical pattern of pas tombés in the opening phrase is also composed principally for the benefit of the Présence. In this context, the temps de courante and tombé facing one's partner become a pleasant result of the design rather than the purpose of the phrase.

Particularly ingenious is Pécour's use of the pas de gaillarde as a traveling step to change position in the third phrase. The dancers must be careful to perform these steps at an angle which allows them to pass over the center line during the pas tombé forward, so that they can execute the second pas de gaillarde to the side while facing each other.

Rameau's arm movements for the pas tombé are essential to the character of "la Conty" because they contribute to the dramatic effect of the unusual step which they accompany. The arm movements for the contretemps de côté may also be considered essential because, as a result of their similarity to those of the tombé, they lend a sense of unity to the first three strains of the dance and the last two.

Rameau's arm movements for the pas de bourrée emboîté and the coupé de mouvement effectively reflect the internal contrast of the steps. Those for the pas de bourrée behind and before and assemblé lead smoothly into the contretemps de côté and were probably intended to be used for this purpose. Rameau's arm movements for the pas de sissonne should be used to mark the moment when the dancer's focus shifts from the Présence to the partner.

The use of the arm movements for the other pas depends upon the context. I use them when they seem to contribute to the sense of movement (e.g., in the pas de bourrée forward) and omit them when they confuse the line or figure (e.g., in the pas de bourrée behind and behind and contretemps ballonnés to the side). Interestingly enough, the cadential combination of the pas de bourrée before and behind and coupé in the second phrase seems to be one place where Rameau's opposition to the glissé of the coupé soutenue works, perhaps because it follows the double opposition of the arms in the pas de bourrée before and behind.

The head position in the pas tombés and contretemps de côté is modified by the position of the partner in the figure. In the first strain, the first temps de courante and tombé should be performed face to face without the turn of the head. In the contretemps de côté, I feel the head should be turned in the wrong direction, both so that the dancers can see each other over the lower arm and so that the similarity to the pas tombé is emphasized.

"La Conty" is not renotated in *Abbrégé,* nor do we find any excerpts from it in Rameau's "Traîté de Cadence," nor any specific references to it in *Le Maître à Danser.* Bonin does include it in his list of figured dances.[5]

In 1824, A.A.F. Baron used the first page of "la Conty" as one of two examples to introduce his student, Sophie, to Feuillet notation.[6] At the beginning of the volume, he includes a copy of that page of choreography, which faithfully reproduces Feuillet's notation. Baron's discussion is a clear exposition of the art of reading the notation, using "la Conty" as an example. Unfortunately, he ignores the problems of the interpretation of those measures ambiguously notated by Feuillet in the original (see above). This passage does indicate, however, that "la Conty" was remembered or revived early in the nineteenth century, and some of Baron's omissions (e.g., the Présence) perhaps shed more light on changes in the ballroom in post-Revolutionary France than they do upon the original performance of "la Conty."

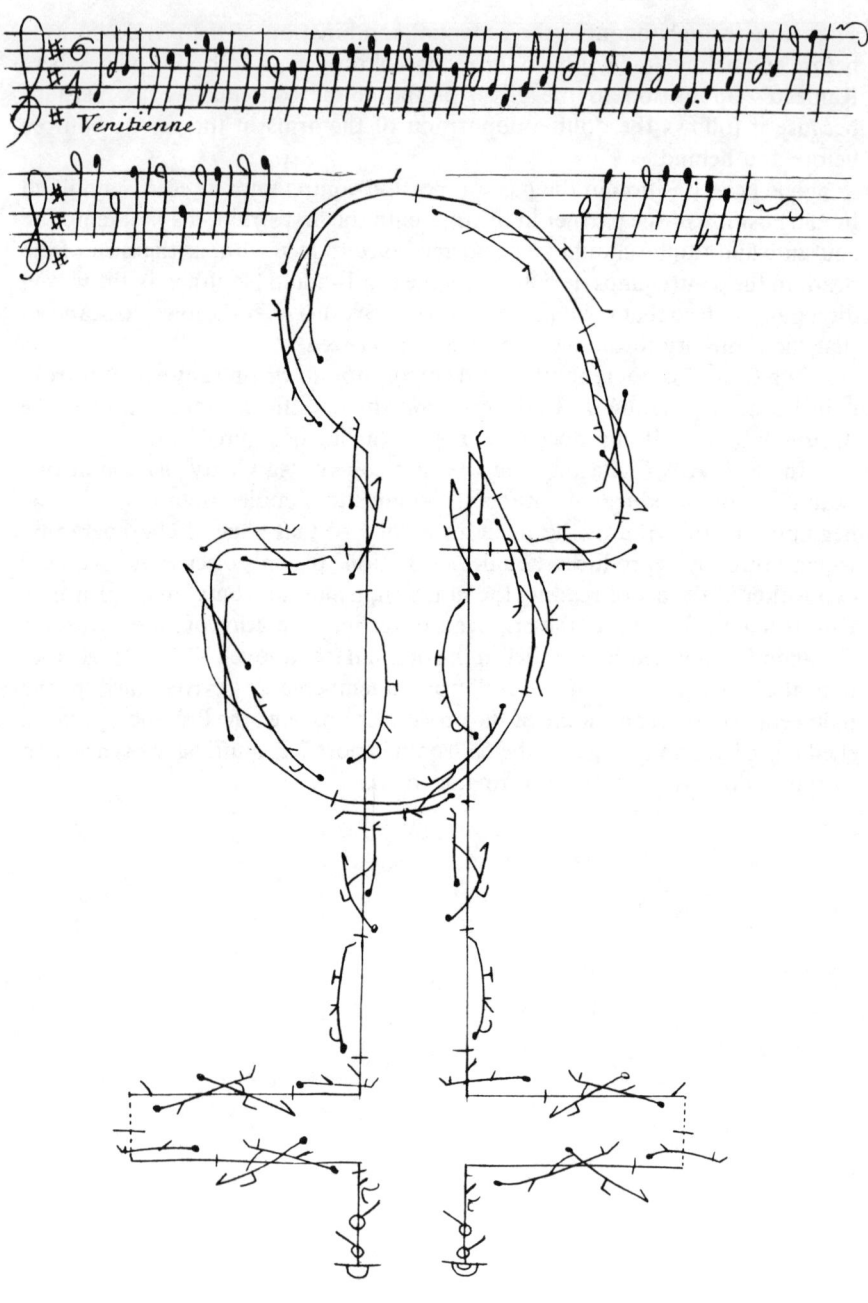

La Conty

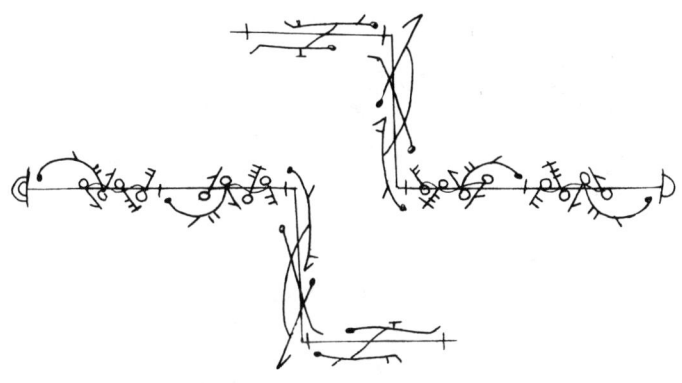

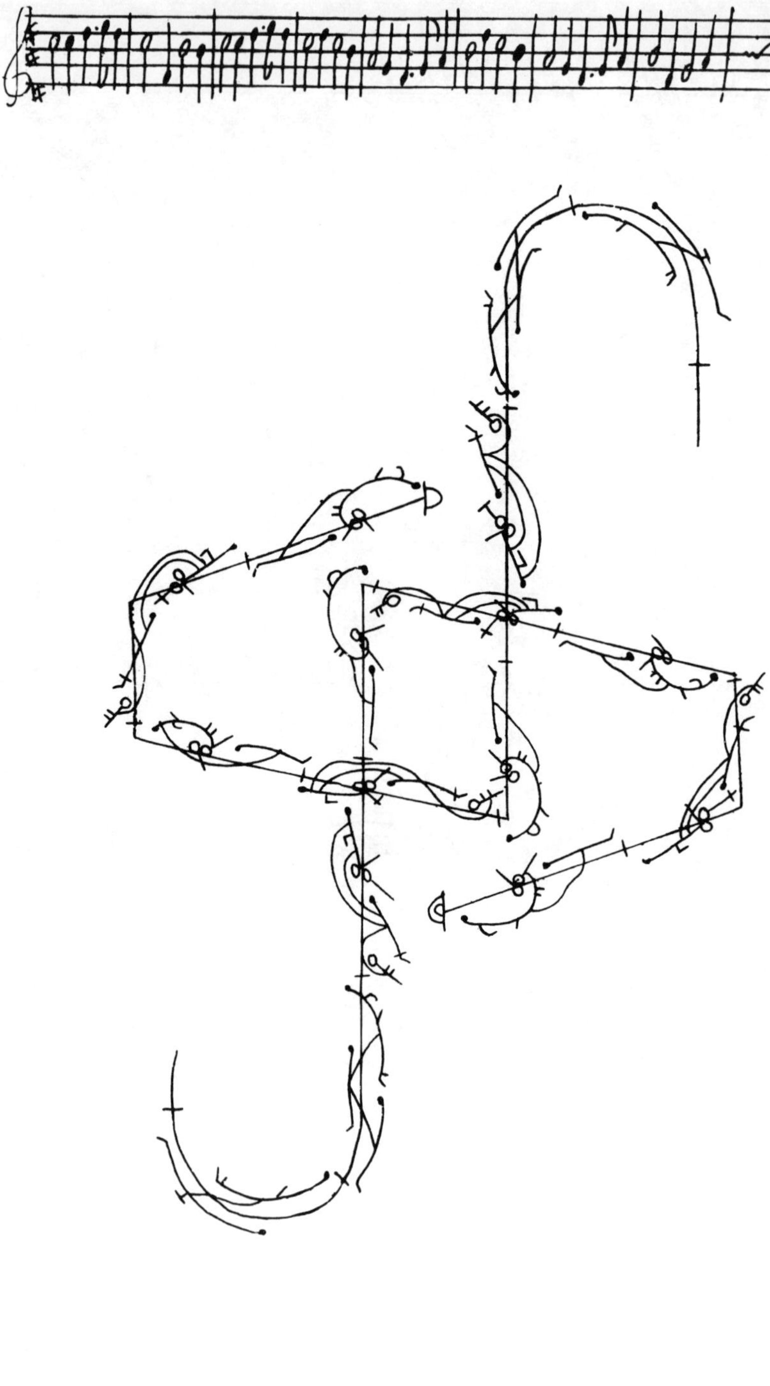

La Conty

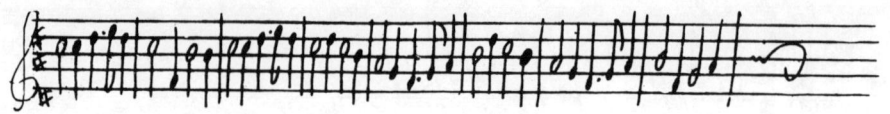

La Conty

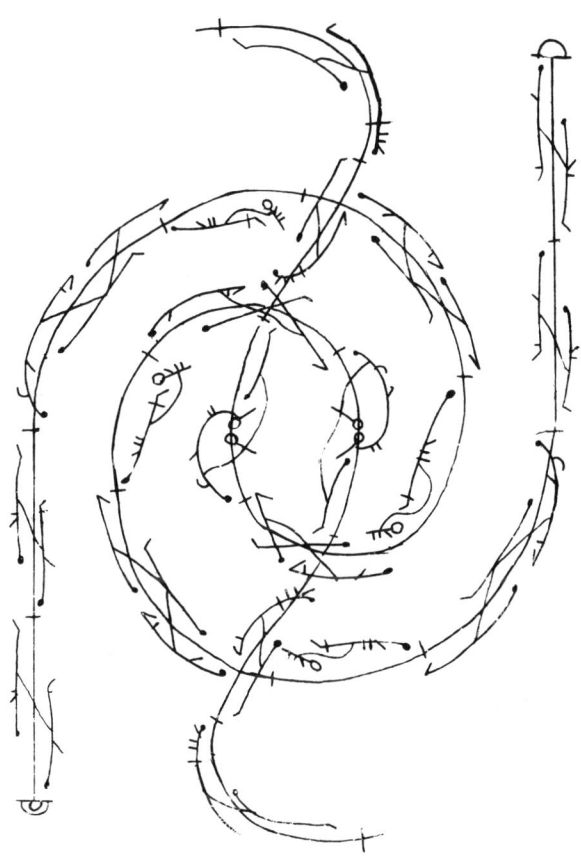

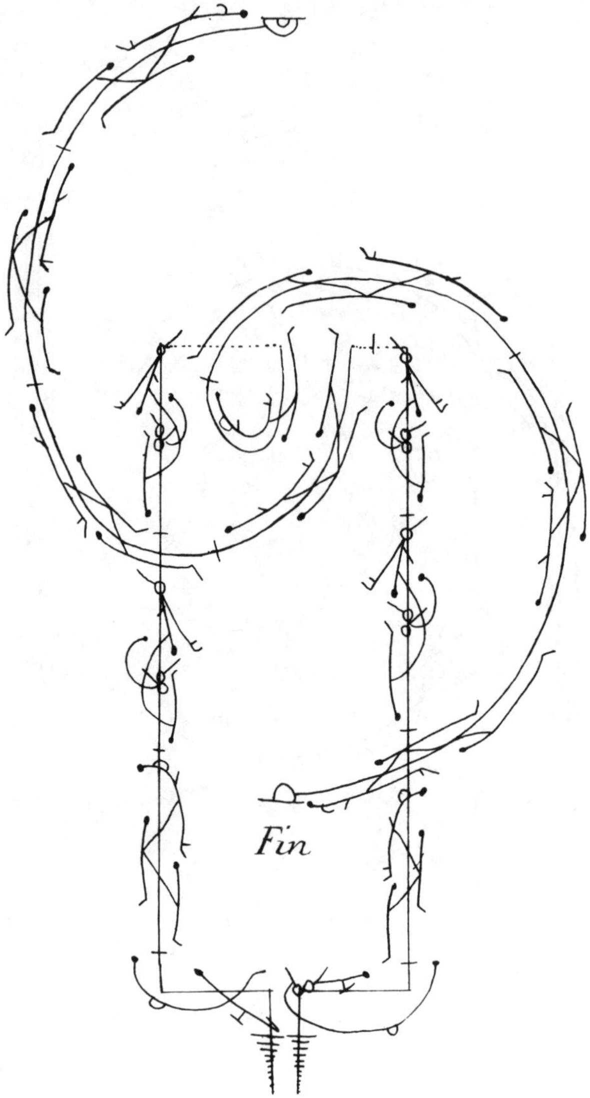

La Conty

Fin

10

Conclusion

Reconstruction

As one might expect in ball dances, as opposed to theater dances, nearly all of the step-units which appear in the choreographies notated by Feuillet can also be found in the tables of step-units in *Chorégraphie*. For the technique and style of movement and the arm movements of step-units, named and unnamed in *Chorégraphie*, one must consult Rameau's *Le Maître à Danser*. Rameau's work also contains detailed discussion of the performance of each named step-unit, including variations which are associated with direction of travel, musical metre, and adjacent step-units.

Part I of Rameau's *Abbrégé* clarifies the timing of the step-units, a topic introduced earlier in *Chorégraphie* and in Feuillet's preface to the 1704 collection of theater dances. Here Rameau also offers a new sign for the demi-jeté.

Rameau's renotation of "la Bourrée d'Achille," "la Mariée," "le Passepied," "la Bourgogne," and "la Forlana" appear in Part II of *Abbrégé*. Here, Rameau corrects some of Feuillet's errors and employs the new sign for the demi-jeté in several places where Feuillet had notated demi-coupés, a convention in the earlier notation.

Rameau's observation in *Le Maître* that, by 1725, the pas de menuet of three movements was no longer in fashion, is borne out by his renotation of all of Feuillet's pas de menuet of three movements forward as pas de menuet of two movements in "la Bourrée d'Achille," "le Passepied," and "la Bourgogne." In addition to this modification, there are also a few adjustments which seem to be the result of Pécour's revision.

Only after exhausting the information provided by Feuillet and Rameau, writers with whom Pécour was familiar, have I turned to the works of other dancing masters in the reconstruction of the dances. On occasion, they supply information which is useful to the dancer where little exists in the French sources, such as Tomlinson's account of the pas tombé forward.

Even the dancer, armed with the foregoing information, faces some decisions. The timing of the few step-units for which Feuillet and Rameau offer no suggestions, certain circumstances in which a shift of weight onto two feet is possible, and some of the arm movements are problems whose solutions rest with the twentieth-century performer.

Rameau gives the arm movements which generally correspond to each step-unit in each direction, followed by specific exceptions and the suggestion that many of the arm movements are finally governed by their context. Thus, it is probable that eighteenth-century dancers also helped to determine the choice of arm movements. At the court of Louis XIV, at least, these dancers' opinions were better-informed than ours can be today, so careful study of Part II of *Le Maître* is essential for the twentieth-century dancer who must eventually add the arm movements to an eighteenth-century court dance.

Analysis

To me, the variety found in Pécour's 1700 *Recueil* is its most remarkable feature: variety of dance type, of technical difficulty, of choreographic construction, and of relationship of music and dance.

This *Recueil* offers the dancer a passepied, a contredanse (gigue), a rigaudon, a bourrée, and a forlana; two titled dances, "la Mariée" and "la Conty (venitienne)"; and two examples of mixed-dance-type choreographies: one bourrée-menuet-bourrée and one courante-bourrée-sarabande-passepied. The sequences of relatively simple step-units found in "la Bourrée d'Achille" would be welcomed by those with a more modest gift for dancing. The brilliant, exuberant "la Mariée," and "la Conty" with its long lines built on tombés and balancés, would challenge the courtier who was pressing his technique to nearly theatrical heights. Such an immediately useful and attractive collection indicates that Pécour and also Feuillet, if it was he who selected the choreographies to be included, were practical anthologists.

Even more intriguing is the variety found in Pécour's choreographic construction and in the relationship of his dances to their music. One might suppose that the social dances of the court of Louis XIV, symbols of an oppressive political regime, were themselves a stilted, codified routine from which any inventive dancer should have been anxious to be liberated. A careful study of the dances of this 1700 *Recueil,* however, reveals that this attitude does not account for Louis Pécour, an artist who found the genre of the danse à deux extremely fertile ground for his creative imagination.

At times, Pécour uses a single step-unit as an organizing element in his choreography: the pas de bourrée emboîté in "le Rigaudon" and the pas tombé in "la Conty" are examples. His use of the pas de bourrée emboîté in "la Mariée" as a kind of motive which he develops throughout the dance may be contrasted with "la Conty," where he has written a pas tombé etude reflected in the arms of the contretemps de côté at its close.

At other times, Pécour exploits a series of step-units. In the simplest use of this technique, a series of four step-units is repeated in a new figure during a musical repetition, as in the bourrées of "la Bourgogne" and "la Bourrée d'Achille" and in the rondo refrains of "la Contredance." "La Savoye" weaves several pairs of step-units and one four-step-unit series into an intricate choreographic exaggeration of a minor inconsistency in the musical structure.

The floor-patterns are also repeated within the course of a dance such as "le Passepied," a dance-type in which the entertainment of the Présence by the design of the floor pattern is traditionally emphasized.

The floor patterns themselves can be the outgrowth of the choice of step-units, as in the opening of "la Conty." The traditional patterns associated with the court menuet and courante are the sources of the floor patterns in the menuet of "la Bourrée d'Achille" and the courante in "la Bourgogne."

A concentration of the dancer's focus on his partner influences the floor patterns in the sarabande from "la Bourgogne," "la Contredance," and "la Mariée."

Finally, there are the mixed-dance-type choreographies, whose purpose seems to be a change of mood within the course of a single dance reflected in a series of dance-types with contrasts of tempo, metre, quality of movement, and structure.

With such a great variety of compositional techniques found in nine ball dances, it is obvious that Pécour did not allow the danse à deux to become a confining genre, nor did he turn out dances carelessly based on a single pattern. Because his dances are anything but routine, however, neither do they provide what some musicians may have hoped to find in his 1700 *Recueil:* the simple dance models for more complicated musical works of art.

In the 1700 *Recueil,* the tunes Pécour chose to choreograph were one very important given element in his creation of a dance. It is worthwhile to survey, briefly, his methods of setting dance to music.

The instances of his strictest adherence to and most straightforward reflection of the music are found in the bourrées of "la Bourrée d'Achille" and "la Bourgogne" and the refrains in the first half of "la Contredance," where musical repetitions in two-reprise form or in a rondo are accompanied by repetition of a series of step-units. The striking danced echo device in "la Forlana" is another example of repeated step-units, which accompany the two-measure musical repetition which is the basis of the forlana.

A more subtle but equally direct reflection of the music is found at the opening of the sarabande of "la Bourgogne," where a sensitive choice of step-units enhances the importance of the second beat of the measure.

In those dance-types whose repertoire of step-units is limited, the relationship of music and dance is determined, in part, by those step-units.

These step-units have a more complicated cadence than any of those dances just described. The pas de menuet, whose cadence influences the menuet from "la Bourrée d'Achille," and, taken at a faster tempo, the passepied of "la Bourgogne" and "le Passepied," is a two-measure step-unit. Its movements on beats 1 and 3 provide an internal counter-rhythm to the musical downbeats, which occur on beats 1 and 4. When Pécour exploits the practice of traveling to the right with a pas de menuet of two movements and to the left with a pas de menuet of three movements, the dancer with the pas of three movements adds a third movement (the demi-jeté on beat 6) to the counter-rhythms already created by his partner and the music.

In the courante, the other limited step-unit dance-type, the step-units which Pécour employs are those which divide the measure into two unequal parts with two movements per measure:

$$\begin{array}{cc} o & d \\ tc & dj \\ c & dj \end{array}$$

and that which divides the measure into three equal parts with one movement per measure:

$$\begin{array}{ccc} d & d & d \\ p & d & b \end{array}$$

Pécour also provides many examples of counter-rhythms or counter-phrasings of his own devising. The simplest of these occurs in those dances whose step-units begin one half-measure later than the musical phrase, as in "la Conty." In "la Contredance," a single pas marché inserted at the beginning of the second half of the tune transforms a very straightforward rondo into a very straightforward rondo danced one half-measure late from that point on.

In certain instances, Pécour consciously avoids mirroring a striking musical rhythm in the dance. His bounds at musical phrase endings in "la Mariée" simply do not let the dancer or audience relax too much. In the places where he choreographs a dancer's tombé over a suspended musical line, as he does in "la Forlana," or has his dancer dance straight through a musical hemiola, as he does at the end of the sarabande from "la Bourgogne," he draws attention to the musical gesture by creating tension between its rhythm and that of the dance.

Finally, we find dance phrases whose boundaries do not correspond to those of the accompanying musical phrase. A simple example is the last dance figure of "la Conty," which uses two musical strains. Pécour's more astonishing examples occur in his setting internal dance phrases against those of the music to create such cross-currents as: $5+7$ over $7+5$ in "le Rigaudon," $5+3$ over $4+4$ in the passepied of "la Bourgogne," $3+3+1$ $[(1+1)/2]$ over 8 in "la Savoye," and $6+2+6$ over $5+4+5$ in "la Mariée."

Each of these phrases serves a specific function in its composition: to provide a shot of contrast in a happy passepied finale, to serve as the climax of a tangled bourrée, or as the initial barrage of "la Mariée."

Appendix A

Rameau's Notation of Five Dances from Pécour's 1700 *Receuil*

In the second partie of *Abbrégé de la nouvelle methode dans l'art décrire ou de tracer toutes sortes de danses de ville,* Rameau renotates, according to his "nouvelle correction et augmentation," twelve dances of Louis Pécour, including five from the 1700 *Recueil de Danses:* "la Bourrée d'Achille," "la Mariée," "le Passepied," "la Bourgogne," and "la Forlana." The *Abbrégé* collection contains the only Rameau notations of Pécour's dances which I have seen, although Rameau indicates he has notated others.[1] Their significance to both scholars and performers is enhanced by their authenticity. Pécour's approbation of *Abbrégé* and the passage in which Rameau refers to his contact with Pécour concerning his renotation of these dances are reproduced below:

Rameau, *Abbrégé,* Part I, pp. 110-11.

Je me fuis fervi pour exemple de plufieurs paffages des Danfes de Mr Pecourt, comme étant connuës, & de plus placées dans toute la précifion de l'air. J'ai même prié cet excellent Auteur de les voir avant que de les écrire, & il les a trouvé conformes à fes intentions, de même que les Danfes contenuës dans cette feconde Partie. J'ai même choifi celles qui ont eu le plus de cours, & je finis par la Roïale qui a été compofée pour feu Madame la Dauphine : mais il feroit inutile de parler de leurs beautez, la memoire que le Public en conferve étant au-deffus de tout ce que l'on en pourroit dire.

Quant aux autres Danfes de Mr Pecour, je les ai toutes écrites à la main, fuivant la correction, & pour la commodité du Public. Elles fe vendront féparément, de même que les Danfes nouvelles que je donnerai tous les ans avant la faint Martin, foit en Recueil ou féparément : elles fe vendront 12. fols, & un Recueil de Menuets nouveaux avec les Baffes qui fera du même prix.

Je donnerai inceffamment avis du Traité general de la Chorégraphie, contenant un nombre infini de tous les Pas qui font en ufage dans la Danfe férieufe ; & de plus des caracteres nouveaux que j'ai inventez pour exprimer les Pas de tous les caracteres comiques. Il fera orné de plufieurs Taille-douces, qui reprefenteront les diverfes attitudes où l'on doit être.

APPROBATION.

J'Ai examiné par ordre de Monseigneur le Garde des Sceaux une *Augmentation à l'ancienne Table de la Chorégraphie*, qui m'a paru très-utile aprés me l'être fait expliquer par celui qui en est l'Auteur : j'ai cru que ceux qui depuis long-tems se servoient de cette maniere y trouveront cette Augmentation trés-juste pour l'intelligence & la facilité d'écrire les Pas de Danse qui sont dans l'ancienne Table avec plus de correction. Fait à Paris le vingt Octobre mil sept cens vingt-cinq.

PECOURT.

Rameau's corrections and augmentations of Pécour's dances as they were notated by Raoul-Auger Feuillet twenty-five years before can be divided into three categories. First, Pécour himself has evidently made a few revisions of step-units and floor-patterns, which Rameau notates. Second, Rameau's system of notation, which has been explained in Part I of *Abbrégé*, attempts to put into the notation some details for which Feuillet had relied upon the dancer's knowledge. Finally, Rameau serves as a proof-reader, catching many, but not all, of Feuillet's minor oversights.

In content, Rameau's notations may be considered a second, revised edition of Pécour's dances. There is also a noticeable difference in Rameau's style of notation, which affects both its efficiency for the sight-reading dancer and its reflection of choreographic and musical structure.

Feuillet's slightly less specific notation is also less cluttered. It is not difficult for the dancer who knows what Feuillet means to use his 1700 *Recueil* in hand to learn a dance, turning the book as he describes in *Chorégraphie*.[2] Rameau's notation, with detached signs for each measure and turn as well as more signs for positions and the demi-jeté, make his book more suitable for study seated at a table.

Furthermore, Rameau's layout differs. Taken as graphic art alone, his work is not as clear as a page of Feuillet, who took greater care to make his steps a standard length. Where Rameau's pagination differs, surprisingly, he puts more of his complicated notation on each page. Where the pagination differs, it also appears that the reflection of choreographic and even musical structure was a far greater consideration for Feuillet than for Rameau, who goes so far as to allow a change of dance type to fall in the middle of a page.

210   Appendix A: La Bourrée d'Achille

In the following pages, I have reproduced Rameau's notation of each of the dances which appear in Pécour's 1700 *Recueil,* followed by a chart indicating the differences between Feuillet's and Rameau's notation and a brief discussion of the changes which appear in *Abbrégé.*

La Bourée D'achille

Pécour's 1725 intentions are reflected in the changes in step-units (pas de menuet of two mouvements forward, replacing those of three movements forward, and the pas de bourrée emboîté replacing a coupé sans poser le corps to the side in measure 88) and in the adjusted floor pattern near the end of the menuet section (measures 69-72).

The clarification which Rameau's notation attempts may be seen in the notation of the sign for the position (fifth) from which temps de courante forward are taken following step-units to the side which end in close position, and in the use of the demi-jeté sign at the end of the pas de menuet of three movements.

The addition of quarter-turn signs and signs to drop hands are the result of Rameau's proof-reading. It is noteworthy that Rameau did not change a pas de menuet of two movements to the left in measures 67-68. Rameau contributes only one original error to "la Bourrée d'Achille:" the extra pas de menuet in the gentleman's part on page 5.

La Mariée

Pécour's decision to take the circles beginning in measures 53 and 57 with steps to the side while holding hands is the most striking change presented in Rameau's renotation of "la Mariée." The unusual high arm position for this passage is illustrated by Rameau at the foot of that page of choreography.

Other minor changes include the single line of liaison in measure 8, another solution to a weight change problem in measures 27-30, and a contretemps de gavotte with point replacing the same step-unit with pied en l'air in measure 101.

Rameau's notation clarifies the raise of the heel before the pas tombé and provides a more accurate indication of the movement of the feet in the pas de bourrée ouvert and in turning pas de bourrée.

His sign for the demi-jeté is employed in his notation of the coupé de mouvement and glissades.

Le Passepied

In Rameau's renotation of "le Passepied," all of Feuillet's pas de menuet of three movements forward are changed to pas de menuet of two mouvements.

In the pas de menuet of three mouvements to the left, Rameau employs his demi-jeté sign.

The other changes are relatively minor. Rameau has both dancers begin with the right foot free. In measures 83-86, the turning steps traveling down the room, the earlier version has a series of quarter-turns, while Rameau notates more half-turns, finishing the turning more quickly. In measures 99-102, the step-units and paths are adjusted to make less angular floor pattern.

La Bourgogne

Rameau's renotation of the courante corresponds to his description of the dance, employing his demi-jeté sign for the third half-note beat of the measure. The final step of the section in the gentleman's part is changed to a pas de bourrée emboîté.

Rameau's notation of the bourrée and sarabande is virtually identical to Feuillet's. Rameau clarifies a confusing weight change in m. 36, corrects the false jeté on the downbeat of m. 43, and omits the double line of liaison in the same measure, which would alter the rhythm of Feuillet's step.

In the passepied, the pas de menuet forward of three movements are changed to pas de menuet forward of two mouvements. The pas de menuet of three mouvements to the left employ the demi-jeté sign for the final mouvement. The section from measure 79-84 is notated by Feuillet with great attention to changes of hands, changes omitted by Rameau.

La Forlana

Rameau's renotation of "la Forlana" presents no major changes in the execution of the choreography notated in 1700. He consistently uses a sign to indicate raising the heel before the pas tombé and uses his demi-jeté sign in the glissades and the coupé de mouvement.

Appendix A: La Bourrée d'Achille

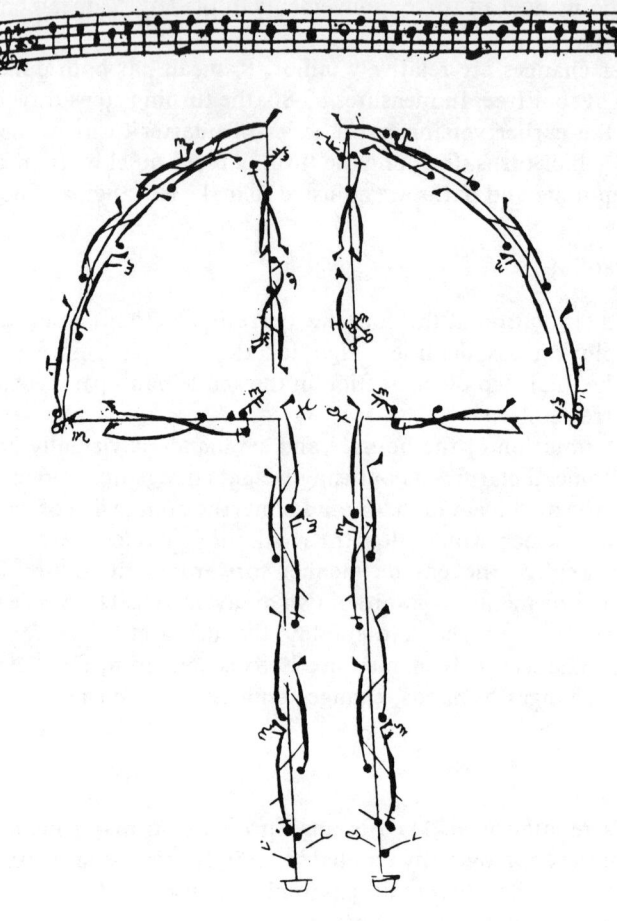

Appendix A: La Bourrée d'Achille

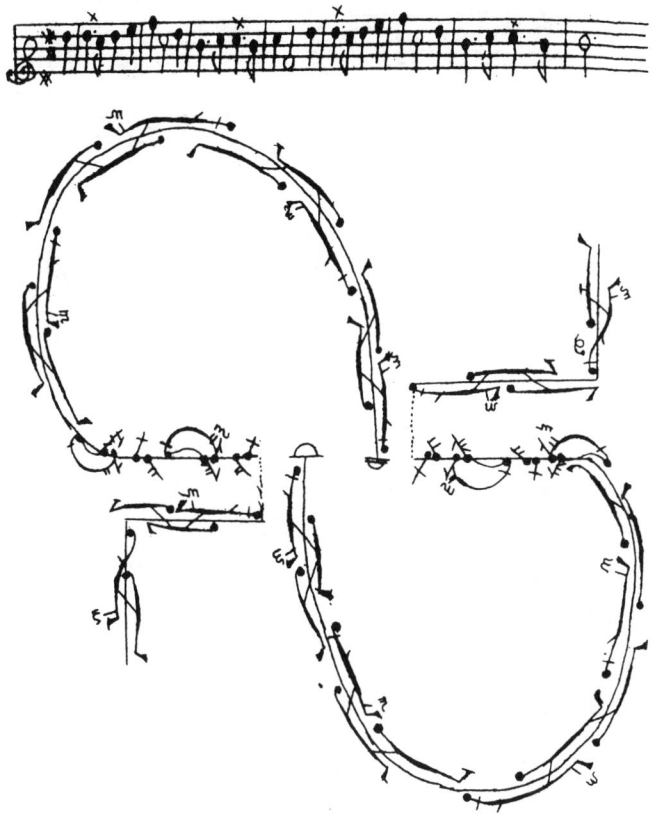

Appendix A: La Bourrée d'Achille

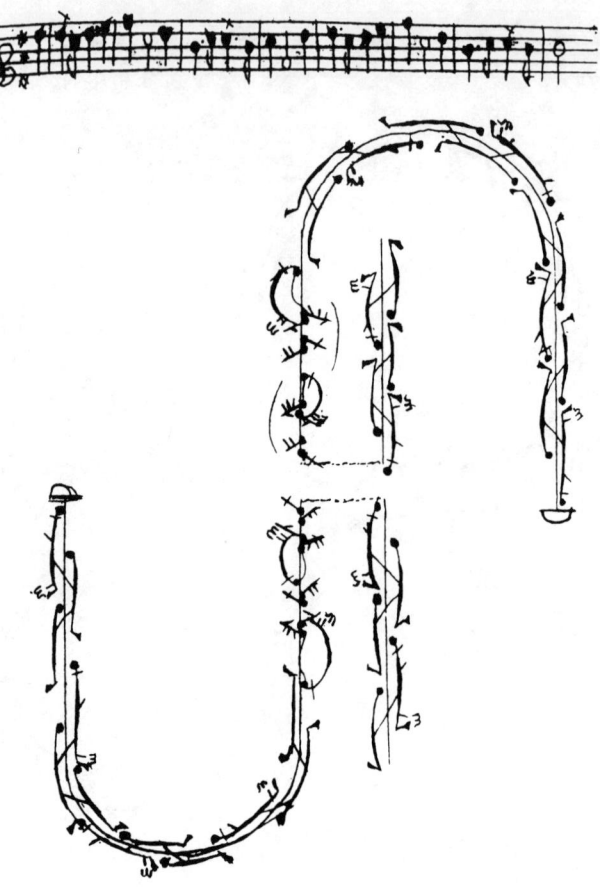

Appendix A: La Bourrée d'Achille

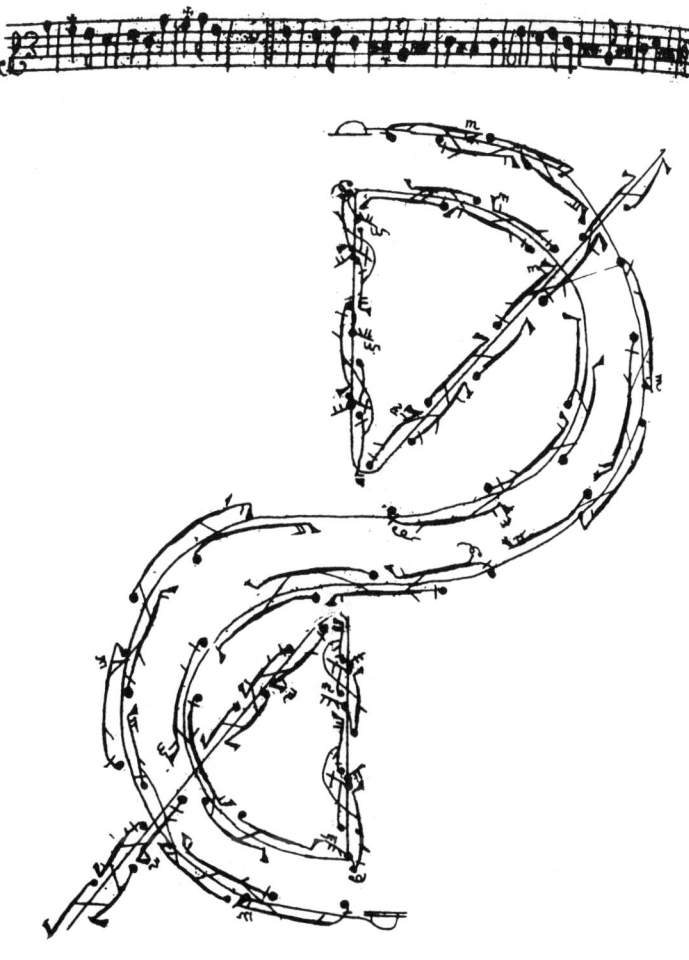

Appendix A: La Bourrée d'Achille

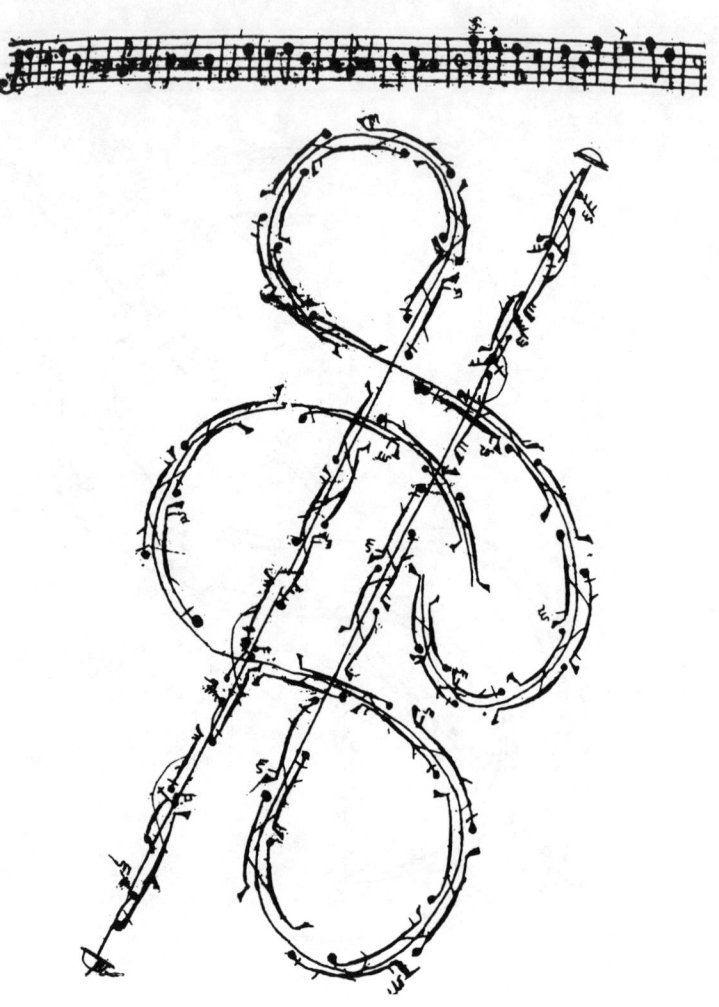

Appendix A: La Bourrée d'Achille

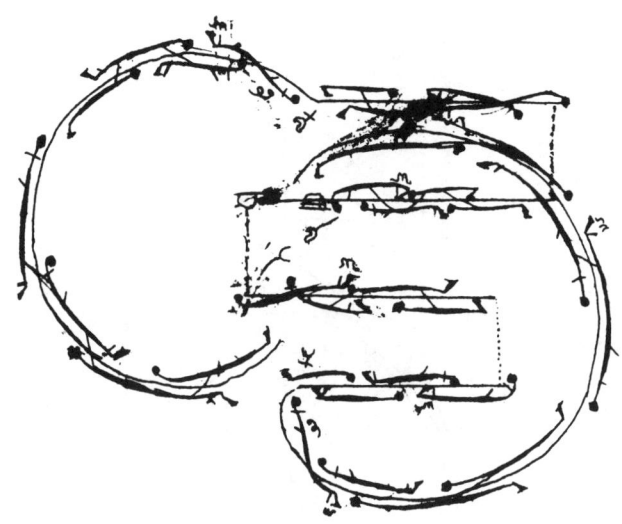

218   Appendix A: *La Bourrée d'Achille*

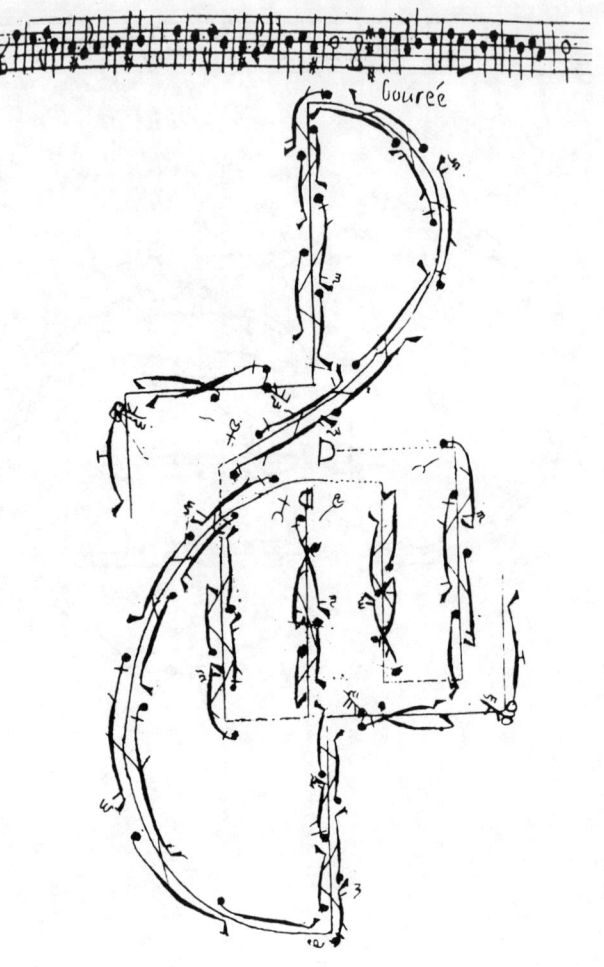

Appendix A: La Bourrée d'Achille

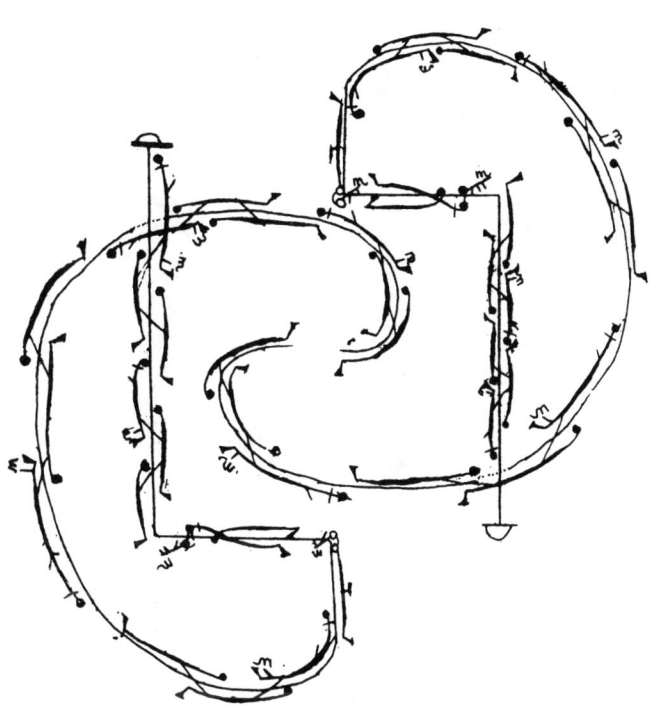

Appendix A: La Bourrée d'Achille

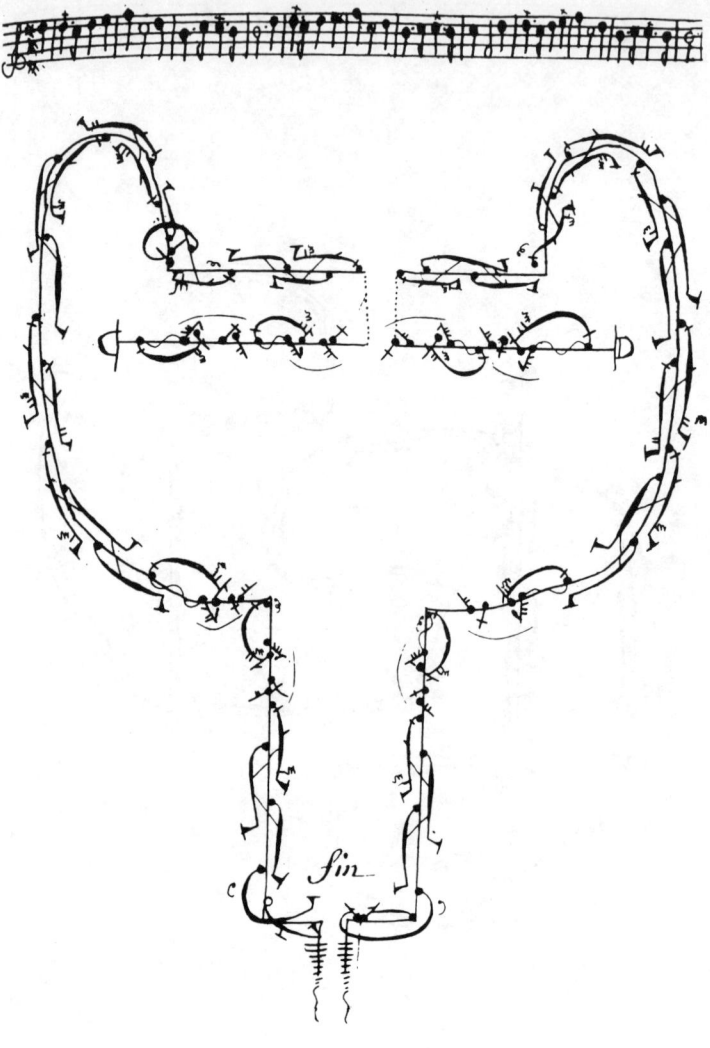

La Bourrée d'Achille

Feuillet 1700 Recueil p. 1 - m. 1-8	Rameau Abbrégé (1725) p. 1 - m. 1-8
m.4 no position given	m.4 fifth position indicated
m.8 no position given	m.8 fifth position indicated in the lady's part
p. 2 - m. 9-16	p. 2 - m. 9-16
p. 3 - m. 17-24	p. 3 - m. 17-24
m.24 (music) dotted half-note	m.24 (music) half-note
p. 4 - m. 25-40	p. 4 - m. 25-40
m.25-26 pas de menuet of three mouvements to the left with final demi-coupé	m.25-26 pas de menuet of three mouvements to the left with final demi-jeté
m.27-28 "	m.27-28 "
m.29-30 pas de menuet of three mouvements forward	m.29-30 pas de menuet of two mouvements forward
m.31-32 "	m.31-32 "
m.33-34 quarter-turn sign omitted in gentleman's part	m.33-34 quarter-turn sign included in both parts
p. 5 - m. 41-48	p. 5 - m. 41-56
m.45-46 pas de menuet of three mouvements forward	m.45-46 pas de menuet of two mouvements forward
m.47-48 "	m.47-48 "
p. 6 - m. 49-56	
m.49-50 pas de menuet of three mouvements forward	m.49-50 pas de menuet of two mouvements forward
m.51-52 "	m.51-52 "
m.53-54 "	m.53-54 "
m.55-56 "	m.55-56 "
	m.55^a-56^a an extra pas de menuet of two mouvements forward is included in the gentleman's part

Appendix A: La Bourrée d'Achille

Feuillet	Rameau
p. 7 - m. 57-64	p. 6 - m. 57-64

m.57-58 pas de menuet of three mouvements to the left with final demi-coupé in the lady's part

m.57-58 pas de menuet of three mouvements to the left with final demi-jeté in the lady's part

m.59-60 pas de menuet of three mouvements to the left with final demi-coupé in the gentleman's part

m.59-60 pas de menuet of three mouvements to the left with final demi-jeté in the gentleman's part

m.61-62 pas de menuet of three mouvements forward

m.61-62 pas de menuet of two mouvements forward

m.63-64   "

m.63-64   "

p. 8 - m. 65-72   p. 7 - m. 65-76

m.65-66 pas de menuet of three mouvements to the left with final demi-coupé in the gentleman's part

m.65-66 pas de menuet of three mouvements to the left with final demi-jeté in the gentleman's part

m.67-68 pas de menuet of two mouvements to the left in the lady's part; no sign to drop hands

m.67-68 pas de menuet of two mouvements to the left in the lady's part; sign to drop hands included

m.69-70 pas de menuet of three mouvements forward; quarter-turn sign in the lady's part

m.69-70 pas de menuet of two mouvements forward; no turn signs, circular path in the lady's part

m.71-72 pas de menuet of three mouvements forward

m.71-72 pas de menuet of two mouvements forward

p. 9 - m. 73-80

m.76 no position given

m.76 fifth position indicated

                                                p. 8 - m. 77-84

m.80 no position given

m.80 fifth position indicated

p.10 - m. 81-84

p.11 - m. 85-96   p. 9 - m. 85-96

m.88 coupé sans poser le corps to the side in the gentleman's part

m.88 pas de bourrée emboîté in the gentleman's part

Appendix A: La Mariée de Rollant

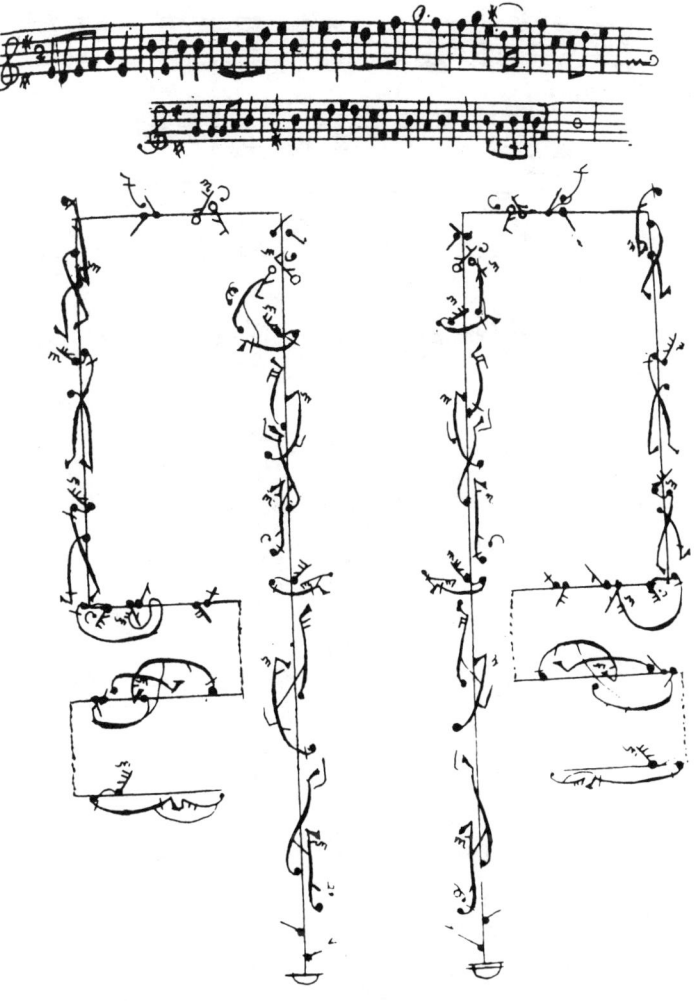

224 *Appendix A: La Mariée de Rollant*

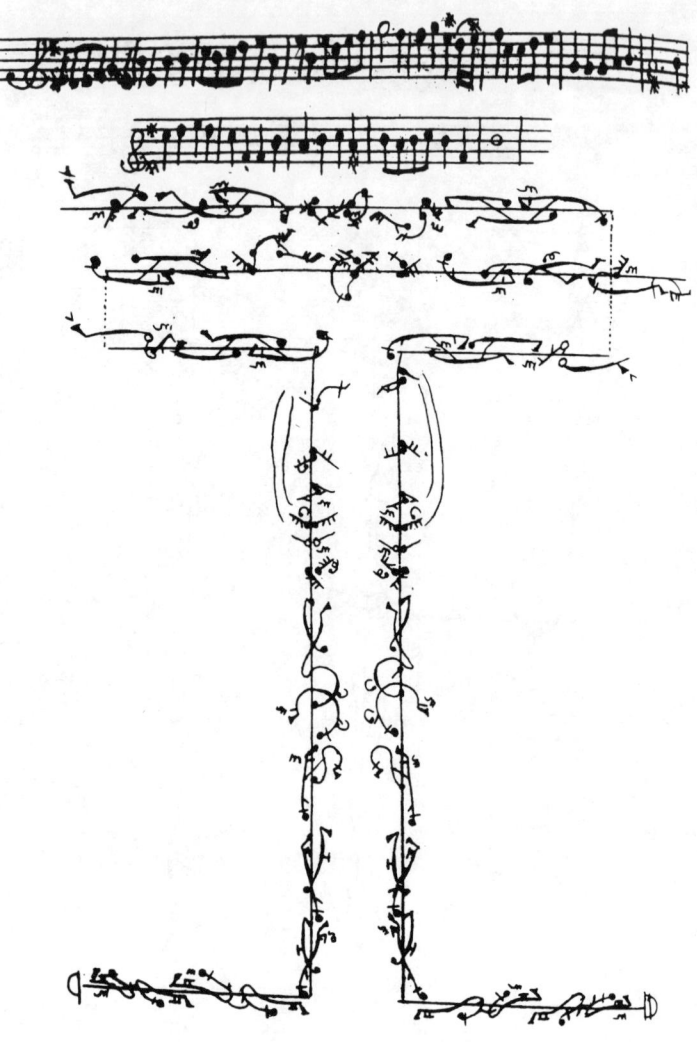

Appendix A: La Mariée de Rollant 225

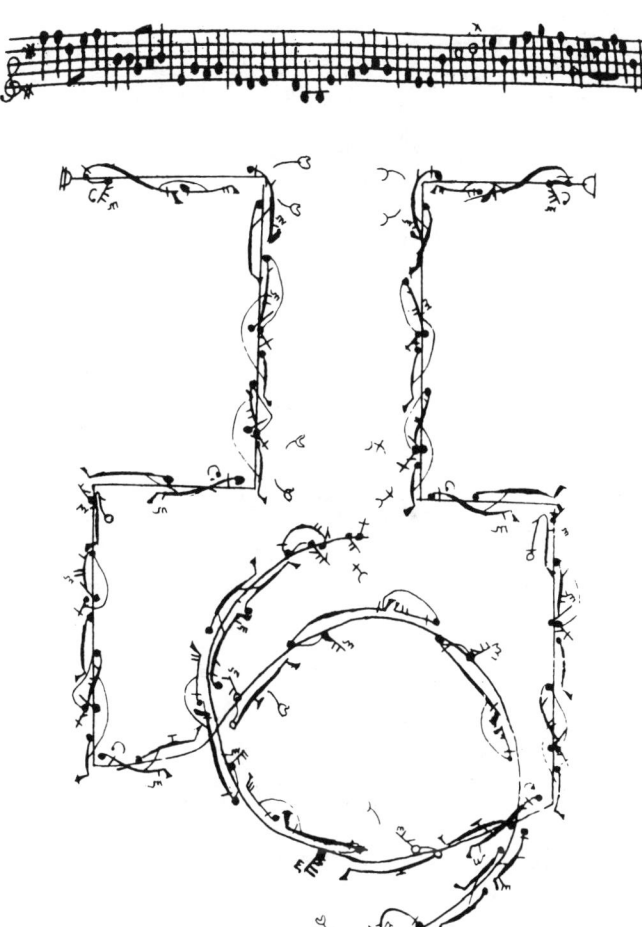

Appendix A: La Mariée de Rollant

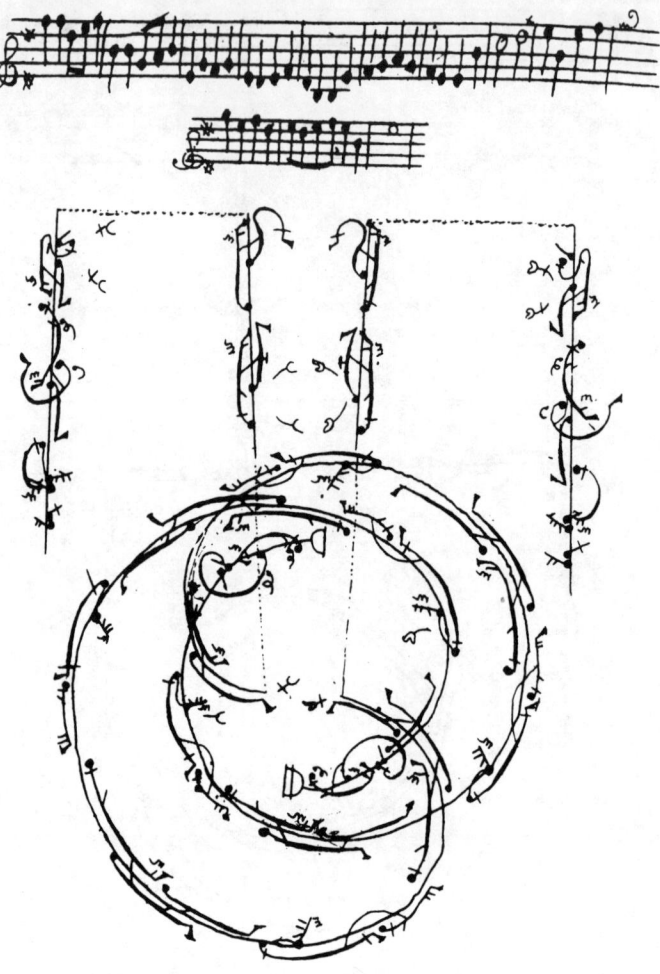

Appendix A: La Mariée de Rollant

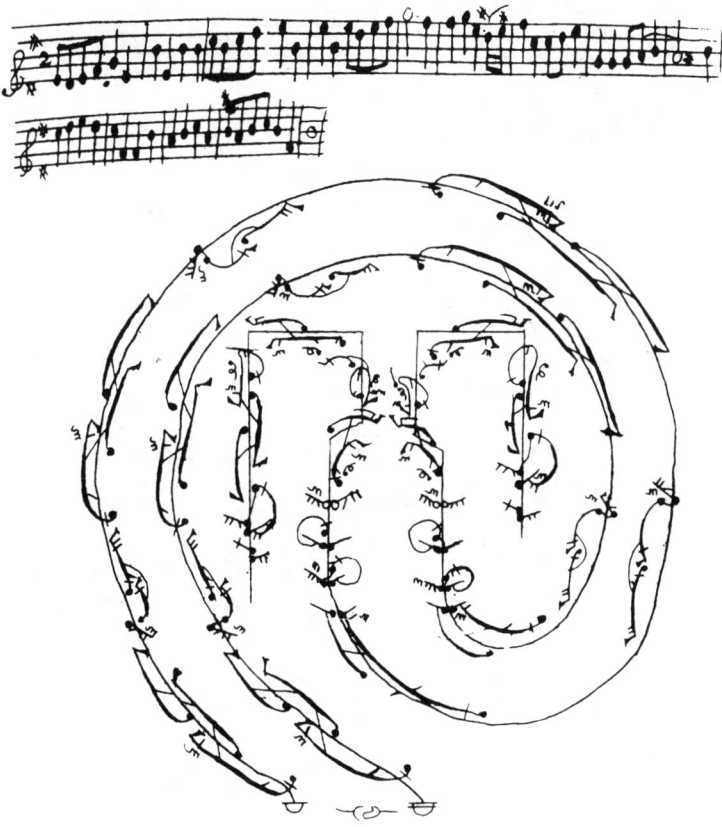

228 *Appendix A: La Mariée de Rollant*

Appendix A: La Mariée de Rollant

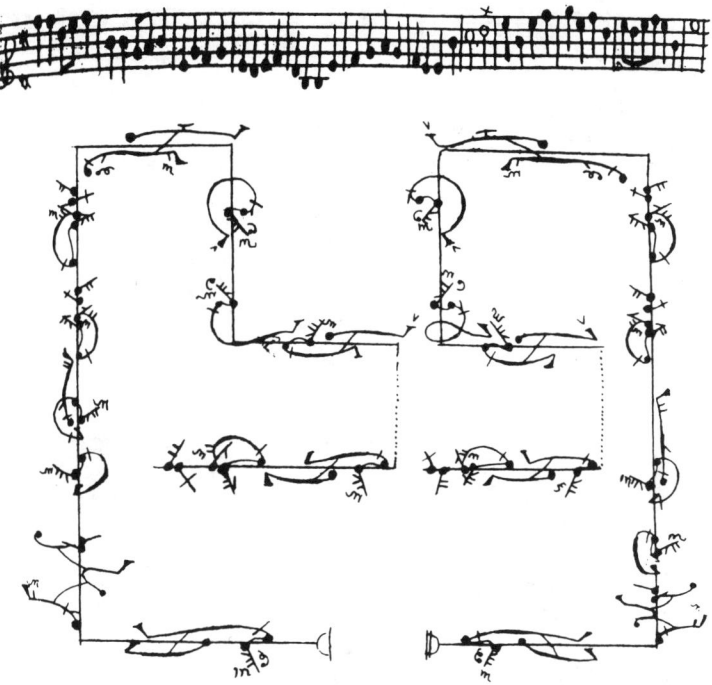

230 *Appendix A: La Mariée de Rollant*

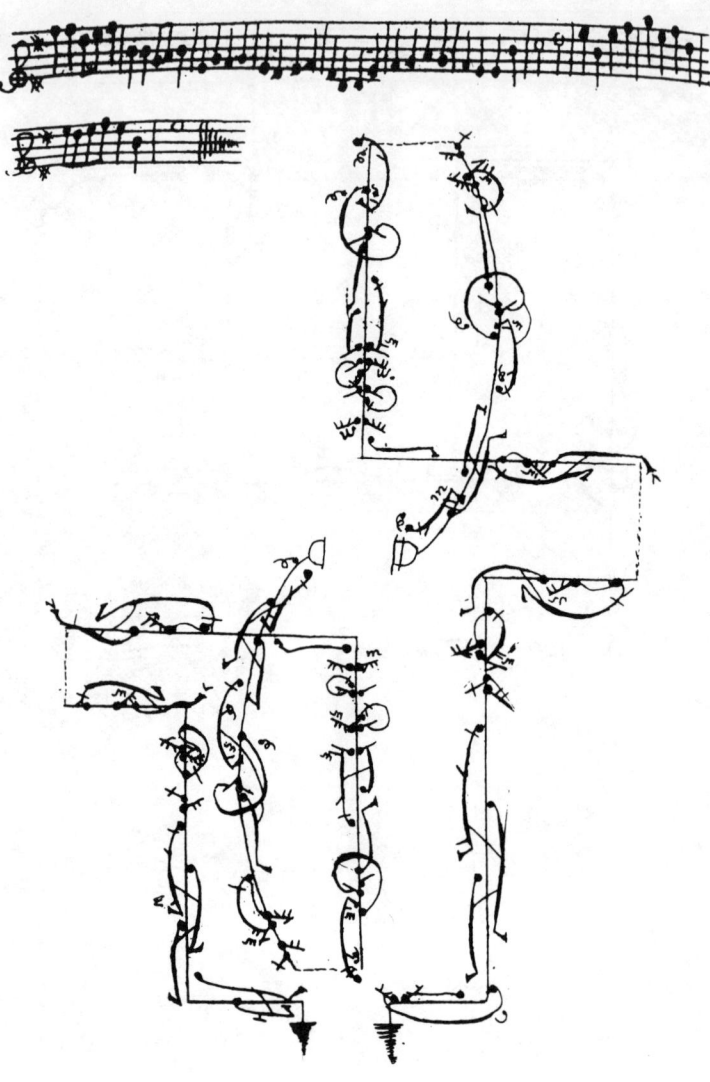

Appendix A: La Mariée de Rollant 231

La Mariée

Feuillet	Rameau
p. 12 - m. 1-14	p. 10 - m. 1-14
m.1 no sign to raise heel	m.1 sign to raise the heel in preparation for tombé included
m.4 "	m.4 "
m.8 pirouette with double lines of liaison to point. (music) no C#, incorrect rhythm	m.8 pirouette with single line of liaison to pied en l'air. (music) no C#, correct rhythm
m.12-13 (music) C#'s included	m.12-13 (music) C#'s omitted
p. 13 - m. 15-28	p. 11 - m. 15-28
m.17 glissades with demi-coupés	m.17 glissades with demi-jetés
m.19 turning pas de bourrée with glissé on last step	m.19 turning pas de bourrée, movement of free foot into fifth position behind indicated before second step; no glissé on last step
m.22 (music) C# included	m.22 (music) C# omitted
m.26 (music) C#'s included	m.26 (music) initial C# omitted
m.27 contretemps ballonné in lady's part. (music) C# included	m.27 contretemps consisting of a saut and a point in lady's part. (music) C# omitted
p. 14 - m. 29-40	p. 12 - m. 29-40
m.29 contretemps ballonné landing first on left in lady's part	m.29 contretemps ballonné landing first on right in lady's part
m.30 pas de gaillard to the side in lady's part	m.30 coupé to the side in lady's part
m.36 (music) no agréments	m.36 (music) agrément on second half-note
p. 15 - m. 41-47	p. 13 - m. 41-52
m.47 coupé soutenue in gentleman's part	m.47 coupé simple in gentleman's part

232 Appendix A: La Mariée de Rollant

Feuillet	Rameau
p. 16 - m. 48-52	
m.48 (music) no agréments	m.48 (music) agrément on second half-note
	m.50 drop hands
m.51 drop hands	
m.52 turning pas de bourrée with half-turn and plié on first step, quarter-turn and élevé on second step	m.52 turning pas de bourrée with quarter-turn, plié, and élevé on first step; half-turn on second step
p. 17 - m. 53-61	p. 14 - m. 53-66
m.53 no sign to take hands; pas de bourrée to the side behind and before	m. 53 sign to take hands included; pas de bourrée to the side behind and behind
m.55 pas de bourrée to the side before and before	m.55 pas de bourrée to the side behind and behind
m.57 pas de bourrée forward	m.57 pas de bourrée to the side behind and behind
m.59 coupé simple to first, rising on toes	m.59 coupé simple to first; no indication of rising on toes
m.60 (music) C# included	m.60 (music) C# omitted
p. 18 - m. 62-75	
m.62 coupé de mouvement with plié-élevé on second step	m.62 coupé de mouvement with demi-jeté on second step; no sign to drop hands
m.64 "	m.64 coupé de mouvement with demi-jeté on second step
m.65 pas de bourrée in lady's part	m.65 coupé soutenue in lady's part
m.66 pas de sissonne backward closing in fifth position before on the first saut in lady's part	m.66 pas de sissonne backward closing in fifth behind on the first saut in lady's part. Includes drawing of couple holding hands to indicate arm position

Appendix A: La Mariée de Rollant 233

Feuillet

Rameau

p. 15 - m. 67-80

m.67 no sign to take hands; pas de bourrée to the side behind and before

m.67 sign to take hands; pas de bourrée to the side behind and behind

m.69 pas de bourrée forward

m.69 pas de bourrée to the side behind and behind

m.71 "

m.71 "

m.73 coupé soutenue to first position, rising onto toes in gentleman's part

m.73 coupé simple to first position; no sign to rise onto toes

m.74 pas de rigaudon landing from the first saut on the inside foot. (music) C# included

m.74 pas de rigaudon landing from the first saut on the right foot. (music) C# omitted

p. 19 - m. 76-80

m.76 glissades with demi-coupés

m.76 glissades with demi-jetés

m.77 coupé to the side with pied en l'air

m.77 coupé soutenue to the side closing behind

m.78 glissades with demi-coupés

m.78 glissades with demi-jetés

m.79 no sign to drop hands

m.79 sign to drop hands

p. 20 - m. 81-92

p. 16 - m. 81-92

m.82 pas de bourrée ouvert with first two steps opening to second position

m.82 pas de bourrée ouvert indicating movement of second step into first position before opening to second position

m.88 (music) no agréments

m.88 (music) agrément on second half-note

p. 21 - m. 93-104

p. 17 - m. 93-104

m.93 pas de bourrée backward

m.93 quarter-turn and pas de bourrée to the side behind and behind

m.97 coupé simple to first, rising onto toes in lady's part

m.97 coupé simple to first, not rising onto toes

234 Appendix A: La Mariée de Rollant

Feuillet	Rameau
m.100 (music) no agréments	m.100 (music) no agréments
m.101 contretemps de gavotte with pied en l'air in gentleman's part	m.101 contretemps de gavotte with point in gentleman's part
m.104 glissé on closing pas in lady's part	m.104 no glissé on closing pas in lady's part

Appendix A: Le Passepied 235

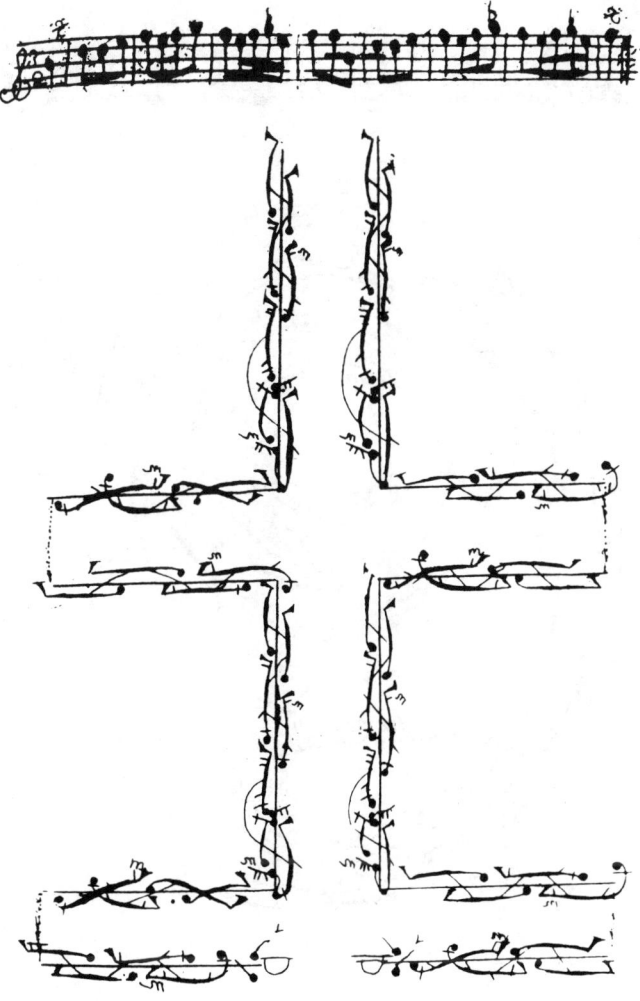

Appendix A: Le Passepied

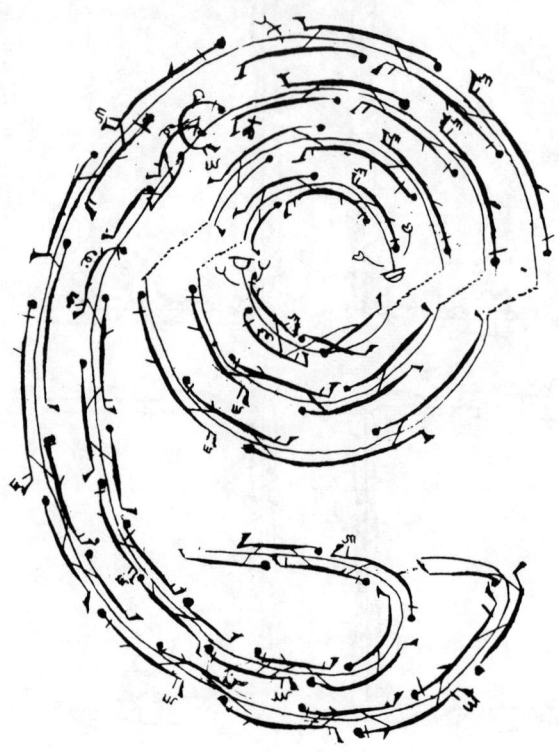

Appendix A: Le Passepied

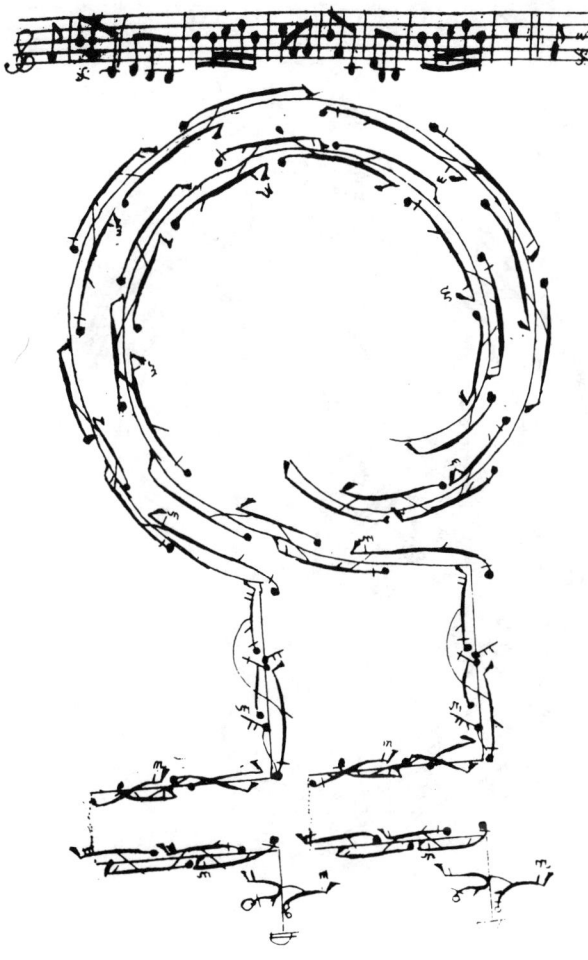

Appendix A: Le Passepied

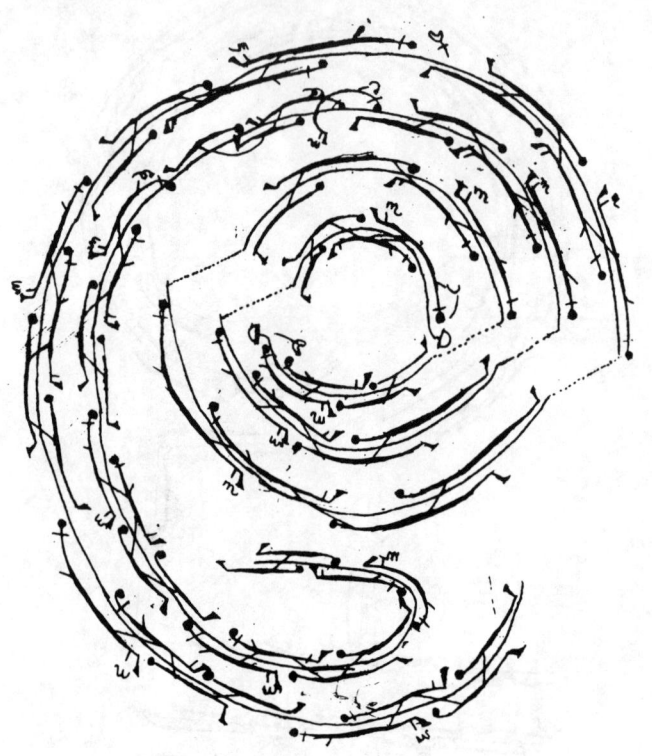

Appendix A: Le Passepied

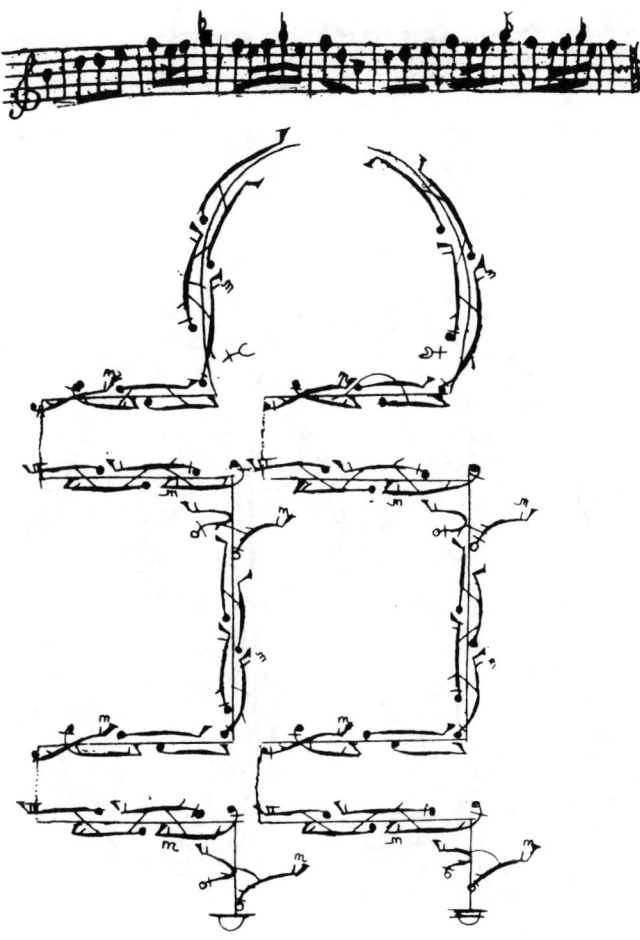

Appendix A: Le Passepied

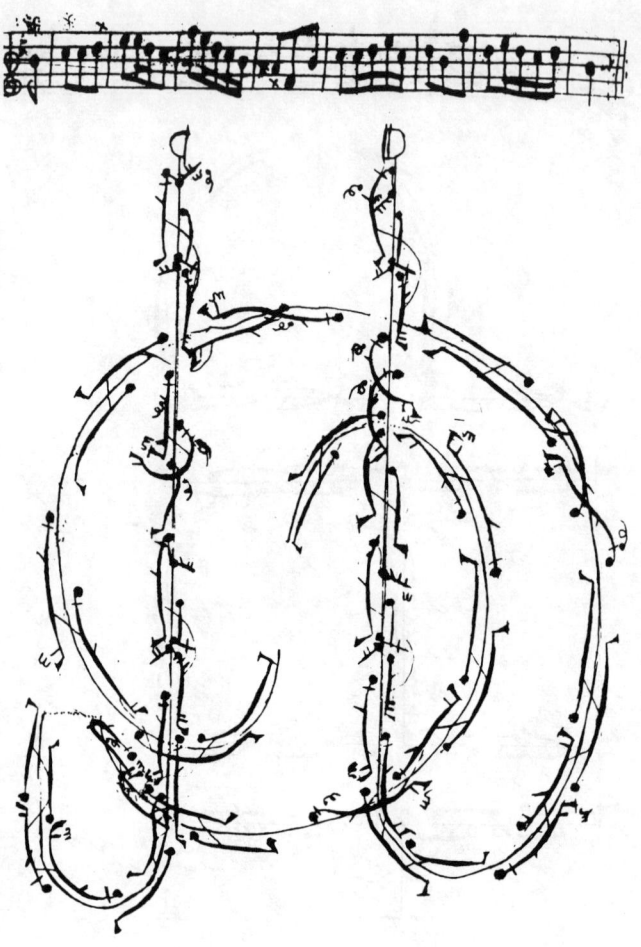

Appendix A: Le Passepied

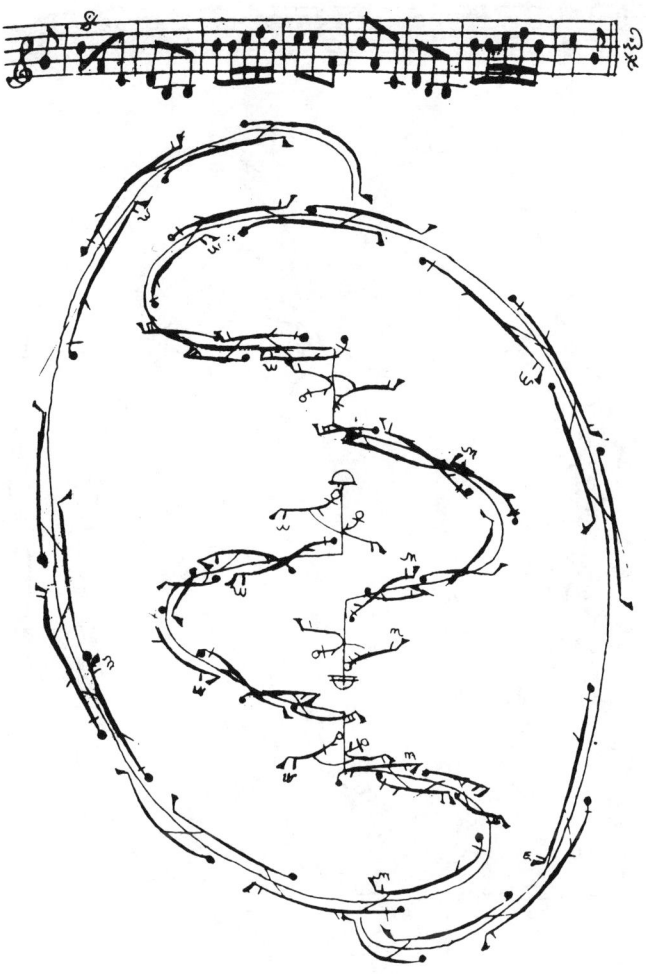

242 Appendix A: *Le Passepied*

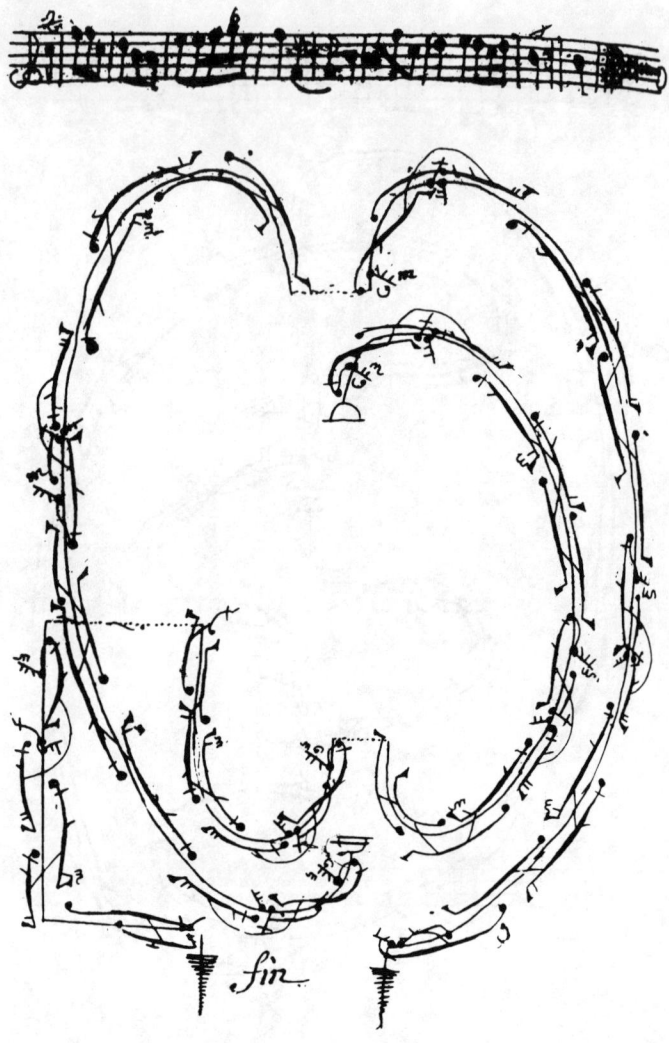

Appendix A: Le Passepied   243

Le Passepied

Feuillet	Rameau
p. 22 - m. 1-16	p. 18 - m. 1-16
m.1-2 starting position with outside foot free; [pas de menuet of three mouvements to the left with a final demi-coupé] in gentleman's part	m.1-2 starting position with right foot free; [pas de menuet of three mouvements to the left with a final demi-jeté] in gentleman's part
m.3-4 see 1-2, in lady's part	m.3-4 see 1-2, in lady's part
m.7-8 pas de menuet of three mouvements forward	m.7-8 pas de menuet of two mouvements forward
m.9-10 see 1-2, in gentleman's part	m.9-10 pas de menuet of two mouvements left, in gentleman's part
m.11-12 see 1-2, in lady's part	m.11-12 see 1-2, in lady's part
m.15-16 see 7-8	m.15-16 see 7-8
p. 23 - m. 17-32	p. 19 - m. 17-32
m.17-18 see 7-8, in both parts	m.17-18 pas de menuet of two mouvements right, in the gentleman's part; see 7-8, in lady's part
(music) 	(music) 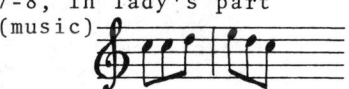
m.19-20 see 7-8	m.19-20 see 7-8
m.21-22 "	m.21-22 "
m.23-24 see 7-8, in gentleman's part; turning pas de menuet of three mouvements left, in lady's part; sign to drop outside hand included in both parts	m.23-24 see 7-8, in gentleman's part; turning pas de menuet of two mouvements left, in lady's part; sign to drop outside hand included in gentleman's part
m.25-26 see 7-8	m.25-26 see 7-8
m.27-28 "	m.27-28 "
m.29-30 "	m.29-30 "

244   *Appendix A: Le Passepied*

Feuillet	Rameau

m.31-32 pas de menuet of two mouvements forward in gentleman's part; pas de menuet of three mouvements left in lady's part

m.31-32 pas de menuet of two mouvements forward with final pas marché left in gentleman's part; pas de menuet of two mouvements left in lady's part

    p. 24 - m. 33-40

    p. 20 - m. 33-48

m.35-36 see 1-2

m.35-36 see 1-2

    p. 25 - m. 41-48

m.41-42 pas de menuet of three mouvements left

m.41-42 pas de menuet of two mouvements left

m.43-44   "

m.43-44   "

m.45-46   "

m.45-46   "

m.47-48   "

m.47-48   "

    p. 26 - m. 49-64

    p. 21 - m. 49-64

m.49-50 see 7-8

m.49-50 see 7-8

m.51-52   "

m.51-52   "

m.53-54   "

m.53-54   "

m.55-56 turning pas de menuet of three mouvements left, in gentleman's part; see 7-8, in lady's part

m.55-56 turning pas de menuet of two mouvements left, in gentleman's part; see 7-8, in lady's part

m.57-58 see 7-8

m.57-58 see 7-8

m.59-60   "

m.59-60   "

m.61-62   "

m.61-62   "

m.63-64 pas de menuet of three mouvements left, in gentleman's part; see 7-8, in lady's part

m.63-64 pas de menuet of two mouvements left, in gentleman's part; see 7-8, in lady's part

    p. 27 - m. 65-80

    p. 22 - m. 65-80

m.67-68 see 1-2

m.67-68 see 1-2

m.71-72 see 7-8

m.71-72 see 7-8

Appendix A: Le Passepied 245

Feuillet	Rameau
m.75-76 see 1-2	m.75-76 see 1-2
m.79-80 see 7-8	m.79-80 see 7-8
p. 28 - m. 81-96	p. 23 - m. 81-96
m.83-84 turning pas de menuet of three mouvements: 1/4 turn right and demi-coupé to fifth before, 1/4 turn right and demi-coupé to second, 1/4 turn right and pas marché to second, demi-coupé into fifth before, in gentleman's part;	m.83-84 turning pas de menuet of two mouvements: 1/4 turn right and demi-coupé to fifth before, 1/4 turn right and demi-coupé to second, 1/2 turn right and pas marché forward, final pas marché omitted, in gentleman's part;
1/4 turn left and demi-coupé to second, 1/4 turn left and demi-coupé to second, pas marché to fifth behind, demi-coupé to second, in lady's part	1/2 turn left and demi-coupé to second, 1/2 turn left and demi-coupé to second, two pas marchés forward, in lady's part
m.85-86 1/4 turn right and contretemps de menuet forward, in gentleman's part; 1/4 turn left and contretemps de menuet forward, in lady's part	m.85-86 contretemps de menuet forward
m.87-88 see 7-8	m.87-88 see 7-8
m.89-90 "	m.89-90 "
m.93-94 "	m.93-94 "
m.95-96 "	m.95-96 "
p. 29 - m. 97-112	p. 24 - m.97-112
m.99-100 pas de menuet of two mouvements directly right behind and behind	m.99-100 pas de menuet of two mouvements diagonally forward/right behind and before
m.101-102 pas de menuet of three mouvements forward with demi-coupé	m.101-102 pas de menuet of three mouvements diagonally forward/left before and behind with demi-jeté
m.105-106 see 1-2	m.105-106 see 1-2
m.107-108 see 7-8	m.107-108 see 7-8

Appendix A: Le Passepied

Feuillet	Rameau
m.109-110 see 7-8	m.109-110 see 7-8
m.111-112 "	m.111-112 "
p. 30 - m. 113-120	p. 25 - m. 113-128
m.115-116 see 7-8	m.115-116 see 7-8
m.119-120 "	m.119-120 "
p. 31 - m. 121-128	
m.123-124 see 7-8	m.123-124 see 7-8
m.127-128 glissé on final step, in lady's part	m.127-128 no glissé on final step, in lady's part

Appendix A: La Bourgogne

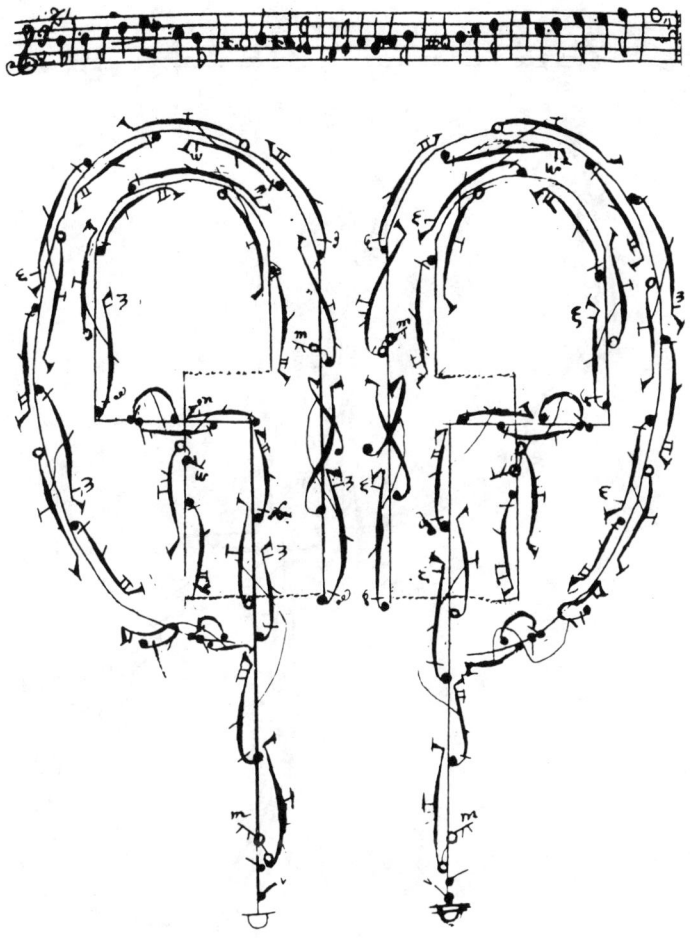

Appendix A: La Bourgogne

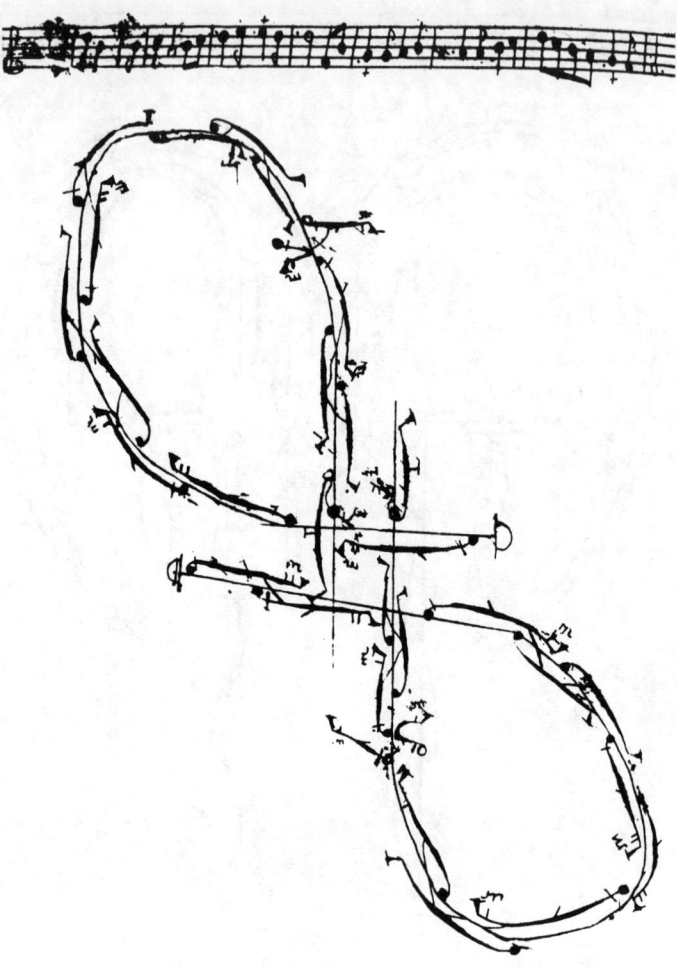

Appendix A: La Bourgogne

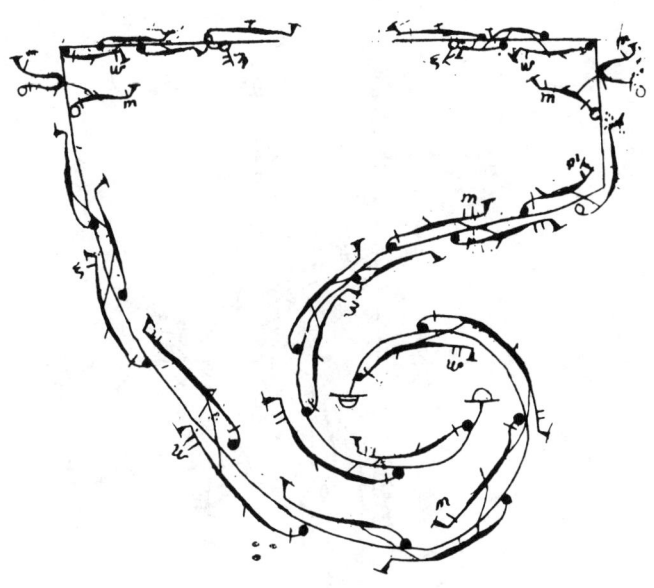

Appendix A: La Bourgogne

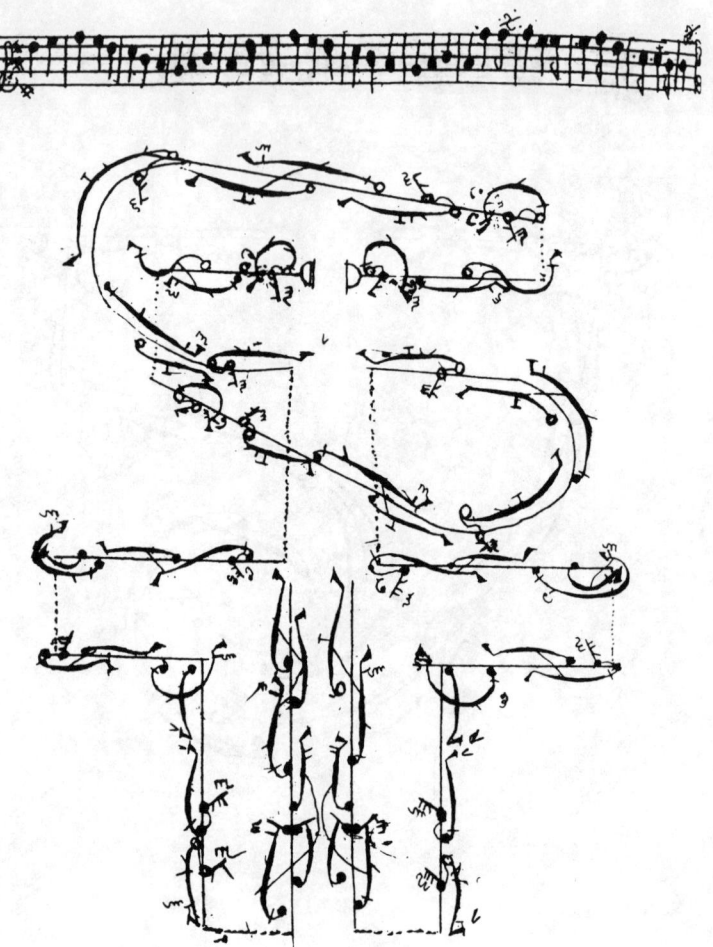

Appendix A: La Bourgogne

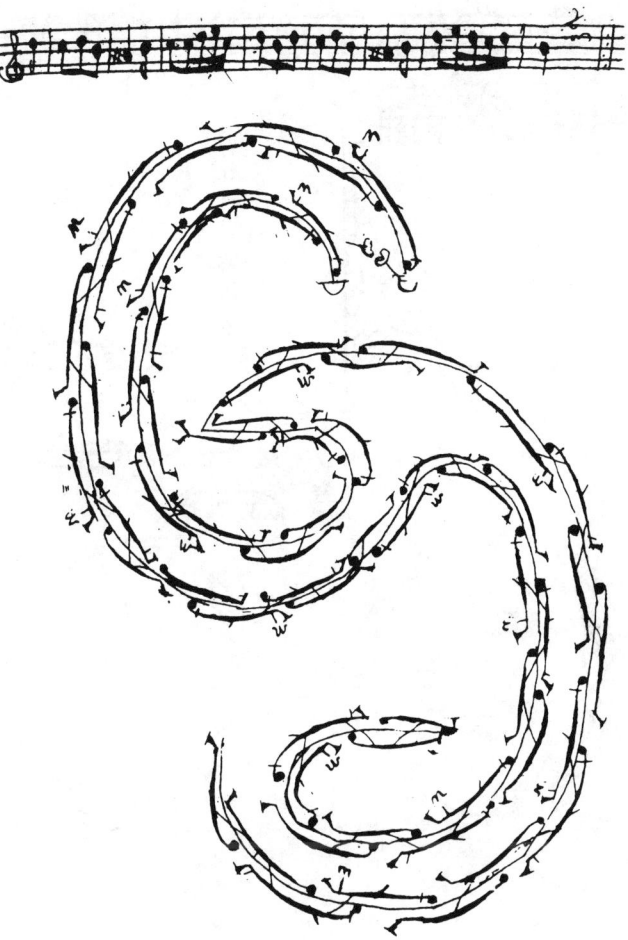

252   Appendix A: La Bourgogne

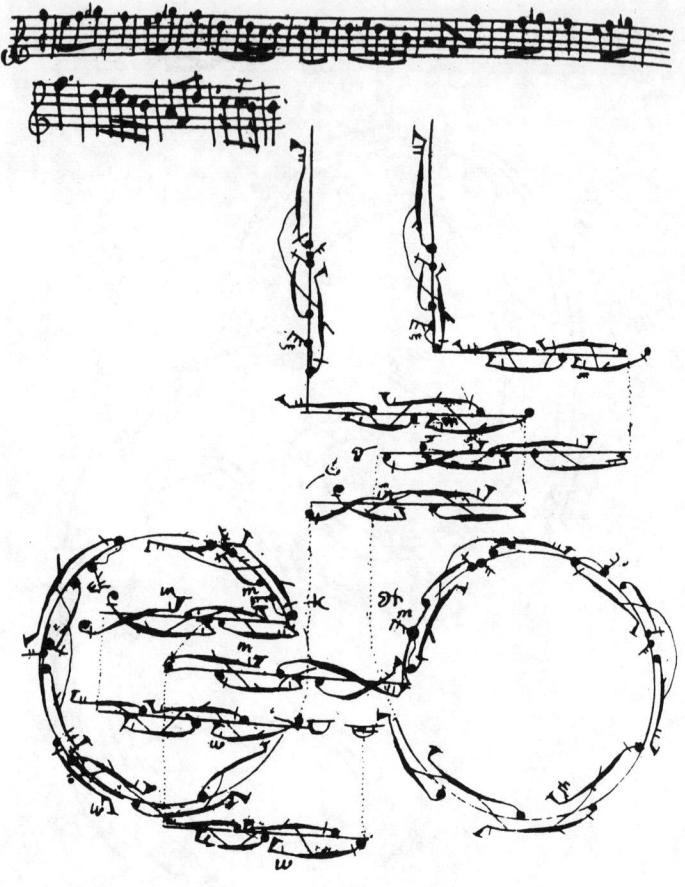

Appendix A: La Bourgogne

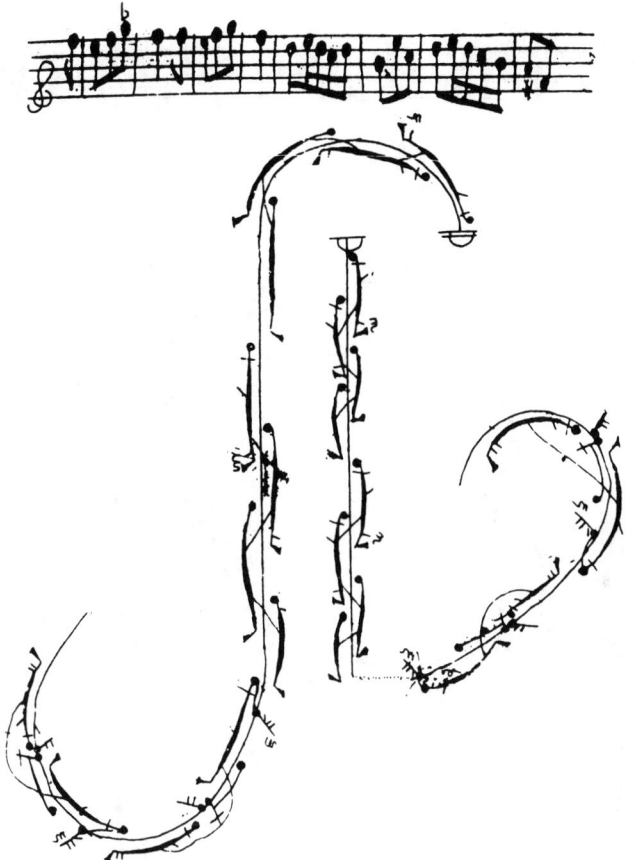

Appendix A: La Bourgogne

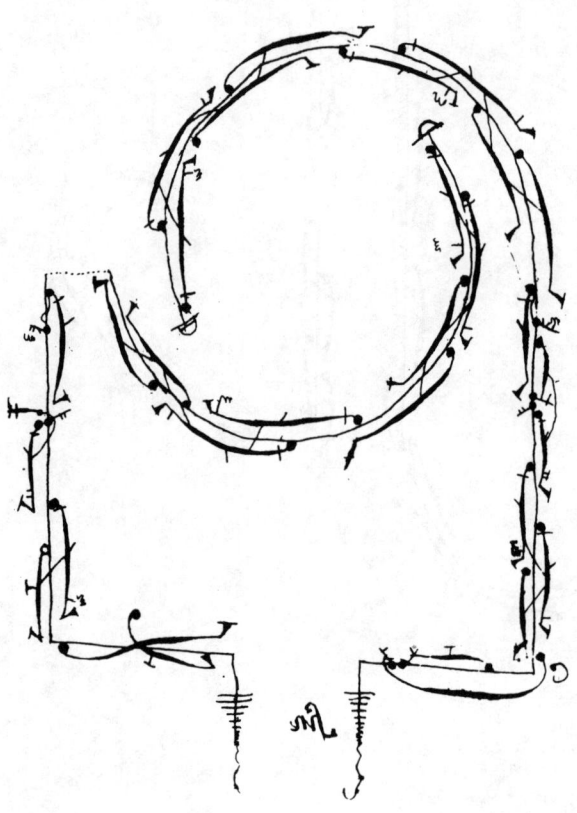

La Bourgogne

Feuillet	Rameau
p. 43 - m. 1-6	p. 26 - m. 1-12

m.1 temps de courante and demi-coupé forward

m.2 coupé soutenue forward, quarter-turn and demi-coupé into fifth before

m.4 coupé soutenue and demi-coupé forward

m.5 see m.4

m.6 see m.1

p. 44 - m. 7-12

m.8 temps de courante to second, quarter-turn and demi-coupé forward

m.9 see m.4; (music) C# omitted on beat 5

m.10 "

m.11 "

m.12 beaten demi-coupé backward, pas marché into third behind, pas marché backward, in gentleman's part (final pas marché should be sans poser le corps); (music) meter signature change to 2

m.15 (music) no agréments

p. 46 - m. 21-28

m.23 see m.15

m.1 temps de courante and demi-jeté forward

m.2 coupé soutenue forward, quarter-turn and demi-jeté into fifth before

m.4 coupé soutenue and demi-jeté forward

m.5 see m.4

m.6 see m.1

m.8 temps de courante to sec-one, quarter-turn and demi-jeté forward (error in direction of foot position sign on temps de courante)

m.9 see m.4; (music) C# included on beat 5

m.10 "

m.11 "

m.12 pas de bourrée emboîté, in gentleman's part (final pas marché should be sans poser le corps); (music) change of meter signature omitted

m.15 (music) agrément on third quarter-note beat

p. 28 - m. 21-28

m.23 see m.15

256   Appendix A: La Bourgogne

Feuillet	Rameau
p. 47 - m. 29-36	p. 29 - m. 29-44

m.36 temps de courante forward

m.36 temps de courante forward sans poser le corps

p. 48 - m. 37-44

m.43 double line of liaison between first two steps. First step is a jeté in lady's part

m.43 single line of liaison between first two steps. First step is a demi-coupé in lady's part

m.44 (music) meter change to $\frac{3}{8}$

m.44 (music) no meter change

p. 49 - m. 45-60

p. 30 - m. 45-60

m.45-46 pas de menuet of three mouvements forward

m.45-46 pas de menuet of two mouvements forward

m.47-48   "

m.47-48   "

m.49-50   "

m.49-50   "

m.51-52   ", in lady's part

m.51-52   ", in lady's part

p. 50 - m. 61-70

p. 31 - m. 61-76

m.61-62 pas de menuet of three mouvements left with final demi-coupé

m.61-62 pas de menuet of three mouvements left with final demi-jeté

m.63-64 pas de menuet of two mouvements right behind and before

m.63-64 pas de menuet of three mouvements right behind and behind (pas de menuet of <u>four</u> mouvements right behind and behind in lady's part is an error)

m.69-70 see m.45-46

m.69-70 see m.45-46

p. 51 - m. 71-76

m.71-72 pas de menuet of two mouvements right behind and behind

m.71-72 pas de menuet of three mouvements right behind and behind with third mouvement on third step, in gentleman's part; pas de menuet of four mouvements right behind and behind with final demi-jeté, in lady's part

Appendix A: La Bourgogne 257

Feuillet

m.73-74 see m.61-62

    p. 52 - m. 77-84

m.77-78 see m.45-46, in lady's part

m.79-80 pas de menuet of three mouvements backward with eighth-turn before final demi-coupé forward, in gentleman's part; see m. 45-46 in lady's part. (music) B♮ included

m.81-82 gentleman drops right hand and takes left hand

m.83-84 dancers exchange left hands for right hands

    p. 53 - m. 85-92

m.85-86 see m.45-46

m.87-88   "

m.91-92 penultimate step a demi-coupé, in gentleman's part

Rameau

m.73-74 see m.61-62

    p. 32 - m. 77-84

m.77-78 see m.45-46, in lady's part

m.79-80 pas de menuet of two mouvements backward, in gentleman's part; see m. 45-46 in lady's part. (music) B♭ omitted

m.81-82 no signs to take nor drop hands

m.83-84 no signs to take nor drop hands

    p. 33 - m. 85-92

m.85-86 see m.45-46

m. 87-88   "

m.91-92 penultimate step a pas marché, in gentleman's part

258 Appendix A: La Forlana

Appendix A: La Forlana

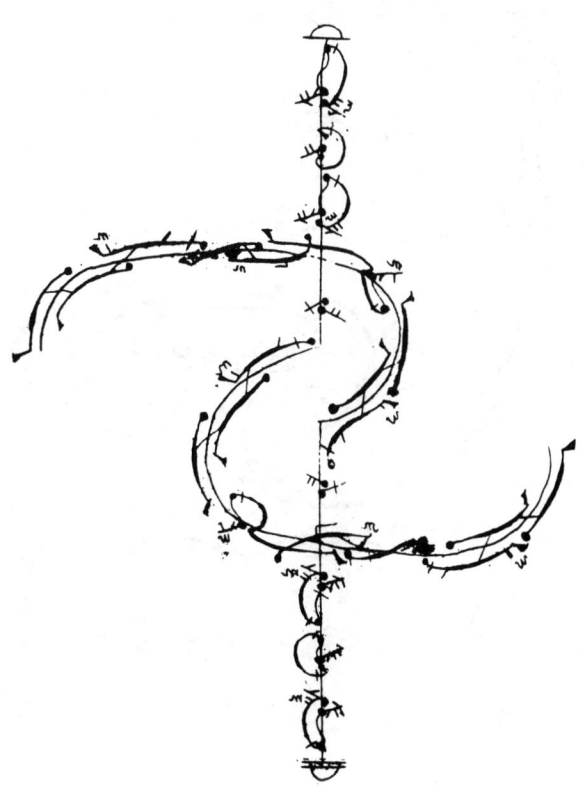

Appendix A: La Forlana

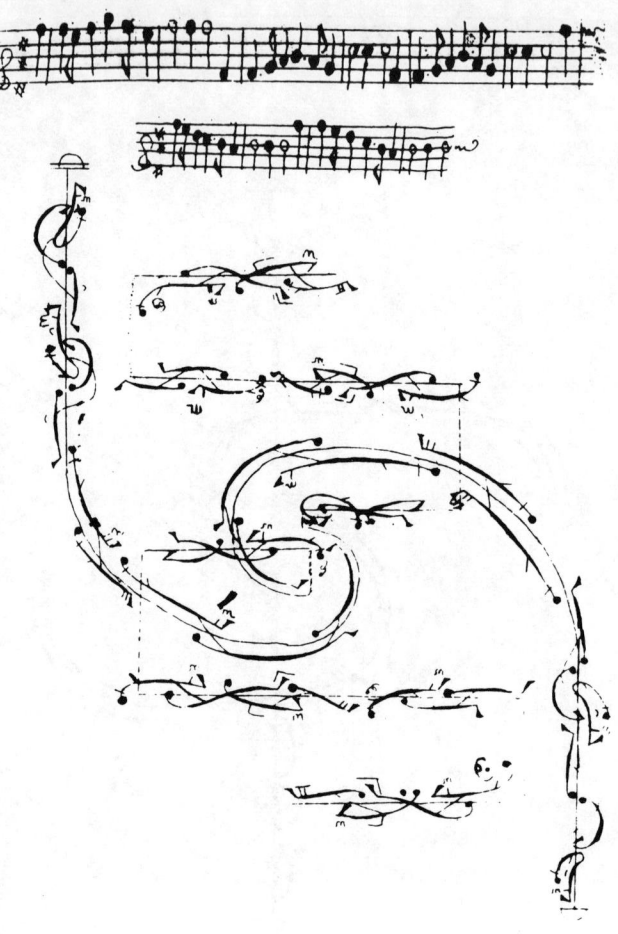

Appendix A: La Forlana

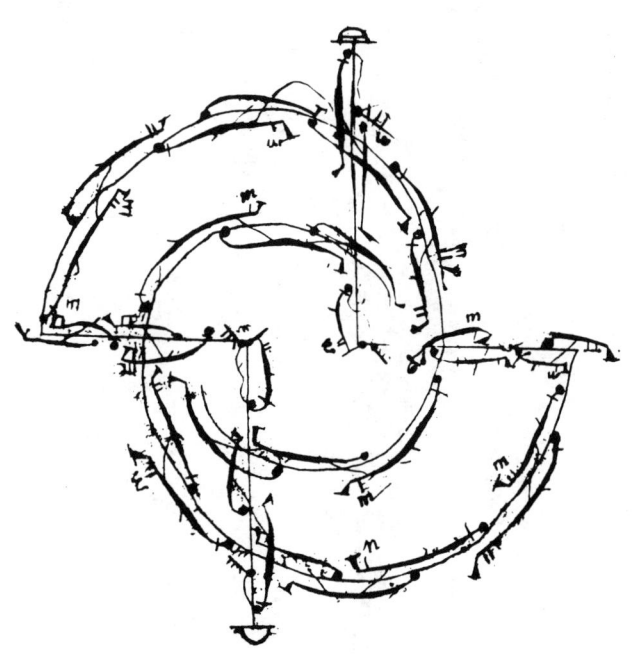

262 *Appendix A: La Forlana*

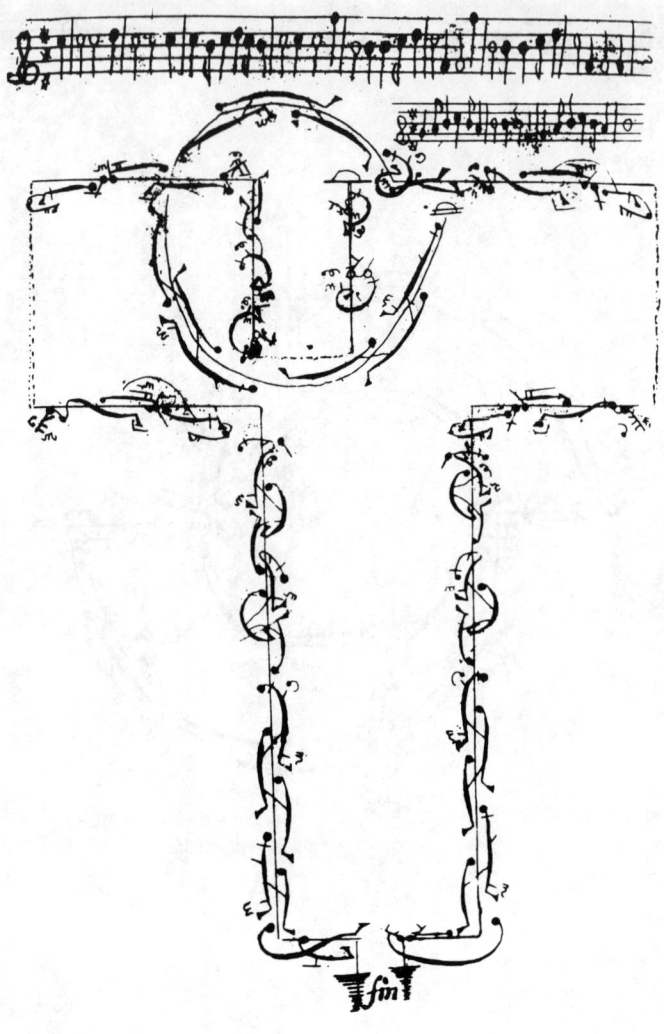

La Forlana

Feuillet	Rameau
p. 62 - m. 1-12	p. 34 - m. 1-12
m.5 glissades with demi-coupés in lady's part	m.5 glissades with demi-jetés in lady's part
m.7 glissades with demi-coupés in gentleman's part	m.7 glissades with demi-jetés in gentleman's part
m.10 (music) no agréments	m.10 (music) agrément on downbeat
m.11 no sign to raise heel (music) no agréments	m.11 sign to raise heel in preparation for tombé (music) agrément on downbeat
m.12 pas tombé, pied en l'air, and jeté	m.12 pas tombé and demi-jeté
p. 63 - m. 13-18	p. 35 - m. 13-18
m.17 see m.12	m.17 see m.12
p. 64 - m.19-28	m. 36 - m. 19-28
m.24 see m.11	m.24 see m.11
m.25 see m.12	m.25 pas tombé and jeté, in gentleman's part; see m.12, in lady's part
m.27 half-turn away from partner and demi-coupé forward, quarter-turn in same direction and pas marché to second. No sign to raise heel	m.27 quarter-turn toward partner and demi-coupé to fifth, pas marché to second with sign to raise heel
m.28 see m.12	m.28 see m.12
p. 65 - m. 29-36	p. 37 - m. 29-36
m.31 coupé de mouvement with final demi-coupé	m.31 coupé de mouvement with final demi-jeté
m.32 see m.31	m.32 coupé de mouvement with final demi-coupé, in gentleman's part; coupé simple, in lady's part

Appendix A: La Forlana

Feuillet	Rameau
p. 66 - m. 37-40	p. 38 - m. 37-48

m.40 quarter-turn and pas de bourrée to the side behind and before, in gentleman's part; pas de bourrée: half-turn right and demi-coupé, quarter-turn and pas marché to second, pas marché to fifth before, in lady's part

m.40 quarter-turn and pas de bourrée forward, in gentleman's part; pas de bourrée: half-turn right and demi-coupé to fifth before, pas marché to second, pas marché to fifth behind, in lady's part

p. 67 - m. 41-48

m.41 quarter-turn and half-contretemps forward, no sign to raise heel

m.41 quarter-turn sign omitted, half-contretemps forward, sign to raise heel in preparation for pas tombé

m.43 half-turn and half-contretemps forward, no sign to raise heel

m.43 half-turn and half-contretemps forward, sign to raise heel in preparation for pas tombé

Appendix B

Sources of the Music in Pécour's 1700 *Recueil*

1. La Bourrée d'Achille, Jean-Baptiste Lully (1632-1687) and Pascal Colasse (1649-1709)
   Achille et Polixène (1687)
      Prologue. "Entrée des Genies de Talie"

   Lully died before finishing *Achille et Polixène*.
   Colasse completed the work.

2. La Mariée, Jean-Baptiste Lully
   A. *Ballet de Temps* (1654)
         "Entrée d'un vieillard"
   B. *Ballet des Plaisirs* (1955)
         IIième Partie: Divertissements de la Ville
            8ième entrée: Un vieillard avec sa famille, à laquelle il donne, après souper, le divertissement des Oublieux, et fair venir pour cela tous ceux que l'on peut rencontrer.
         "Air pour le Vieillard et sa Famille"
   C. *Ballet des Noces de Village* (1633)
         This tune appears in at least these three works of Lully. The title of the dance in Rameau's *Abbrégé*, "La Mariée de Rollant," may be related to a source mentioned in Wotquenne, II, 12:
            "Air de *la Noce de Roland* dans le ballet *les Plaisirs* (1655) ensuite dans celui des *Noces de Village* (1663) Notre Philidor p. 50-Ecorch. I, 202; IV, 176; V, 67.

3. Le Passepied
      One of three tunes in this collection for which I have no theatrical source. Carol Rowan sent me copies of bass-lines for these tunes which she found in *Airs de danses angloises, hollandoises, et françoises, a deux parties. Nouvellement recueillies par Antoine Pointel.* Amsterdam & Paris, C. Ballard, 1700. (RISM 1700^5)

4. La Contredance, Jean-Baptiste Lully
   Serse (1660)
      I^{iere} entrée "2e AIR, Rondeau"

   From ballet music which Lully composed to accompany a production of Cavalli's opera. This tune is from a group of dances for an ensemble of Basques, which follows the Prologue.

5. Le Rigaudon des Vaisseaux
    La Baguette de Vulcain (1693)
    "Puis qu'il le faut"

    I have not seen this work and can provide no late seventeenth-century bass for the tune. Alfred Wotquenne identifies this as the source of the tune and refers to its performance at the "ancien th. Italien" in his manuscript catalogue of Ballard publications, "Thèmes des Petits Recueils Ballard (1695-1743)," which I consulted at the Library of Congress.

6. La Bourgogne
    No theatrical source. Bass-line from the Pointel collection (RISM 1700^5).

7. La Savoye
    No theatrical source. Bass-line from the Pointel collection (RISM 1700^5).

8. La Forlana, André Campra (1660-1744)
    L'Europe Galante (1699)
    Entrée III, Scene II

9. La Conty, André Campra
    Le Carnaval de Venise (1699)
    Act I, Scene 4

Appendix B   267

La Bourrée d'Achille

268 *Appendix B*

Appendix B 269

La Mariée

270   Appendix B

Le Passepied

Deuxième Air.

Appendix B   271

La Contredance

Appendix B

Appendix B 273

La Bourgogne

274   Appendix B

La Savoye

Appendix B 275

La Forlana

276 *Appendix B*

Appendix B 277

La Conty

278 *Appendix B*

Notes

Introduction

1. The term "step-unit" will be used in the present work to refer to both *pas composés* and *temps*, dance steps comparable in duration to a musical measure.
2. A bow for the gentleman and a courtesy for the lady.
3. Johann Pasch, *Beschreibung wahrer Tanz-Kunst* (Franckfurth: Wolfgang Michabelles und Johann Adolph, 1707).
4. Louis Bonin, *Die Neueste Art zur Galanten und Theatralischen Tantzkunst* (Franckfurt und Leipzig: Job. Christoff Lochner, 1711).
5. Gottfried Taubert, *Der Rechtschaffener Tantzmeister* (Leipzig: Friedrich Lanckischens Erben, 1717).
6. John Weaver, *An Essay Toward an History of Dancing* (London: Jacob Tonson, 1712).
7. Kellom Tomlinson, *The Art of Dancing* (London: printed for the author, 1735).
8. Pemberton, *An Essay for the Improvement of Dancing* (London: 1711).
9. Pablo Minguet, *El Noble Arte de Danzar a la Francesca* (Madrid: Pablo Minguet, n.d.).
10. Giambatista Dufort, *Trattato del Ballo Nobile* (Napoli: Felice Mosca, 1728).
11. P. Rameau, *Le Maître à Danser* (Paris: Jean Villette, 1725); and *Abbrégé de la Nouvelle Methode, dans l'Art d'Ecrire ou de Tracer Toutes Sortes de Danses de Ville* (Paris: chez l'auteur, 1725).

Chapter 1

1. As a result of the inconsistencies in spelling in the original sources, I have employed modern spellings for the step-units when possible.
2. In those measures in which the lady and gentleman do not perform the same step-unit, the gentleman's step-unit is indicated first, followed by a slash and the lady's step-unit.
3. When the dancers are side by side, the "inside foot" refers to the foot closest to the partner.
4. Feuillet, *Chorégraphie,* p. 14; Rameau, *Abbrégé,* Part I, p. 20.
5. Rameau, *Le Maître,* Part I, Chapter 27.
6. Rameau, *Abbrégé,* Part II, p. 1.

Notes for Chapter 1

7. In these tables, I have determined the direction of the pas de sissonne by the movement of the free foot on the first assemblé following Feuillet's example in *Chorégraphie*, p. 81.

8. The original opera score has the same change from bourrée to menuet, but does not repeat the bourrée after the menuet.

9. The sign for the quarter-turn is omitted in the gentleman's part, an error which is corrected in Rameau's *Abbrégé*, Part II, p. 5.

10. Rameau, *Le Maître*, Part I, Chapter 21.

11. The sign to drop hands is omitted by Feuillet, another error corrected by Rameau in *Abbrégé*, Part II, p. 7.

12. See Appendix A of the present work.

13. Taubert, *Der Rechtschaffener Tantzmeister*, pp. 615-74 (also Angelika Gerbes, "Gottfried Taubert on Social and Theatrical Dance of the Early Eighteenth Century," unpublished Ph.D. dissertation, Ohio State University, 1972; and her translations of portions of Taubert's writings on the menuet in *Dance as a Theatre Art*, Selma Jean Cohen, editor, pp. 42-51).

14. Tomlinson, *The Art of Dancing*, pp. 103-41.

15. Dufort, *Trattato del Ballo Nobile*, "Trattato del Minuetto," pp. 117-49.

16. Rameau, *Le Maître*, Part I, chapters 21-25 (also Anne Witherell, "Pierre Rameau's French Menuet," unpublished M.A. project, Stanford University, 1973; and Wendy Hilton, *Dance of Court and Theatre: The French Noble Style* [Princeton: Princeton Book Company, 1981]).

17. Rameau, *Le Maître*, Part I, Chapter 21.

18. Rameau, *Abbrégé*, Vol. 1, p. 54.

19. Feuillet, *Chorégraphie*, "Supplement de pas."

20. Tomlinson, *The Art of Dancing*, p. 109, Plate U.

21. Taubert, *Der Rechtschaffener Tantzmeister*, "Die hauptfigur von der Menuet," p. 658.

22. Helen Meredith Ellis, "The Dances of J.B. Lully," p. 72.

23. Rameau, *Abbrégé*, Vol. 2, p. 7.

24. Rameau, *Le Maître*, Part I, Chap. 21.

25. Rameau, *Abbrégé*, Vol. 2, "Le Passepied" and "La Bourgogne."

26. Taubert, *Der Rechtschaffener Tantzmeister*, p. 624.

27. Rameau, *Abbrégé*, Vol. 1, p. 104.

28. Ibid., p. 110.

29. Rameau, *Le Maître*, Part I, Chap. 24.

30. Rameau, *Le Maître*, Part I, Chap. 24.

31. Ibid.

32. Dufort, *Trattato del Ballo Nobile*, pp. 130-33.

33. Bonin, *Die Neueste Art zur Galanten und Theatralischen Tantzkunst*, 1711, p. 147.

34. Taubert, *Der Rechtschaffener Tantzmeister*, pp. 554-56.

35. Tomlinson, *The Art of Dancing*, pp. 126, 130, 132, 136.
36. Rameau, *Le Maître*, Part I, Chap. 10.
37. Taubert, *Der Rechtschaffener Tantzmeister*, pp. 647-49.
38. Tomlinson, *The Art of Dancing*, pp. 126, 130, 132, 136.
39. Ibid, p. 130.
40. Ibid.
41. Taubert, *Der Rechtschaffener Tantzmeister*, pp. 647-49.
42. Rameau, *Le Maître*, Part I, Chap. 22.
43. Taubert, *Der Rechtschaffener Tantzmeister*, pp. 647-49.
44. Rameau, *Le Maître*, Part I, Chap. 22.
45. Tomlinson, *The Art of Dancing*, pp. 126-28, Plate U.
46. Rameau, *Le Maître*, Part I, Chap. 22.

Chapter 2

1. Rameau, *Le Maître*, Part I, Chapter 42.
2. Tomlinson, *The Art of Dancing*, p. 88.
3. Rameau, *Le Maître*, Part I, Chapter 29.
4. Tomlinson, *The Art of Dancing*, p. 54.
5. Rameau, *Le Maître*, Part I, Chapter 28.
6. Rameau, *Le Maître*, Part I, Chapter 27.
7. Tomlinson, *The Art of Dancing*, pp. 34-35, Plate VI and Figure E.
8. Rameau, *Le Maître*, Part I, Chapter 27.
9. Rameau, *Abbrégé*, Part I, pp. 106-7.
10. For a thorough discussion of the term "pas de gaillarde," see the chapter "La Forlana" of the present work. In "la Mariée," Pécour employs only Feuillet's pas de gaillarde.
11. Rameau, *Le Maître*, Part I, Chapter 39.
12. Open positions are second and fourth; first, third, and fifth are closed.
13. Tomlinson, *The Art of Dancing*, Part I, pp. 64-65, 73.
14. Ibid., p. 73.
15. Rameau, *Abbrégé*, Part I, p. 72.
16. See above, p.
17. Tomlinson, *The Art of Dancing*, p. 56.
18. Rameau, *Le Maître*, Part I, Chapter 41.
19. Rameau, *Le Maître*, Part I, Chapter 32.
20. Pécour, 1704 *Recueil*, "Traité de la Cadence," "Suitte des Exemples pour les mesures à deux et à trois temps."

21. Rameau, *Abbrégé*, Part II, p. 16.
22. Rameau, *Le Maître*, Part I, Chapter 32.
23. Rameau, *Le Maître*, Part II, Chapter 19.
24. Johann Mattheson, *Der vollkommene Capellmeister*, 1736, II. Theil, XIII. Capitel, p. 92. Mattheson does not mention that the title of the dance is actually derived from the Lully ballet in which the music originally appears, *Ballet des Plaisirs*, 1655, where the tune, "Air de la Noce de Roland," accompanies a ballet for eight dancers. Lully employs this tune again in his *Ballet des Noces de Village*, 1663.
25. Louis Bonin, *Die Neueste Art zur galanten und theatralischen Tantzkunst*.... Franckfurt und Leipzig: Joh. Christoff Lochner, 1711, pp. 135-36.
26. Rameau, *Le Maître*, Part II, Chapter 14.
27. Ibid., Part II, Chapter 19.
28. Tomlinson, *The Art of Dancing*, p. 39.
29. Rameau, *Le Maître*, Part I, Chapter 27.
30. The eighth and final strain closes with a closing coupé, to lead into the final bows.

Chapter 3

1. Sebastien de Brossard, *Dictionnaire de musique*, 1703.
2. Rameau, *Abbrégé*, Part II, pp. 18-25.
3. Louis Bonin, *Die Neueste Art*..., Franckfurt, 1711, pp. 135-36.
4. Pablo Minguet, *El Noble Arte de Danzar a la Francesca y Española*, Madrid, 1758, p. 27.
5. Rameau, *Abbrégé*, Part II, p. 18.
6. "La Bourgogne," measures 48 and 52.
7. See discussion in the chapter "La Bourrée d'Achille" of the present work.
8. Rameau, *Le Maître*, Part I, Chapter 33, and *Abbrégé*, Part I, p. 104.
9. Rameau, *Abbrégé*, Part II, p. 23.
10. For a detailed comparison of the *Abbrégé* "Passepied" and that in the 1700 *Recueil*, see Appendix A of the present work.
11. See the chapter "La Bourgogne" of the present work.
12. See the chapter "La Bourrée d'Achille" of the present work.
13. Rameau, *Le Maître*, Part I, Chapter 28.
14. Shirley Wynne, "The Minuet," *CORD* (Institute of Court Dances of the Renaissance and Baroque Periods) (© 1972), pp. 41-57.
15. Erich Schwandt, "L'Affilard on the French Court Dances," *The Musical Quarterly* 60 (1974), pp. 389-400.
16. Wye Jamison Allanbrook, "Dance as Expression in Mozart Opera," Ph.D. dissertation, Stanford University, 1974.
17. Michel de Pure, *Idée des Spectacles*, pp. 177ff.

18. Johann Mattheson, *Der Vollkommene Capellmeister*, p. 229.
19. Rameau, *La Maître*, Part I.
20. Rameau, *Abbrégé*, Part I, p. 104.
21. Rameau, *Le Maître*, Part I, Chapter 25.
22. Ibid., Part I, Chapter 37.
23. Wendy Hilton, interview, 1976.
24. Tomlinson, *The Art of Dancing*, p. 114.
25. Rameau, *Le Maître*, Part I, Chapter 25.
26. This situation may be contrasted with the repetitions of sequences of pas composés with changing floor patterns in "la Bourrée d'Achille."
27. Compan, *Dictionnaire de Danse*, "passepied."
28. Meredith Ellis, "The Dances of J.B. Lully," Ph.D. dissertation, Stanford University, 1968, p. 75.

Chapter 4

1. Pécour, 1704 *Recueil*, "ENTRÉE—Aimons tout nous y convie," p. 64.
2. Pécour, 1700 *Recueil*, "La Bourrée d'Achille," p. 4.
3. Pécour, 1700 *Recueil*, "Le Passepied," p. 24.
4. Feuillet, *Recueil de contredanses*...(Paris, 1706).
5. Dezais, *2e Recueil de nouvelles contredanses*...(Paris, 1712).
6. Guilcher, *La Contredanse* (Paris: 1969)
7. Rameau, *Le Maître*, Part I, Chapter 25.
8. Feuillet, *Quatrième Recueil de danses de bal* (Paris, 1708). See also Guilcher's discussion of "le Cotillon" in *La Contredanse*, pp. 75-79.
9. Rameau, *Le Maître*, Part I, Chapter 25.
10. Rameau, *Le Maître*, Part I, Chapter 38.
11. For a detailed discussion of the pas de gaillarde, see the chapter "La Forlana" of the present work.
12. See the chapter "La Conty" of the present work.
13. Rameau, *Le Maître*, Part I, Chapter 38.
14. Rameau, *Le Maître*, Part II, Chapter 16.
15. Rameau, *Le Maître*, Part II, Chapter 14.

Chapter 5

1. "La Savoye" uses the same transition in measures 11-15.
2. Rameau, *Abbrégé*, Vol. I, p. 71, "autre ballonné scavoir au ler mouvement un quar. et au 2e un quar."

3. See discussion of demi-jetés in glissades in the chapter "La Mariée" of the present work.
4. See the chapter "La Savoye" of the present work.
5. Rameau, *Le Maître*, Part II, Chapter 26.
6. Rameau, *Le Maître*, Part II, Chapter 12.
7. This opening is found in a few other ball dances by Pécour; "Pavane des Saisons" from the *Recueil de danses de bal pour l'année* is one example, but it is clearly exceptional.
8. See above, p. 118.
9. I have not located the original music. In his manuscript catalogue of Ballard publications, "Thèmes des Petits Recueils Ballard (1695-1743)," Alfred Wotquenne identifies the source of the tune as "la Baguette de Vulcain (ancien th. Italien, 1693) avec la texte: Puis qu'il le faut."
10. See the chapter "La Savoye" of the present work.

Chapter 6

1. Rameau, *Abbrégé*, Part II, p. 26.
2. See the chapter "La Bourrée d'Achille" of the present work.
3. Rameau, *Le Maître*, Part I, Chapter 27.
4. Rameau, *Abbrégé*, Part II, p. 26.
5. Rameau, *Abbrégé*, Vol. II, p. 29.
6. Ibid.
7. Rameau, *Abbrégé*, Vol. II, p. 29.
8. Rameau, *Abbrégé*, Part II, p. 32.
9. Rameau, *Abbrégé*, Part II, p. 32.
10. Meredith Ellis Little, "The Contribution of Dance Steps to Musical Analysis and Performance: La Bourgogne," *Journal of the American Musicological Society*, Vol. 28, No. 1, Spring 1975. Wendy Hilton, "A Dance for Kings: the 17th-century French Courante," *Early Music*, Vol. 5, No. 2, April 1977, pp. 160-72.
11. Rameau, *Abbrégé*, Part II, p. 25.
12. As pointed out in earlier chapters, the timing of the pas de menuet was subject to numerous local variations.
13. The pas de menuet takes two measures of passepied music in 3/8.

Chapter 7

1. Leonard Ratner, " 'Ars Combinatoria'. Chance and choice in eighteenth-century music." *Studies in Eighteenth-Century Music: A Tribute to Karl Geiringer on his Seventieth Birthday.* Ed. H.C. Robbins Landon, in collaboration with Roger E. Chapman. New York: Oxford University Press, 1970, pp. 343-63.
2. A brief discussion of syntax in eleven French ball dances including "la Savoye" is found in Francine Lancelot, "Écriture de la danse—le système Feuillet," *Revue d'ethnologie française*, Vol. 1, No. 1 (1971), pp. 29-50.

3. Rameau, *Le Maître,* Part I, Chapter 34.
4. Tomlinson, *The Art of Dancing,* pp. 44-45 and Plate V.
5. Rameau, *Le Maître,* Part I, Chapter 28.
6. Feuillet, *Chorégraphie,* p. 67. Feuillet does give an example of this step-unit on p. 64, calling it "autre, dont le dernier d'ouvre droit a coté."
7. Rameau, *Le Maître,* Part I, Chapter 28.
8. See the chapters "La Forlana" and "La Conty" in the present work.
9. Feuillet, *Chorégraphie,* p. 92.

Chapter 8

1. Rameau, *Le Maître,* Part 1, Chapters 29 and 42.
2. Rameau, *Le Maître,* Part 1, Chapter 31.
3. Rameau, *Abbrégé,* p. 59.
4. Tomlinson, *The Art of Dancing,* p. 48.
5. See example, p. 175.

Chapter 9

1. Open positions are second and fourth; closed are first, third, and fifth.
2. The rise, shift, and fall constitute the pas tombé itself and are designated by the single sign:
3. The only exceptions to the rule that every musical measure has a corresponding choreographic measure are menuets and passepieds in 3/4 or 3/8. In these dances, every pas composé is two musical measures long, and those choreographic measure lines which fall in the middle of a pas composé may be omitted.
4. See below, page 195.
5. Bonin, *Die Neueste Art zur Galanten und Theatralischen Tantzkunst,* pp. 135-36.
6. Baron, *Lettres et Entretiens sur la Danse,* pp. 197-202.

Appendix A

1. Rameau, *Abbrégé,* Part I, p. 111.
2. Feuillet, *Chorégraphié,* "De la maniere quel'on doit tenit le Livre pour déchiffrer Les Dances qui sont écrites," pp. 33-35.

Bibliography

Primary Sources

Bickham, George, Jr. *AN EASY/INTRODUCTION/TO/DANCING:/OR THE/MOVE-MENS in the MINUET/FULLY/EXPLAINED./ADORN'D WITH/Twelve FIGURES drawn from the Life, representing the different/Attitudes of young Gentlemen and Ladies, from which all the Steps/are to be taken, and performed, in that Celebrated Dance./WITH/An additional PLATE, representing the Form or Figure of the said/DANCE./AS ALSO/Six New MINUETS and RIGADOONS, likewise their proper Basses, for the/Harpsichord, Spinnet, Violin, &c. Curiously Engraved on Copper-/Plates,/LONDON:/*Printed and Sold in May's Buildings, near Covent Garden [1738].

Bonin, Louis. *DIE NEUESTE ART/Zur Galanten und Theatralischen/Tantz-Kunst:/Worinnen/Gründliche Nachricht anzutreffen(/)wie dieses höchst-nützliche/EXERCITIUM/Souol vor Alters(/)als anjetzt(/)beschaffen;/Auch wie man zur richtigen Erlernung dessel-bigen(/)und zu/manirlichen Aufführungen(/)sowol unter seines gleichen(/)als/unter fürneh men Personen(/)gelangen Kan-/Deme beygefüget(/)/Was für Requisita zu einen rechtscahf-fenen Tantz-Meister gehören(/)damit/er einen guten Scholaren machen(/)sich selbsten aber bei Hofe(/)in Assembleen, Ballen(/)/Redouten und Masqueraden(/)&c. desgleichen in Opern und Comoedien/auf dem Theatro will sehen lassen./*Der heutigen galanten Welt zum Nutzen und Ergötzen an das Liecht gestellet(/)/Von/LOVIS BONIN,/Fürstl. Sachsen-Eisenachischen privilegirten Tantz-Meister auf der/Welt-berühmten Universität JENA./Samt einer Vorrede von/MELETAON./Franckfurt und Leipzig(/)zu finden bei Job. Christoff Lochner(/)Buch-händler. Anno 1711.

Brossard, Sebastien de. *DICTIONAIRE/DE MUSIQUE,/CONTENANT UNE EXPLICA-TION/Des Termes Grecs, Latins, Italiens & François les plus/usitez dans la Musique./A l'occasion desquels on rapporte ce qu'il y a de plus/curieux, & de plus necessaire a sçavoir;/Tant pour l'Histoire & la Theorie, que pour la Composition, & la Pratique/Ancienne & Modern, De la Musique Vocale,/Instrumentale, Plaine, Simple, Figurée &c./ENSEMBLE,/UNE Table Alphabetique des Termes François qui sont dans le corps de L'Ouvrage,/sous Les Titres Grecs, Latins & Italiens; pour servir de Supplément,/UN Traité de la maniere de bien prononcer, surtout en chantant, les Termes/Italiens, Latins, & François,/ET un Catalogue de plus de 900. Auteurs qui ont écrit sur la Musique,/en toutes sortes de Temps, de Pays, & de Langues. A PARIS,/Chez CHRISTOPHE BALLARD,/M.DCCIII.*

Burette. "Histoire de la Danse des Anciens," *Memoires de Litterature,* v. 1, 1717.

Cahusac. *LA DANSE/ANCIENNE/ET/MODERNE/OU/TRAITÉ HISTORIQUE/DE/LA DANSE,/A LA Haye/Chez Jean Neaulme [1754].*

Compan. *DICTIONNAIRE/DE DANSE,/CONTENANT l'histoire, les regles & les/principes de cet Art, avec des Réflexions/critiques, & des Anecdotes curieuses concer-/nant la Danse* ancienne & moderne;/Le tout/tiré des meilleurs Auteurs qui ont/écrit sur cet Art. A PARIS,/Chez Cailleau,/1787.

Desboulmiers, Jean-Auguste Julien. *Histoire Anecdotique et Raisonnée du Théâtre Italien.* Paris: 1769. Reprinted, Slatkine reprints, 1968.

Dezais, Xe *RECÜEIL/DE/DANSES/POUR L'ANNÉE/1712,/ ... /A* PARIS/Chez le Sr DEZAIS.../1712.

———. *XIII RECÜEIEL* [sic]...*pour*...*1715.* Ibid. [n.d.].*

———. *2e Recueil de nouvelles contredanses.* Paris: 1712. Reprinted, Gregg International Publishers, Ltd., 1972.

Dufort, Giambatista. *Trattato del Ballo Nobile.* Napoli: 1728. Reprinted, Gregg International Publishers, Ltd., 1972.

du Manoir, Guillaume. *Le/Mariage/de la/Musique/avec la Dance;/contenant/la Reponce au Livre/des treize pretendus Academi/stes, touchant ces deux Arts.* A Paris,/Guillaume de Luyne/1664.

Duni, Egidio. *Minuetti e Contridanze/in segno d'ossequiosa gratitudine/*Londra M.DDC. XXXVIII.

Edinburgh. University Library. Manuscript collection. "A Collection of New Ball- and Stage Dances Compos'd by Several Masters. vis The Montaigu [etc.] All writ down in Characters by F. Le Roussaü Dancing-Master [1720].

Feuillet, Raoul-Auger. *CHOREGRAPHIE/OU/L'ART DE DE CRIRE/LA DANCE,/PAR CARACTERES, FIGURES/ET SIGNES DEMONSTATIFS,/Avec lesquelles on apprend facilement de soy-meme toutes/sortes de Dances./Ouvrage tres-utile aux Maîtres à Dancer & à toutes les personnes qui/s'appliquent à la Dance./ ... /Seconde édition, augmentée.* A Paris:/Chez l'auteur,.../Et chex Michel Brunet,.../M.DCCI.

———. *For the Further Improvement of Dancing.* Translated by John Essex. London: 1710. Reprinted, Westmead: Gregg International Publishers, Limited, 1970.

———. *ORCHESOGRAPHY./OR, THE/ART/OF/DANCING,/BY/Characters and Demonstrative Figures./WHEREIN/The whole Art is explain'd; with compleat/Tables of all Steps us'd in Dancing, and Rules for the/Motions of the Arms, &c./WHEREBY/Any Person (who understands Dancing) may of himself/learn all manner of Dances./BEING/An Exact and Just Translation from the/French of Monsieur Feuillet./By JOHN WEAVER, Dancing-Master./*LONDON: Printed by H. Meere,.../1706.

———. *Recueil de contredanses.* Paris: 1706: Reprinted, Broude Brothers, 1968.

———. *RECUEIL/DE DANCES,/ ... /A* PARIS,/Chez l'Auteur,.../Et chez MICHEL BRUNET,.../M.DCC.

———. *IIII. RECÜEIL/de/DANCES DE BAL/pour l'Année/1706./Recüeillies et mises au Jour/PAR Mr FEUILLET Mre DE DANCE/Auteur/de la Chorégraphie./ ... /à Paris/Chez le Sr Feüillet Rüe de Bussi/Faubourg Saint Germain à la Cour Imperiale./ ... 1705.*

———. *Vme RECÜEIL...pour...1707.* Ibid. 1706.

———. *VIme RECÜEIL/DE/DANSES/ET DE?CONTREDANSES/POUR L'ANNÉE 1708./* Recüeillies et mises au jour/par Mr FEÜILLET Me de Danse/se vend 30... broché./Et 40. relié en Veau./A PARIS/Chez l'Auteur, Rüe de Bussy/Faubourge Saint Germain./AVEC PRIVILEGE DU ROY. 1707.

———. *VIIe RECÜEIL...pour...1709.* Ibid. 1709.

Furetière, Antoine. *DICTIONAIRE/UNIVERSEL, CONTENANT GENERALEMENT/ TOUS LES MOTS FRANÇOIS/TANT VIEUX QUE MODERNES/Et les Termes de toutes les Sciences & des Arts;/SÇAVOIR/La Philosophie, Logique, & Physique; la Medecine, ou Anatomie; Pathologie, Terapeutique, Chirurgie,/Pharmacopée, Chymie, Botanique, ou l'His-*

---

*Recueils de danses were published for each year in the first quarter of the eighteenth century by Feuillet and, after his death, by Dezais.

toire naturelle des Plantes, & celle des Animaux, Mineraux,/Metaux & Pierreries, & les noms des Drogues artificielles:/*LA JURISPRUDENCE CIVILE ET CANONIQUE, FEODALE ET MUNICIPALE,/& sur tout* celles des Ordonnances:/Les Mathematiques, la Geometrie, l'Arithmetique, & L'Algebre; la Trigonometrie, Geodesie, ou l'Arpentage, & les Sections/ coniques; l'Astronomie, L'Astrologie, la Gnomonique, la Geographie; La Musique, tant en theorie qu'en pratique,/Les Instrumens à vent & à cordes; l'Optique, Catoptrique, Dioptrique, & Perspective; l'Architecture/civile & militaire; la Pyrotechnie, Tactique, & Statique:/Les Arts, la Rhetorique, la Poësie, la Grammaire, la Peinture, Sculpture, &c. La Marine, le Manege, l'Art de faire des armes,/le Blason, la Venerie, Fauconnerie, la Pesche, L'Agriculture ou Maison Rustique,/& la plus-part des Arts mechaniques:/Plusieurs termes de Relations d'Orient & d'Occident, la qualité des Poids, Mesures & Monnoyes; les Etymologies des mots,/L'invention des choses, & l'Origine de plusieurs Proverbs & leur relation à ceux des autres Langues:/Et enfin les noms des Auteurs qui ont traitté des matieres qui regardent les mots, expliquez avec quelques Histoires,/Curiositez naturelles, & Sentences morales, qui seront rapportées pour donner des exemples/de phrases & de constructions./Le tout extrait des plus excellens Auteurs anciens & modernes.* Recueilli & complilé par feu/Messire ANTOINE FURETIERE/.../NOUVELLE EDITION CORRIGÉE ET AUGMENTÉE./.../A LAHAYE ET A ROTTERDAM/Chez ARNOUT ET REINIER LEERS./M.DC.XCIV.

Gallini, Giovanni-Andrea. *A/TREATISE/ON THE/ART/OF/DANCING.* London:/Printed for the Author;/And sold by R. & J. Dodsley,...,/T. Becket,.../And W. Nicholl,.../ MDCCLXII.

L'Abbé. *A NEW/COLLECTION/OF/DANCES/Containing a great Number of the best/Ball and Stage Dances:/.../That have been performed both in Drury-Lane and Lincoln's-/Inn-Fields, by the best Dancers, VIZ,/Monsieur BALON, Mons' L'ABBE, Mons' LA GARDE, Mons' DUPRE, Mons' DESNOYER, Mrs. ELFORD, Mrs. SANTLOW, Mrs. BULLOCK, Mrs. YOUNGER. A Work very Useful to all Masters, and other Persons that apply themselves to Dancing.* Recollected, put in Characters, and engraved, by Monsieur ROUSSEAU, /Dancing-Master. To be sold at Mr. Barreau's...; and at Mr. Rousseau's...[n.d.]

———. *THE/Prince of Wales's/Saraband/A New Dance/For Her Majesty's Birthday/1731/*By Mr Labbe/Writt by Mr Pemberton. And sold by him.

Landrin. *Potpourri françois/de contredanse ancienne/Tel qu'il se danse chez/La Reine/.../*A PARIS/Lahante [n.d.]

Masson, Charles. *NOUVEAU TRAITÉ/DES REGLES/POUR LA COMPOSITION/DE LA/MUSIQUE/Par lequel on apprend à faire facilement un/Chant sur des Paroles; à composer à 2. 3. & 4./Parties, &c. Et à chiffrer la Basse-Continue,/suivant L'usage des meilleurs Auteurs./Ouvrage tres utile à ceux* qui jouent de L'Orgue,/du Clavessin, & du Théorbe, /.../SECONDE EDITION,/Revuë, corrigée, & augmentée./A PARIS,/Chez CHRISTOPHE BALLARD,.../M.DC.XCIX./Reprinted with an Introduction by Imogene Horsley. New York: Da Capo Press, 1967.

Mattheson, Johann. *Der vollkommene Capellmeister.* Hamburg: 1739. Reprinted, Bärenreiter-Verlag, 1954.

Menestrier, Claude François. *DES/BALLETS/ANCIENS/ET MODERNES/SELON LES REGLES/DU THEATRE./*A PARIS,/Chez RENÉ GUIGNARD, rue Saint/Jacques, au grandSaint Basile./M.DC.LXXXII./Avec Privilege du Roi.

Mersenne, F. Marin. *HARMONIE/UNIVERSELLE,/CONTENANT LA THEORIE/ET LA PRATIQUE/DE LA MUSIQUE.* Paris: Cramoisy, 1636.

Minguet e Yrol, Pablo. *EL NOBLE/ARTE DE DANZAR A LA/FRANCESA, Y ESPAÑOLA:/ADORNADO CON, LX.L AMINAS/finas, que enseñan al modo de ha-/cer todos los passos de las Dan-/zas de Corte, con sus reglas, y de/conducir los brazos en cada passo;/y por Chorografia demuestran/como se deben escribir otras./*Con Licencia: En Madrid, por Pablo Minguet [n.d.].

Paris, Bibliothèque Nationale, Ms. FR 14.884. Collection of dances in Feuillet notation.
Paris. Opéra. Bibliothèque, archives et musée. Ms. C. 2454. Collection of dances in Feuillet notation.
Pasch, Johann. *Beschreibung wahrer Tanz-kunst.* Franckfurth: 1707. Reprinted, Heimeran Verlag, 1978.
Pécour, Louis Guillaume. *La Pavanne des Saisons*/DANCE NOUVELLE/DE LA COMPOSITION DE MONSr PECOUR/Pensionnaire des menus plaisirs du Roy,/et Compositeur des Balets de la Cade-/mie [sic] Royale de Musique de Paris./et mise au Jour/Par Mr FEÜILLET Me de Dance/Autheur de la Chorégraphie/se vend dix sols./A PARIS/Chez le sieur FEUILLET Rüe de Bussy/Faubourg Saint Germain à la Cour Imperiale/et Chez/Michel Brunet dans la grande salle du Palais/au Mercure galand./Avec Privilége du Roy 1700.
_____. *RECUEIL/DE DANCES,/COMPOSEES/Par M. PECOUR, . . . /Et Mise sur le Papier Par M. Feuillet, Maître de Dance.* A PARIS,/Chez l'Auteur . . . /Et chex MICHEL BRUNET . . . /M.DCC.
_____. *RECUEIL DE DANCES/contenant/un tres grand nombres des meillieures/ENTRÉES DE BALLET/DE Mr PECOUR./tant pour homme que pour femmes,/dont la plus grande partie/ont été dancées à L'Opéra./*Recüeillies et mises au jour./PAR Mr FEUILLET Me DE DANCE./A PARIS/Chez le Sieur FEUILLET . . . 1704.
Pemberton. *An Essay for the Improvement of Dancing.* London: 1711. Reprinted, Gregg International Publishers, Ltd., 1970.
_____. *Mr Caverly's/Slow/Minuet./A New Dance for a Girl*/The Tune Composed by/Mr Firbank/Writt by/Mr Pemberton:/And sold by Him [n.d.].
Pure, Michel de. *IDÉE/DES/SPECTACLES/ANCIENS/ET/NOVVEAVX./Des/Anciens(:)/Cirques./Amphitheatre./Theatres./Naumachies./Triomphes./NOVVEAVX./Comedie./Bal./Mascarades./Carosels./Courses de Bagues/& de Testes.(:)/Joustes./Exercices & Reveuës/Militaires./Feux d'Artifices./Entrées des Rois & des/Reynes./*Par M.M.D.P. A PARIS,/Chez MICHEL BRUNET, à l'entrée de la/grand' Salle du Palais, du costé de S. Barthe-/lemy, au Loüis d'Or./
_____. *Idée des Spectacles.* Paris: 1668. Reprinted, Minkoff, 1972.
Rameau, P. *ABBREGE'*[sic]/ *DE LA NOUVELLE METHODE, DANS/L'ART D'ECRIRE ou DE TRACER/TOUTES SORTES DE/DANSES DE VILLE/ . . . /Ouvrage/très utile pour toutes Personnes qui ont sçu/ou qui apprennent à Danser, puis que par le/Secour de ce livre, on peut se remettre facile-/ment dans toutes les Danses que l'on à appris./*A PARIS/chez l'Auteur, le Sr Boivin, le Sr Le Clerc [1725].
_____. Ibid. . . . With different dances in Rameau's revised Feuillet notation.
_____. *LE MAÎTRE/A DANSER/Qui enseigne la maniere de faire tous/les differens pas de Danse dans toute/la regularité de l'Art, & de conduire/les Bras à chaque pas./Enrichi de Figures en Taille-douce servant/de demonstration pour tous les differens/mouvemens qu'il convient faire dans/cet exercice./Ouvrage très-utile non-seulement à la Jeunesse qui/veut apprendre à bien danser, mais encore aux per-/sonnes honnêtes & polies, & qui leur donne des/regles pour bien marcher, saluer & faire les reveren-/ces convenables dans toutes sortes de compagnies./ . . . /*A PARIS,/Chez JEAN VILLETTE/M.DCCXXVI.
_____. *The Dancing Master.* Translated with an introduction by Cyril W. Beaumont. London: E.W. Beaumont, 1931. Reprinted, New York: Dance Horizons, 1970.
_____. *THE/Dancing-Master:/OR,/The whole ART and MASTERY of/DANCING/EXPLAINED;/And the Manner of Performing all STEPS in/Ball-Dancing made short and easy./In TWO PARTS/The First, Treating of the proper Positions and different/Attitudes for Men and Women, from which all the Steps are/taken and performed; adorned with instructive Figures: And/a Description of the Minuet-Figure, shewing the beautiful/Turns of the Body in that Dance: As also the Manner how/Men and Women ought to walk gracefully with a genteel/Behaviour upon all Occasions. Likewise the Ceremonial, as/used at the King's Great*

Ball, and of behaving genteely at Regulated Balls. The Second, Of the Use and agreeable Motions of the Arms/and Legs in taking their proper Movements, and forming/the Contrast. With Figures for their better Explanation;/In Sixty Draughts, done from the Life, and Engraved on/Copper Plates,/This WORK will be very Useful to all Gentlemen and Ladies who take Delight in this Exercise, and to those which keep Boarding-/Schools; for this will give their Scholars a just Notion of Address, a good Carriage, and genteel Behaviour./.../The SECOND EDITION./LONDON, Printed and Sold by him [John Essex]...,/and J. Brotherton. MDCCXXXI. Translated with an introduction by John Essex. Plates by G. Alsop.

————. Ibid.... Plates by George Bickham, Junior.

Rousseau, Jean Jacques. *DICTIONNAIRE/DE/MUSIQUE.* Paris: chez la Veuve Duchesne, 1768.

Taubert, Gottfried. *Rechtschaffener Tantzmeister/oder gründliche Erklärung/der Frantzösischen Tantz-Kunst/bestehend in drey Büchern,/deren/das Erste historice/des Tantzens Ursprung, Fortgang, Verbesserung, unterschiedlichen/Gebrauch, Zuläzzigkeit, vielfältigen Nutzen, und andere Eigenschafften mehr/untersuchet;/Das Andere methodice/des so wol galanten als theatralischen/Frantzösischen Tantz*=Exercitii Grund-Sätze/Ethice, Theoretice und Practice, das ist: was in dem Prosaischen/Theile zu der äusserlichen Sitten-Lehre und gefällig-machenden Ausführung: was in/dem Poëtischen Theile zu der theoretischen Wissenschafft und Betrachtung so wol der niedrigen Kammer—als hohen theatralischen Täntze: und was in Praxi so wol zu der Regel-mä igen/Composition, und geschichtilichen Execution, also gründlichen Information dieser beyden/Haupt-Theile gehöret, deutlich zeiget;/Anbey wird, nebst einer Ausführlichen Apologie für die wahre Tantz-Kunst, der/Haupt-Schlaessel zu der Choregraphie, oder Kunst alle Taentze durch Characteres, Figuren,/und allerhand Zeichen zu beschreiben, als welche ingeniöse Werck vormals dürch Msr. Feuillet/Tantzmeister in Paris, ediret, anitzo aber, nebst den Kupfferstichen, von dem Autore als/dem Frantzösischen in das Teutsche, und in diesen Format gebracht worden,/zu finden seyn;/Und das Dritte discursive/Derer Maitres, Scholaires, Assemblees, Balls, Hochzeit=Täntze,/und andere Tantz=Compagnien Requisita, wie sie nemlich beschaffen seyn sollen,/und unterweisen beschaffen sind, zulänglich erörtert. Endlich ist ein vollständiges Register aller eingebrachten Sachen/beygefüget worden. Leipzig, bey Friedrich Lanckischens Erben, 1717.

Tomlinson, Kellom. *THE/ART/OF/DANCING/Explained by/READING and FIGURES/Whereby the/Manner of Performing the STEPS/IS MADE EASY/By a NEW AND FAMILIAR METHOD;/BEING the/ORIGINAL WORK/First Design'd in the YEAR 1724,/And now Published by/KELLOM TOMLINSON, Dancing-Master./In Two BOOKS. /.. /LONDON/Printed for the AUTHOR:/.../MDCCXXXV.*

————. *The Art of Dancing and Six Dances.* London: 1735 and 1720. Reprinted, Gregg International Publishers Limited, 1970.

Weaver, John. *AN/ESSAY towards an/HISTORY/OF/DANCING.,/In which the whole ART and its Various Excel-/lencies are in some Measure explain'd./CONTAINING/The several Sorts of DANCING, AN-/TIQUE and MODERN, SERIOUS,/SCENICAL, GROTESQUE, &c. with/the Use of it as an Exercise, Qualification,/Diversion, &c.*/London:/Printed for Jacob Tonson.../1712.

Secondary Sources

Allanbrook, Wye Townsend Jamison. For works by this author, see Jamison, Wye Townsend (Allanbrook).

Baron, A.A.F. *Lettres et Entretiens sur la Danse.* Paris: Dodey-duprés, père et fils, 1824.

Beaumont, Cyril William. *A Bibliography of Dancing.* London: The Dancing Times, Ltd., 1929.

Bobillier, Marie, (Brenet, Michel). *Dictionnaire Pratique et Historique de la Musique.* Paris: Librarie Armand Colin, 1926.

Bukofzer, Manfred F. *Music in the Baroque Era from Monteverdi to Bach.* New York: W.W. Norton & Company, Inc., 1947.

Cohen, Selma Jean. *Dance as a Theatre Art: Source Readings in Dance History from 1581 to the Present.* New York: Dodd, Mead & Company, 1974.

deMoroda, Friderica Derra. "Choregraphie—The Dance Notation of the Eighteenth Century: Beauchamp or Feuillet?" *The Book Collector,* Winter 1967.

_____. "A Spanish book of 1758: another eighteenth-century book discovery." *The Dancing Times,* New series number 250, July 1931.

Desrat, G. *Dictionnaire de la Danse.* Paris: Librairies-Imprimeries Réunies, 1895.

Écorcheville, Jules, editor. *Vingt Suites d'Orchestre du XVIIe Siècle français.* Paris. L. Marcel Fortin & Cie, 1906.

Ellis, Helen Meredith (Little). "The Contribution of Dance Steps to Musical Analysis and Performance: La Bourgogne." *Journal of the American Musicological Society,* Vol. 28, No. 1, Spring 1975.

_____. "The Dances of J.B. Lully (1632-1687)." Unpublished Ph.D. dissertation, Stanford University, 1967.

Goldmann, Helmut. *Das Menuet in der deutschen Musikgeschichte des 17. und 18. Jahrhunderts.* Nürnberg, 1956.

Guilcher, Jean-Michel. *La Contredanse et les renouvellements de la danse française.* Paris: Mouton & Co., 1969.

Guthrie, John. *Historical Dances for the Theatre: The Pavan and the Minuet.* Worthing, Sussex: Aldrich Brothers, 1950.

Hilton, Wendy. *Dance of Court & Theater: The French Noble Style, 1690-1725.* Princeton: Princeton Book Company, 1981.

_____. "A dance for kings: the seventeenth-century French Courante," *Early Music,* Vol. 5, No. 2, April 1977.

Hutchinson, Ann. *Labanotation.* New York: New Directions Books, 1954.

Jamison, Wye Townsend (Allanbrook). "Dance as Expression in Mozart Opera." Unpublished Ph.D. dissertation, Stanford University, 1974.

_____. "The Minuet in the Eighteenth Century." Unpublished M.A. thesis, Stanford University, 1965.

Kunzle, Régine. "Pierre Beauchamp: The Illustrious Unknown Choreographer." *Dance Scope,* Vol. 8, No. 2, Spring/Summer 1974; and Vol. 9, No. 1, Fall/Winter 1974/75.

Lancelot, Francine. "Écriture de la danse—le système Feuillet." *Révue d'ethnologie française,* Vol. 1, No. 1, 1971.

Leslie, Serge. *A Bibliography of the dance collection of Doris Niles & Serge Leslie.* Annotated by Serge Leslie. Edited by Cyril Beaumont. London: C.W. Beaumont, 1966.

Little, Helen Meredith Ellis. For works by this author, see Ellis, Helen Meredith (Little).

Marcel-Dubois, Claudie. "Menuett." *Die Musik in Geschichte und Gegenwart,* Band 9. Edited by Friedrich Blume. New York: Bärenreiter Kassel, 1961.

Martens, Heinrich. *Musikalische Formen in Historischen Reihen: Das Menuett.* Wolfenbüttel: Möseler, 1958.

Moore, Lillian. "The Great Dupré." *Dance Magazine,* June 1960.

Nettl, Paul. "Forlane." *Die Musik in Geschichte und Gegenwart,* Band 4. Edited by Friedrich Blume. New York: Bärenreiter Kassel, 1961.

Ratner, Leonard. " 'Ars Combinatoria.' Chance and choice in eighteenth-century music." *Studies in Eighteenth-century Music: A Tribute to Karl Geiringer on his Seventieth Birthday.* New York: Oxford University Press, 1970.

Sachs, Curt. *Eine Weltgeschichte des Tanzes.* Berlin: Dietrich Reimer/Ernst Vohsen, 1933.

_____. *World History of the Dance.* Translated by Bessie Schönberg. New York: Bonanza Books, 1937.

Schwandt, Erich. "L'Affilard on the French Court Dances." *The Musical Quarterly*, Vol. 60, No. 3, July 1974.
Skeaping, Mary. "Ballet under the three crowns." *Dance Perspectives*, No. 32, Winter 1967.
Sorrell, Walter. *The Dance through the Ages*. New York: Grosset & Dunlap, 1967.
Vuillier, Gaston. *La Danse*. Paris: Hachette et Cie, 1898.
_____. *A History of Dancing from the Earliest Ages to Our Own Times*. Translated. London: William Heinemann, 1898.
Winter, Marian Hannah. *The Pre-Romantic Ballet*. Brooklyn: Dance Horizons, 1975.
Wood, Melusine. *Advanced Historical Dances*. London: The Imperial Society of Teachers of Dancing, C.W. Beaumont, 1960.
_____. *Historical Dances*. London: The Imperial Society of Teachers of Dancing, Incorporated, 1964.
_____. *Some Historical Dances (Twelfth to Nineteenth Century): Their Manner of Performance and Their Place in the Social Life of the Time*. London: the Imperial Society of Teachers of Dancing, C.W. Beaumont, 1952.
Wotquenne, Alfred. "Thèmes des Petits Recueils Ballard (1695-1743)." Unpublished catalogue.
Wynne, Shirley. *Bibliography. Dance in France and England from 1676 to 1750: Manuals*. Unpublished, 1969.
_____. "The Minuet." Institute of Court Dances of the Renaissance and Baroque Periods. *CORD* (c) 1972.

Index

Baron, A.A.F., 195
Beauchamp, Pierre, 5
Bonin, Louis, 4, 18, 22, 57, 195, 282
Brossard, Sebastien de, 71

Campra, André, 1, 171, 187, 193
carriage, 50
Cavalli, Francesco, 95
choreographic construction, 15, 58-60, 82-83, 96-97, 119-22, 137-40, 153-54, 160-62, 171, 173, 179-80, 190-95, 202-5
Colasse, Pascal, 1, 7
Compan, 283

dance types
    bourrée, 15-16, 137-38
    bransle, 2
    contredanse, 2, 95-97, 103, 187
    courante, 78, 131-32, 138
    forlana, 171, 187
    gavotte, 187
    gigue, 95-97
    menuet, 16-23, 71, 78-83, 96
    passepied, 71, 78-83, 139
    sarabande, 138-39
    venitienne, 187, 192-93
danse à deux, 2-4, 95-97, 103
Dezais, 5, 95
Dufort, Giambatista, 4, 16, 17, 18, 22, 54

Ellis, Helen Meredith (Little), 280, 283, 284

Feuillet, Raoul-Auger, 5
floor patterns, 82, 137, 160-62, 179-80, 194, 203
focus (partner or Présence), 59-60, 96, 103-4, 162, 180, 194
folk dance, 79

Guilcher, Jean-Michel, 96

hands ("la Mariée"), 50, 51
hat (menuet), 18, 22
Hilton, Wendy, 8, 283, 284

Jamison, Wye (Allanbrook), 282

King's Grand Ball, 2

Lambranzi, 4
Lancelot, Francine, 284
Lully, Jean-Baptiste, 1, 7, 60, 95

Mattheson, Johann, 56, 50
Minguet e Yrol, Pablo, 4, 71
movement, 50-52
music and dance (including cadence of step-units), 4, 7-8, 11-12, 14, 35, 41, 60, 82-83, 96, 120-22, 139, 154, 157, 158, 160-62, 171-72, 179-80, 191-93, 203-5

Nettl, Paul, 187

Pasch, Johann, 4
Pécour, Guillaume Louis, 4-5
Pemberton, 4
Pure, Michel de, 50

Rameau, P., 5
Ratner, Leonard, 284

Schwandt, Erich, 282
step-units
    chassés, 47, 57-58
    contretemps ballonné, 114-15
    contretemps de chaconne, 35
    contretemps de côté, 56, 104, 195
    contretemps de menuet, 77-78, 81-82
    coupé battu, 173
    demi-contretemps, 101

demi-jeté, 131
glissades, 41-42, 53
pas de bourrée, 41-42, 59, 176-77
pas de bourrée emboîté, 48, 55, 157
pas de courante, 138
pas de gaillarde, 46-47, 171, 174-75, 191
pas de menuet, 12, 16-22, 139
pas de sissonne, 98, 156, 175
pas de sissonne bâtu, 38-39, 56, 57
pas tombé, 37, 161, 188, 190-91
pirouette, 118-19, 158
pirouette avec saut, 54-55, 119

temps, 43
temps de courante, 10, 132

Taubert, Gottfried, 4, 16, 17, 18, 22, 23, 41, 54
technique, 2, 4, 58, 97
tempo, 78, 79-82
Tomlinson, Kellom, 4, 16, 17, 18, 22, 41, 43, 47, 53, 54, 82, 175

Weaver, John, 4, 41-42
Wotquenne, Alfred, 284
Wynne, Shirley, 282